STAGING LIFE

Annie Horniman, founder of Manchester's Gaiety Theatre and
inspiration to its playwrights.
(*Manchester Library and Archives.*)

STAGING LIFE

The Story of the Manchester Playwrights

JOHN HARDING

To Joyce, With Best Wishes! John

GE

Greenwich Exchange
London

Acknowledgements

I would like to thank Jeanette Martin and the staff at Manchester University's John Rylands Library for all their help. I would also like to thank Duncan McCormick at Salford Local Library (The Harold Brighouse Collection) and Ian Johnston at Salford University's Archives and Special Collections (The Houghton Collection).

Two unpublished PhD theses have been of immense importance: the late Alasdair F. Cameron's *The Repertory Theatre Movement, 1907–1917* (University of Warwick, 1983) and Paul Mortimer's *The Life and Literary Career of W. Stanley Houghton, 1881–1913* (University of Salford, 1984).

A particular thank you goes to Harriet Monkhouse, granddaughter of Allan Monkhouse, for her invaluable help and encouragement.

Greenwich Exchange, London

First published in Great Britain in 2018
All rights reserved

© John Harding, 2018

Printed and bound by imprintdigital.com
Cover design by December Publications
Tel: 07951511275

Greenwich Exchange Website: www.greenex.co.uk

Cataloguing in Publication Data is available
from the British Library

ISBN: 978-1-910996-17-1

Contents

PROLOGUE

A Repertory Revolution

> When we speak of a repertory, we mean a number of plays always ready for perform-ance, with nothing more than a 'run through' rehearsal, which, therefore, can be, and are, acted in such alternation that three, four or five different plays may be given in the course of a week. New plays are from time to time added to the repertory, and those of them which succeed may be performed fifty, seventy, a hundred times, or even more, in the course of one season; but no play is ever performed more than two or three times in uninterrupted succession.[1]

STAGING LIFE IS NOT A HISTORY of British drama, although one or two points concerning theatre chronology and terminology need to be established from the outset.

Frustration with the generally sad state of British theatre towards the end of the 19th century was widespread. In London, the market forces of supply and demand as interpreted by commercial managements had led to stale, limited and repetitious programmes, while beyond, the gradual decline of the touring system dominated by anachronistic 'actor-managers' had led to the decay of the once vibrant provincial theatre.

On the Continent, the new, challenging and often disturbing dramas of modern life appearing from the pens of Ibsen, Strindberg

9

and other writers led to inevitably invidious comparisons with what British writers were producing. The occasional touring company from abroad also gave home audiences tantalising glimpses of what could be.

Change came slowly and in small increments. Grein's Independent Theatre in 1891, followed by William Archer's New Century Theatre in 1897 and finally the Stage Society in 1899 gave the so-called 'New Drama' a start.

However, the Royal Court project under the direction of actor turned director Harley Granville Barker with the aid of his business manager, J.E. Vedrenne, during the three seasons from 1904 to 1907 was the major catalyst for far-reaching theatrical change.

Barker's plan was to take the relatively small Court Theatre and run 'a stock season of the uncommercial drama, staking everything upon the plays and the acting and eschewing lavish "productions"'.

There were three main aims: to prepare the way for public acceptance of 'the repertory idea' and particularly of a National Theatre; to encourage a wider interest in the new avant-garde drama of Europe; and to present such plays simply and unpretentiously, allowing them to make their full impact, unhampered by elaborate sets or star performers.

'In presenting no less than eleven plays by Bernard Shaw the management triumphantly established Shaw's reputation as the major British dramatist of the day; a remarkable range of new or 'uncommercial' drama was introduced to the English theatre; through Barker's work as a director new standards of acting and production were set on the London stage; and, not least, a powerful impetus was given to the repertory theatre movement.'[2]

The advantage of repertory was that it provided for a wide range of plays to be kept constantly before the public for as long as interest was shown in them; at the same time it avoided the evils of the 'long-run' system by ensuring a frequent change of bill, never allowing one production to play for more than three or four performances in succession. Such variety was of particular value to actors, enabling them to progress through a large number of widely different roles and preventing performances from becoming stale.

In July 1907, when the Court seasons ended, Barker, summed up what he believed to have been the most significant aspects of their artistic policy:

> At the Court we have by no means started a repertory theatre or anything like it, but we have introduced a system which may prove the artistic necessity of such institutions.[3]

Only months later, Britain's first permanent repertory theatre company, the Gaiety Theatre, opened in Manchester. Organised on the 'short-run system' and drawing much of its inspiration, several of its actors and a good deal of its early repertoire from that pioneering Court venture, it was a pioneering institution that would have far-reaching effects for drama in the United Kingdom.

Notes

[1] George Rowell and Anthony Jackson, *The Repertory Movement: A History of Regional Theatre in Britain* Cambridge University Press, 1984 p18

[2] ibid p16

[3] ibid p16

1

Annie Horniman and Manchester

We must all take courage and look our difficulties full in the face, neither magnifying them nor avoiding them; and we shall find in many cases that a little self-denial, a little exertion of Will, or even a little commonplace prudence will vanquish them completely.[1]

ANNIE HORNIMAN (HEREAFTER AH) CAME TO Manchester in 1907 aged 47 years old and founded the Gaiety Theatre repertory company: a resident company of actors producing new and old plays on a regular basis for an 'intelligent public'. She would also be responsible for the development of the first regional movement of dramatic writing in the United Kingdom, the 'Manchester School' of playwrights, who would reflect in their work the lives and preoccupations of ordinary men and women living in the North of England.

Yet she herself had never been an actor, wasn't a playwright and didn't possess the necessary skills to be either a producer or a director. In fact, she had never had a proper job in her life. She was a woman, however, with fixed views and a determination to make something out of her life. She wrote some twenty years prior to arriving in Manchester, 'Not one of us has any time to lose. Youth and strength do not last us very long and the present opportunities may never arise again. Work done to please or gain approbation from another is not what we want, but real enthusiasm which overcomes difficulties and grows the stronger because of them.'[2]

Though lacking artistic talent, she took great delight in helping others succeed where she could not. Her wherewithal to do this stemmed from the eponymous family tea business founded by her Quaker grandfather. Her predilection for utilising her inherited wealth to fund artistic endeavours and creative individuals would be an enduring feature of her life. Some observers have suggested that AH used her money to buy credibility as an artist but she was not the sort of person to delude herself. Though she had spent some four years from the age of 22 at the Slade School of Art, she always admitted that she possessed no real artistic talent. ('I spent five years at the Slade School where I learnt that I never should learn to draw.')[3]

However, it was as an art student that she'd been released from her privileged but restricted home environment to travel widely, especially to Germany. She became a Germanophile, steeping herself in German culture; she spoke the language and was a devotee of Richard Wagner, missing only one Bayreuth Festival between 1884 and 1914.

Being fluent in three European languages, she took an educated interest in the avant-garde continental theatre, especially the work of Henrik Ibsen. She claimed to have seen her first Ibsen play, *An Enemy of the People*, in 1889 at the Residenz Theatre, Munich and in 1891, in the same theatre, she was present at the very first performance of *Hedda Gabler* in Munich where she saw the author called on stage afterwards. In 1891, in London, she joined the Independent Theatre Society, a subscription-only organisation (thus enabling it to evade State censorship) which first produced Ibsen's *Ghosts*. Though sometimes depicted unfairly as straight-laced and puritanical, she was well ahead of the times where her dramatic tastes were concerned.

In fact, as early as 1893, after her grandfather had died and left her a legacy of some £40,000, she offered Florence Farr, an avant-garde actress friend, enough money to promote her burgeoning acting career. Farr booked the Avenue Theatre on London's Embankment and asked the three men in her life – George Bernard Shaw, W.B. Yeats and John Todhunter – to write new plays for her to produce and appear in. Yeats would write *The Land of Heart's Desire*, the first of his Irish plays to be professionally staged. Todhunter wrote *A Comedy of Sighs* and Shaw *Arms and the Man*.

Aubrey Beardsley, then just beginning his career as a graphic artist of startling originality, was commissioned to produce a poster for the shows and it caused a small sensation. His first-ever colour lithograph, it doubled as a programme cover illustration and while many critics admired his clever use of outline and the poster's overall decorative effect, they found the woman depicted on it disconcerting. There were outraged responses from the popular press. Despite – or perhaps because of – the ensuing publicity, this seminal theatrical event in March 1894 almost failed completely. Though it helped to launch Shaw's play writing career, it failed to recoup any of the money invested in it. It had been what AH would later term a 'fruitful failure'.[4]

The Avenue Theatre event didn't deter her, however. In 1903 she decided to bank-roll her friend W.B. Yeats' endeavour to establish an Irish National Theatre in Dublin, to create, in her own words, 'a powerful and prosperous theatre with a high artistic purpose.'[5]

She would ultimately be forced to retreat, firstly by the forces of Irish nationalism that felt bitter about receiving her financial largesse and secondarily by those within the theatre itself who resented what they considered to be her misguided interference in its day-to-day running. She was also regularly mocked by Dublin society for what was perceived as her romantic obsession with Yeats. It would not be until 1910 that her financial involvement with the Abbey came to an acrimonious end,

Therefore, her arrival in Manchester in 1907 owed a great deal to a sense of injustice burning fiercely within her. As she told her Manchester producer, Iden Payne, 'I want to teach those impossible people in Dublin that I have other fish to fry.'[6]

II

A Civilized Theatre means that a city has something of cultivation in it, something to make literature grow; a real theatre, not a mere amusing toy.[7]

Exactly why AH chose Manchester needs a little explaining, however. Much has been made of the perfect fit Manchester was for the establishment of a new 'intellectual' theatre. It possessed one of the largest centres of population in the country; it had well-established universities and was an important commercial centre; it boasted newspapers favourable to drama which were respected throughout the country and widely read in the local area; it had a long tradition of theatre-going and was in fact a 'Number One' touring destination for theatrical companies; what's more, it had an active theatre society interested in recent developments in the drama and which was sympathetic to Horniman and her ambitions.

Despite all this, AH made great efforts to find a London theatre for her new enterprise before settling on the Cottonopolis. Three men were instrumental in changing her mind. The first was W.B. Yeats who had wanted her to put her money into a second theatre somewhere in England to showcase his plays. When he refused to leave Ireland, however, AH decided to let him go.

Then there was Alfred Wareing, the London-born advance manager for the legendary Beerbohm Tree dramatic touring company. Ironically, given AH's aversion to what was happening in Dublin, Wareing had visited the Abbey soon after it had been founded, and liked what he saw. He was thrilled both by the productions and by the sight of the company doing everything from building their own scenery to sewing their costumes. It mirrored his own desire to form a 'stock' company: an acting company permanently resident in a particular town in order to give its theatre a strong local identity. He'd already tried the idea twice in East London but lacked sufficient money of his own to make it work.

When he heard that the Abbey players were to tour England, Wareing offered them the use of his extensive network of theatrical contacts, and it was during the tour that Wareing met AH. He put his 'stock' company idea to her and, impressed by his professionalism, she asked him to see if he could secure a suitable venue somewhere in England for such a venture.

Wareing initially tried Liverpool, but the premises were not right. He then thought of Glasgow, but by then someone else had intervened to sway AH's mind: her newly appointed producer/director, 26-year-old Ben Iden Payne.

Iden Payne was one of AH's few positives from the Abbey days, yet at the start of 1907 he'd been a mere jobbing actor, touring Ireland with Benson's second theatrical company. When AH was looking for a new manager for the Abbey Theatre to replace Willie Fay, she had sought advice from John Vedrenne at London's Court Theatre who in turn asked actor Harvey Granville Barker for suggestions. Barker had met Payne just once – in the ABC tearooms in Sloane Square opposite the Royal Court theatre when Payne had asked for a job. He'd been impressed by Payne's enthusiasm for the 'new drama' and thought he might be the man for AH.

Yeats was then sent to track Payne down and invited him to join the Abbey Company.

As we have seen, Payne's tenure at the Abbey lasted no more than six months, when the in-fighting and political wrangling had become too much and he'd resigned.

Within days, he received a summons from AH, asking him to visit her at her London apartment.

> I did so, wondering why she should wish to see me. This was the first of seemingly innumerable times that I was to walk along the dark corridor, past closely shut doors, to where one was faced by an electrically lighted portrait of Yeats. There one turned right into Miss Horniman's comfortably old-fashioned sitting room, with armchairs at each side of the fireplace and a sofa facing it. This was also the first of many times that I partook of Miss Horniman's scented China tea, served with toasted tea cakes.[8]

AH regaled him with a catalogue of the wrongs done to her in Dublin. 'She had ceased,' she said, 'to go to Ireland only to be insulted.'[9] She then announced to the startled Payne that she had a sum of £25,000 to spend and she wanted Payne to undertake the task of setting up a new theatre company for her somewhere in England. It was a dream come true for Payne.

Payne had been born in Newcastle upon Tyne on 5 September 1881 but his family left for Manchester before he was one. His father, the Rev Alfred Payne, was minister of the Strangeways Unitarian Chapel. Payne won a Foundation Scholarship to Manchester Grammar School but eschewed going on to university in favour of a career in the theatre. He first joined F.R. Benson's theatrical touring company in 1899 and worked as an actor in various other touring companies up and down the British Isles for some eight years.

Payne was idealistic and ambitious. The actor Basil Dean described how, when they first met:

> He spoke about William Morris and the beginnings of Socialism.

Thoreau's *Walden* was the first book he lent me, then Walt Whitman's *Leaves of Grass*. Soon he had me reading Blatchford's *Britain for the British,* Prince Kropotkin's *Field, Factory and Workshop,* and Samuel Butler's *Erehwon.* He introduced me to Ibsen, the early Shaw, H.G. Wells, and a world of free-thinking literature previously unknown to me.[10]

The playwright and novelist Arnold Bennett, who met Payne during his early days at the Gaiety, described him as, 'like a little original wild member of the Fabian Society. Cape instead of coat, held on by bands crossing the chest.'[11]

Payne expressed what might be called his personal credo in an article he wrote for the Gaiety Annual in 1909:

The drama is as important to a community as its religion. It is not, as it has been regarded for so long, a mere extraneous amusement, quite negligible in comparison with the serious things of life. Indeed the drama may sometimes be the same thing as religion – the drama expressed in the religion or the religion expressed in the drama.[12]

AH's offer could not have come at a better time for him, but he had doubts:

At first thought it may seem that I should have been overjoyed at being offered such an extraordinary opportunity. In fact, far from being elated, I was taken aback. It was not that I feared the responsibility, weighty though it would be for a young man of twenty-six. I was too brash to feel such qualms. But I had gone on the stage because I enjoyed acting. Anything that frustrated that ambition depressed my spirits. Directing and managerial work had not been my choice; they had been thrust upon me.[13]

Nevertheless, he accepted the offer, because

I saw this stroke of fortune as a step toward creating the kind of theatre that I had longed for but never found. My reading of Ibsen and Shaw ... had made me eager for a chance to experience, and to help advance, the New Drama. Just how intense that eagerness had been I did not quite know myself until suddenly I was offered the chance to make the vision real.[14]

According to Payne, it was he who nudged AH towards Manchester. At an informal conference at AH's London flat attended by Yeats, AH's lifelong friend Miss Ida Gildea, and Payne, AH claimed 'it was settled in ten minutes discussion which of the great cities she should come to.'[15]

Payne's own recollection is very different. Only after a good deal of discussion, he said, was Manchester preferred to London.

> Miss Horniman, who often spoke of her Scottish grandfather, suggested trying to found a Scottish national theatre. Glasgow and Edinburgh were talked of as possible homes for our undertaking. I maintained, however, that the Scots themselves should be the prime movers in any national venture. In view of Miss Horniman's Dublin experience, I argued, she should be leery of any enterprise that bore a nationalistic tag.[16]

This may have been retrospective wisdom. AH's aversion to things Celtic had been amply demonstrated in Dublin. It might also be noted that part of her anger at McGregor Mathers back in the Golden Dawn era had to do with his political machinations on behalf of a Scottish independence movement.

Payne knew Manchester well, however, having grown up in the city and so Wareing, much against his wishes, was tasked with finding a venue there while Payne set out to gather together a company of actors. They moved extremely fast.

On 11 July, 1907 the following letter appeared in several Manchester papers:

> Sir—I am writing to inform you of a scheme, which, it is possible, may form the nucleus of a city theatre, the idea of which, I am informed, has been mooted recently in Manchester. Miss A.E.F. Horniman, with myself as her general manager, hopes to form a repertory theatre in Manchester and we shall commence our work

in the coming autumn with a series of productions, probably at the Midland Hotel Theatre. This, however, will only be a beginning and we hope in time to have our own theatre.

We have, tentatively, given the name of the Manchester Playgoers' Theatre to our work, and we intend to produce no plays, which are not sincere works of art. We shall seek to produce good new plays, to revive old masterpieces and to present translations of the best works of foreign authors. We have chosen Manchester because we feel that of all towns it is the one most ready for such an undertaking, and that there, if anywhere, there will be the support necessary for the success of our scheme. I hope very shortly to give much fuller particulars.

Yours, etc.,

B. Iden Payne[17]

Four weeks later, on 31 August, the concept had been developed further. In the *Manchester City News* it was explained that the new company would be:

(a) A Repertoire Theatre with regular changes of programme no matter how successful the play – no 1,000 nights' runs! – not wedded to any one school of dramatists, but thoroughly catholic, embracing the finest writings by the best authors of all ages ... and with an especially widely open door to present-day British writers

(b) A permanent Manchester stock company of picked front rank artistes ... At present most touring companies consist of a 'star' whose name fills the placards and

announcements supported by a lady (in small type) and generally a nondescript collection of inadequately paid people.

(c) Efficient production, a matter of vital importance; Mr Granville Barker's genius in this direction has made the Court Theatre famous. Manchester's Barker will be Mr B. Iden Payne.

(d) Popular prices. The company is fully alive to the many grievances, which playgoers have endured for a long time, and intends to do all it can to attend to their physical comforts at reasonable rates.[18]

With no appropriate venue immediately available, Wareing arranged for Payne's hastily assembled company to appear at the

Midland Hotel Theatre, 'a venue not suited to the kind of plays she wished to produce. Although conveniently situated in the centre of Manchester, it was little more than a large, rectangular, rather draughty hall with a raised platform at one end.'[19]

A few days before the season opened Payne lectured to the Manchester Playgoers' Club on 'The Advantages of a Repertoire Theatre' with Miss Horniman on the platform for support. He criticised long runs in the theatre and said that there were dangers in too much rehearsal, as spontaneity might be lost. Another evil was that actors were constantly engaged to play over and over again the same type of part and found themselves fixed in it for life. His hope was to have a true repertoire theatre, with changes of play two or three times a week. Only a repertoire theatre, he contended, could become a part of the civic life of the town.

The company's first five-week season was not a financial success, with the audiences so sparse that the actors feared they would soon be out of a job. AH, however, 'seemed quite unperturbed, sitting in one of the side-boxes at every performance and staring at the rows of empty seats with a grim smile'.[20]

She swiftly pressed on with her plans to buy a permanent theatre in Manchester. In November 1907, she wrote to W.B. Yeats, 'The Gaiety is one of the well-known theatres, in a splendid position ... Everyone is glad to hear that I am buying it and that I intend if possible to arrange for all the seats to be booked.'[21]

Her confidence was based on two factors. First, the enthusiastic reception accorded the experiment by the *Manchester Guardian*, the newspaper, 'representing all that the Manchester intelligentsia which does not go to the play might be supposed to think if it did'.[22]

Second, Yeats had cast a horoscope for the Gaiety. He found, perhaps to his disappointment, that all the omens were good ones.

Notes

[1] Mary K. Greer, *Women of the Golden Dawn* (Park Street Press. 1995), p69.

[2] Ibid., p136

[3] *The Woman Worker,* 23 June 1909.

[4] Greer, *op. cit.*, p147.

[5] Edward Malins, 'Annie Horniman: Practical Idealist', *Canadian Journal of Irish Studies*, 3/2 (1977), 22.

[6] Ben Iden Payne, *A Life in a Wooden O* (Yale University Press 1977), p78.

[7] Annie Horniman, 'The Manchester Players', *Poet Lore*, XXV/3 (1914), 212.

[8] Iden Payne, *op. cit.*, p. 78.

[9] Ibid., p. 76.

[10] Basil Dean, *Seven Ages: An Autobiography, 1888–1927* (Hutchinson. 1970), pp38–40.

[11] Arnold Bennett, *Journal*, vol. 1: *1896–1910,* ed. Newman Flower (Cassell, 1932).

[12] *The Gaiety Annual* (1909).

[13] Iden Payne, *op. cit.*, p78.

[14] Ibid., p79.

[15] Annie Horniman, 'A Talk about the Drama' (Manchester Historical Society, 1911), p83.

[16] Iden Payne, *op. cit.*, p79.

[17] *Manchester Courier*, 11 July 1907.

[18] *Manchester City News*, 13 August 1907.

[19] Dean, *op. cit.*, p50.

[20] Ibid., p52.

[21] A.E.F. Horniman, letter of 3 November 1907, in *Letters to W.B. Yeats*, ed. Finnerhan, Harper and Murphy (Macmillan 1977).

[22] James Agate, *A Short View of the English Stage 1900–1926* (Herbert Jenkins, 1926), pp72-3.

2

Iden Payne: The Power
Behind the Throne

She paid the piper; the solid work was done by others. It was
principally done in the first years of the Gaiety by Iden Payne.[1]

With his long fair hair, fresh complexion and pince-nez glasses, he
looked more like a medical student than an actor.[2]

IDEN PAYNE'S ACHIEVEMENT IN THE FIRST few weeks of
the Manchester experiment depended heavily on the ability to
produce something to impress a small, intellectual and already
sophisticated theatre public. To keep such an audience interested,
he knew he would have to vary the bill frequently, but if he gave
shoddy or hurried productions that same audience would desert
the theatre.

If a great deal of the drama was new, the company could not
fall back on traditional 'business', as actors in the old stock
companies had done. In the traditional touring company – the
kind in which Payne had served a long apprenticeship – it was
sufficient for an actor to learn his lines and acquire a stock of
stage tricks which could be adapted to any part. This was not
what Payne wanted. He was by instinct a teacher and he set about
creating a style of performance that would help to transform the

way drama in Britain would henceforth be presented.

Although he had only been at the Abbey Theatre for a short period of time, Payne had learned from the much-maligned Willie Fay. Fay was trying to initiate a realistic, ensemble style of acting. 'Ensemble' implies that an actor has crafted his or her performance to best serve the story, rather than trying to stand out and be noticed individually. For Fay, the company was totally subservient to the play. Payne would instinctively develop a similar directorial technique with the advantage that he would be employing professionals drawn from companies he had worked with or was familiar with.

The selection of a suitable company was thus extremely important, as the bulk of the proposed repertoire of the theatres comprised new and recently written plays. The kind of actor needed for these plays was one who would act well in an ensemble and who would work for the sake of the play. 'The play is the thing,' wrote Alfred Wareing when describing his ideal acting company, and Payne recruited actors who understood this. (See Appendix)

The new theatre had also to prove that its standards of production were far above those of the touring companies it so deprecated. With many new plays to produce, a new repertoire to establish, and frequent changes of bill promised, there had to be someone in overall artistic control – a director – something that was also relatively new to the theatre.

With the actor's theatre of the late nineteenth century giving way to the writer's theatre of the early twentieth, an efficient director was necessary to make sure that the dramatist's meaning was conveyed to the audience and that the actors were made to serve the play. Payne, in his autobiography, explained how a director became necessary with the plays of Ibsen and Shaw, which required the consequent need to analyse a text and relate all actions to the whole. He realised that the new type of stage director must always search for the deeper meaning of the play.

Playwrights such as Ibsen and Shaw though their plays were rarely performed had a profound influence upon playwrights who began to write plays with much more psychological import. Motives for action were less obvious than they had been; they were frequently veiled and so required explanation and guidance for the actors. Then too there were more plays in which atmosphere was of the utmost importance. A guiding hand became indispensable to its achievement.

Payne swiftly developed a flexible directorial method suitable to all plays, giving them a 'finish' while leaving details, such as characterisation, to the actors. He concentrated on analysing his texts in order to evoke for his actors what he termed the 'atmosphere' of each play, giving them the limits within which they could develop their parts. Payne's evocation of 'atmosphere' appeared to mean the ability to make the actors believe in what they were doing and in turn to convince the audience that what they were witnessing was in some way real.

The Gaiety actress Sybil Thorndike perceived a similarity between Payne's directorial methods and that of Stanislavsky when she said that Payne's directorial methods were very close to the system of 'method' acting based on Stanislavsky's theories. Payne, for example, insisted that his actors, like method actors, should really believe in what they were doing, that they should 'be' rather than just 'do' ...

Basil Dean tells of a rehearsal for *Cupid and the Styx* early in 1909:

> In one of the acts Lewis and Sybil had a scene together while I and another character had to stand about with nothing to say, so we retired to the back of the stage gesticulating wildly in make-believe conversation. 'What on earth are you doing' came Payne's clear high-pitched voice, I turned round rather offended 'Just keeping up the

scene.' But what are you saying, 'Nothing really,' I replied. 'Well if its not in the play, don't play it,' said Payne.[3]

F. Sladen Smith, watching the company perform Bernard Shaw's *Widowers' Houses* understood that Payne was doing something new and radically different:

> Astonishing! It was alive, it was astoundingly alive. There was no breakneck rush to the footlights – the players actually acted for the sake of acting and for the sake of the play and the result was an astonishing unity. And the joy of seeing a play that was a play and not a mere peg to hang mannerisms on![4]

Not everyone was impressed. The critic James Agate wrote:

> The so-called Manchester school demanded actresses of respectability rather than glamour, a quality with which Welsh dressers do not consort. Lacking glamour, and knowing that they lacked it, Miss Horniman's leading ladies cottoned on to soul. I remember a scene in a Galsworthy play in which an ultra-soulful creature used to go to the window, open it, and flap her arms like the wings of a fowl. When I asked what this grotesque nonsense was supposed to mean, the actress – who was quite well known – said sepulchrally, 'It's the soul in the act of liberating itself.'[5]

'Ensemble' acting was particularly important because of the large number of modern 'realistic' plays the Gaiety would produce, such as those of Arnold Bennett, John Galsworthy and particularly those of the soon-to-become, 'Manchester School'. These plays demanded realistic behaviour on the stage, a realism that extended to details of set dressing such as having real roast beef on the table or chrysanthemums rather than just any flowers for a particular scene.

Pogson later remarked:

> Considering Payne's youthfulness – he was only twenty-six when the venture started – and the complete absence of anything approaching assertiveness or domination in his character, the control

he had over his company was astonishing. Invariably he was good-tempered, patient, even gentle, yet there was never any doubt who was in command. His secret lay in sincerity and the gift of inspiring confidence in his abilities; actors worked well for him because they liked him and because they knew he was capable in his job.[6]

His command and control are all the more remarkable when one considers that he was working in close tandem with AH, a woman who had declared when setting up her new Manchester company that she would be in total control. She made this plain in a letter written in August 1908, just before the newly refurbished Gaiety theatre opened. She would not, she declared, make the mistakes she had made in Dublin, and was determined to keep strict control over all aspects of the theatre:

> Everyone paid and open to dismissal for good reason, no one allowed to feel indispensable. If two men come to blows just before the curtain rises they will 'get the sack'. If the leading man refuses to rehearse with the leading lady, well he won't be allowed another chance. If the stage manager orders me off the stage because I give him a necessary message from the paying public there will be ructions.[7]

Rex Pogson admitted, 'Technically her knowledge of the theatre was small when she went to Manchester and it was at no time large … The truth was that her approach to the theatre was almost naively simple.'[8] The possibilities for conflict were thus crystal clear. What's more, Iden Payne, though initially somewhat in awe of AH ('At first encounter I had felt almost that I was in the presence of a prophetess') soon realised that she was not the ogre she appeared.

She could, of course, strike any stranger as intimidating, not least on account of her flamboyant dress style. The actress Sybil Thorndike described AH as wearing, 'beautiful stuff that you would only think of for curtains' as she often used drapery brocades from Liberty's of London to make her distinctive loose, flowing Pre-Raphaelite gowns.

'She must have been aware of the amused interest her appearance excited,' commented the writer St John Ervine, 'but she was indifferent to what was said about her, going the way she wanted to go, despite all attempts to prevent or impede her ... But odd though her style of dress was, it was not ugly ... She was, I insist, a stylish woman, and she illuminated any place in which she appeared.'[9]

Her dress style wasn't simply caprice, however. The Gaiety Theatre biographer Rex Pogson wrote of her:

> In appearance Miss Horniman was striking. Although not much above average height, her unusual thinness made her appear taller than she was. An early attack of typhoid fever left her thin to the point of emaciation, and nothing would increase her weight. The unusual mode of her evening dress, variously attributed to eccentricity and showmanship, was in fact dictated by her inability to wear the low-cut gowns fashionable in the period. For the same reason she always wore a lace neckband with piping of black velvet, creating an old-maidish appearance which was very misleading.[10]

There was also her trademark gold chain that featured an opal cat-like dragon with little pointed ears, a whiskery ruff, and pointed claws. It measured five inches across, contained 300 opal 'scales', and glared at the observer through flashing ruby eyes. She claimed it was a likeness of herself, but it may have been her 'witch's familiar', a kind of magical companion.[11]

If one adds her, at times, peculiar cat-like behaviour, purring when she was pleased, hissing and scratching when she was annoyed, then it's no wonder Iden Payne was initially taken aback.

Writing many years later, however, he made the point that although AH might have sounded profound and her speech was direct and in practical matters always to the point, 'I soon became aware that the rest of her conversations consisted of flat commonplaces. These were uttered as if they were almost pontifical pronouncements, but often ended with an amusing twist of assumed modesty.'[12]

In fact, 'It was disconcerting to find, as I soon did, that there was simply no common ground on which we could discuss the artistic aspects of the work in which, ostensibly, we were both engaged.'[13] In particular, he pointed out that AH's ability to appraise the worth or otherwise of a play was limited.

> Miss Horniman had a curious way of regarding the drama. She was the only person I have ever met who could see a play only from the visual point of view! 'I asked her if she had not in her travels seen any European plays that might be translated for our use. After a pause for cogitation she said she could remember one play that might be useful, but all she could tell me about it was that in one scene there was a courtyard, that in the courtyard there was a well, and that when women lowered pots into it, water was seen to be dripping from their sides when they were raised. This realistic touch had impressed her deeply. It was useless to try to discover anything about the plot of the play. I did succeed in getting as far as an admission that the subject was more or less biblical, but every further question always brought her back to the dripping water pots.[14]
>
> A little later, the London production of a play by Mrs W.K. Clifford was announced. Since this writer had previously had a play produced by the Stage Society, an organisation noted for its modern outlook, I thought that it might possibly suit our purposes. Miss Horniman still maintained her apartment in London, so I suggested that she report on the new play. She was delighted to do so. In due course she declared that it was useless. The plot was laid in Italy in the month of October, yet there had been green grass-mat covering the stage. 'Everyone knows,' said Miss Horniman, 'that in Italy the grass is burnt brown in the autumn!' This was the last time I attempted to procure information from Miss Horniman about the plays she had seen.[15]

Although somewhat self-effacing and never a martinet, Payne was soon irked by what he felt was the undue praise AH was receiving: 'Because I was very young for such a responsible position and had no knowledge of life beyond the limited experiences of a touring actor, I could not help resenting the way in which she received all the credit for our artistic activities, although she had no share whatever in them.'[16]

Which seems a trifle overstated, given that whenever she was asked, AH always praised her young director. Georgina Pearce, writing in *The Woman Worker* in June 1909, was adamant:

> I am to be sure and say that praise for the present productions ... the stage management and the acting is entirely due to Mr Iden Payne. 'The papers have, none of them, emphasised that,' complained Miss Horniman. 'I have the initiative force and the capital, but that's all.'[17]

Nevertheless, Payne revealed that very early on in the enterprise, he had taken some advice from Yeats, a man Payne admired immensely:

> I happened one day to be with Yeats in his little London apartment. He asked me what agreement I had signed with Miss Horniman. I had to confess that, with my usual lack of business acumen, I had not given any thought to the matter. He advised me that, when the subject came up, I should make the contract a tight one, laying down definite limits beyond which Miss Horniman should have no authority or right to interfere. 'You know,' Yeats explained, 'she is a vulgarian.' This attitude surprised me greatly for the moment. It did make me speculate, however, that perhaps there might be two sides to the perpetual rows between her and everyone connected with the Abbey Theatre, from the directors to Willie and Frank Fay.[18]

'Vulgarian' was a strong word to use. However, Payne did not contradict him. Instead,

> I took Yeats's advice, and learned to be grateful for it ... I insisted on a contract with Miss Horniman that gave me an almost completely

free hand in the choice of actors and the selection of plays as well as in their method of production. It did not take long to discover how sound Yeats's advice had been. Miss Horniman often attributed her strong principles to her Scotch Presbyterian ancestry. No doubt these principles lent the authority that could make even her most commonplace remark seem impressive – an effect heightened by those medievally inspired costumes of brocaded silk.[19]

Pogson was certainly sure that AH,

adhered scrupulously, in spirit as well as letter, to every detail of any contract she made ... So punctilious was she in avoiding any appearance of interfering in the production side that members of the company in the early years rarely saw her. Payne, in fact, asked her not to attend rehearsals, since the company would flock around her and so be distracted from their work, and she observed this most faithfully. On the rare occasions when she did enter the theatre during rehearsals, she tip-toed, as someone has said, as though she were entering a cathedral during service.[20]

As Muriel Pope told listeners to a radio programme in 1958, 'It was no use going to her with complaints about parts or if you'd had words with the producer. She would never listen.'[21]

AH later commented: 'But while I am owner and manager of a theatre I am not the "producer", a word which often seems to be misunderstood. I keep to my own side of the business but I resolved to learn that thoroughly and to master every detail.'[22]

Basil Dean attributed this surprising meekness to AH's 'masculine' trend. 'This may explain in part the affinity she felt for sensitive minds like W.B. Yeats, and the strong regard, not to say affection, she had for Iden Payne. In the light of modem psychology her later disagreements with Lewis Casson, a more definite and masculine character, become understandable.'[23]

In the new Gaiety Theatre, the producer was king, and for the next four years that king would be Iden Payne ...

Notes

[1] Harold Brighouse, *What I Have Had: Chapters in an Autobiography* (Harrap, 1953).

[2] Dean, *op. cit.*, p39.

[3] Basil Dean, '50 Years of Repertory', ABC Television, 14 September 1958.

4F Haden Smith, 'Memories of a Manchester Playgoer', *Drama* (October 1919), 42–3

[5] James Agate. *Selective Ego: The Diaries of James Agate,* 3, ed. Tim Beaumont (Harrap, 1976), p87.

[6] Pogson, *op. cit.*, p109.

[7] Ibid., p23.

[8] Ibid., p20.

[9] St John Ervine, 'Introduction', in Pogson, *op. cit.*

[10] Pogson, *op cit.*, p14.

[11] Ibid., p15.

[12] Ibid., p76.

[13] Ibid., p92.

[14] Ibid., p108.

[15] Ibid., p109.

[16] Ibid., p92.

[17] *Women Worker*, 23 June 1909.

[18] Iden Payne *op. cit.*, p. 80.

[19] Ibid., p. 92.

[20] Pogson, *op. cit.*, p. 110.

[21] Muriel Pope, BBC interview, 1953

[22] Annie Horniman. 'Woman's Place in the Drama', *Daily Mail*, 18 February 1914.

[23] Dean, *op. cit.*, p. 168.

3

Horniman's Challenge

Miss Horniman will find out more about us from the booking office than from anything we can tell her about our tastes and sympathies ... Who knows whether we may not even develop our own school of dramatists?[1]

There has been an idea that I go out of my way to encourage local talent, but this case is simply a coincidence. I do not mind where the dramatist belongs to, or who he is, so long as his work is good.[2]

IT WAS ALWAYS GOING TO BE the case that the new theatre would mix established works and classics while awaiting the emergence of new writers. In the first Gaiety season at the Midland Hotel, the plays produced included those of French poet and dramatist Edmund Rostand, Belgian playwright Maurice Maeterlinck, Herman Sudermann, Euripides, Beaumont and Fletcher, and Shakespeare. George Bernard Shaw's *Widowers Houses* was also produced (though none of his most popular plays could be afforded) along with works by contemporary playwrights such as George Paston and Sir John Hankin.

Mixing popular classics and those of well-known playwrights with new local drama would continue throughout the theatre's existence. After all, the Gaiety had not been established to produce new drama. Its purpose was, first and foremost, to reproduce the professional standard of production of 'good' plays similar as in continental theatres.

It was also intended to make money, enough to allow it to survive. It was never a philanthropic undertaking. Payne would later write that 'catholicity' had always been the watchword: 'There was no special axe to grind, no particular theory of production or playwriting to be exploited.' and 'It would be a mistake to imagine that the Manchester Theatre in any way specialises in local plays.'[3]

Nonetheless, before the new season started, AH thought it necessary to go give the Manchester public what the *Manchester Evening Chronicle* called a 'nudge'. In a letter circulated to all the Manchester newspapers, she said there still seemed to be some doubts about the aims of her repertory company:

> Rumours of philanthropy and a desire to 'raise the drama' have reached me and I feel that these rumours may cause prejudice to arise. I care for the drama in the same way as many care for painting and so they collect pictures, but the drama is even a wider art, it falls dead unless the public give their aid. So I have bought and redecorated the Gaiety hoping to make a theatre there which will be something for Manchester to be proud of in the future.
>
> Unless I am supported so that it can pay its way my scheme must soon come to an end. The plays will be carefully selected so as to interest intelligent people of different tastes and they will be acted and mounted with all possible care. I hope to bring forward new authors as well as to revive classics, but it depends on the people of Manchester whether or not this can be done.[4]

She later wrote:

> One thing I want to do is to encourage young English playwrights. I want to find English dramatists who will write better than the Irish. We ought to be ashamed of ourselves. If Lancashire playwrights will send their plays to me I shall pledge myself to read them through. Let them write not as one dramatist does, about countesses and

duchesses and society existing in imagination, but about their friends and enemies – about real life.[5]

Iden Payne certainly appeared to have this possibility in mind when he came to Manchester – initially at least. Just before the Midland Theatre season had started in August 1907, Dr Haden Guest in an article advocating the creation of municipal theatres had included the plea that 'We must have our Manchester playwrights as we have our Irish playwrights, and this means our Manchester Managers.'

In reply Payne wrote that he and his 'Manchester manager', Miss Horniman, 'hoped to create our school of Manchester dramatists'. He added: 'In my preliminary announcement of the opening of our company I had expressed the hope that the presence of a repertory theatre would stimulate local authors to write plays.'[6]

As the seasons progressed, new plays did start to arrive. Exactly who chose them, however, is debatable. Despite Payne's assertion that he was in complete control of everything that happened where the artistic side of things was concerned, the comments of both AH and others rather contradict this.

Lewis Casson, who became the director of plays after Payne resigned in 1912, recalled that AH was 'an absolute dictator in the choice of plays'.[7]

Gaiety historian Rex Pogson was in no doubt:

> During the whole of her time in Manchester a good portion of every day was devoted to reading plays submitted. With unflagging enthusiasm she read every one, made a short synopsis of it, whether accepted or rejected, and filed the reference. The stream of plays submitted flowed unchecked, steadily increasing until the outbreak of war in 1914. For long periods the postman was delivering an average of forty manuscripts a week – and received free tickets for the Gaiety as a reward.[8]

AH often spiced her talks to local societies and the press with examples of the types of material that was soon flooding into the Gaiety. She described plays that needed 'swarming bees' and 'children chasing butterflies'; there was a play submitted about Venice in which one character announced that he had just had 'a row with the cab man'...[9]

> Some two or three years ago she had a play sent which she would never forget. It was very thick and was in writing. She looked at the list of characters there were twenty-eight; two armies, a crowd of citizens, and a letter with it which explained that she might consider it was rather long, but a subject like the Monmouth rebellion required a large canvas (laughter) – rather ... It was in nine acts and in verse. She wrote a nice letter back, which she thought would prevent any more such specimens coming. She explained that her company consisted of only twenty-one or twenty-two actors, and she did not think the municipality of Manchester would let her have the loan of Albert Square as an addition to her theatre, by which means alone she could put up the play. The writer did not send it back. (Laughter)[10]
>
> Miss Horniman also pointed out that bad plays came from all sections of society: There was no class that had not sent her plays of different degrees of impossibility. She had had them from cousins of Royalty, she would not mention which country; she had had them from workpeople; and she had had rubbish from the Universities, from ships of war, from factories, from doctors, and from clergy.

To everyone who submitted a play she replied personally, sometimes setting out at length the reasons for rejection. When she felt an author was too insistent or too conceited, her reply was less courteous, as in the case of Marie Stopes; sometimes she gave vent to her feelings in private correspondence, as, 'I need hardly say that Victoria Cross's play was more impossible than even her unspeakable novels.'[11]

One aspiring playwright who much later became a business manager in the theatre, wrote of his own experience:

Iden Payne

Lewis Casson

Basil Dean

(*Author's collection*)

Three important Manchester Gaiety figures.

It was not long before I was sending MSS to Miss Horniman ... Miss Horniman firmly and not always too kindly rejected all my efforts at playwriting. My first one-acter, *Youth Disposes* she said 'failed because I had left out a critical incident in the play which should have (been) made by the entrance of an actor. So yes, she was very helpful in her criticism – there was never a letter she sent me, however terse – and some of them were extremely terse – never a letter without some valuable advice. My second play *The Deliverer* was too short and contained characters which were not sufficiently of the kind to be convincing. Then came *Liddy* which she rejected on the ground that it had a coffin in full view of the audience all the time and coffins she said always unnerved the actors ... [12]

Often her interest in dramatists having their first play produced was almost touchingly maternal. If a new writer could not attend the performance, she would write him at length, telling of the reception and the size of the audiences.

A letter from the playwright H.F. Rubinstein, written after the acceptance of his play *Consequences* in 1914, indicates how her methods were appreciated:

When I sent up my play, my friends assured me I need expect to hear nothing of it for a year or so; when I got your letter (about two weeks later) they warned me you would endeavour to steal all my rights in it; when the almost incredibly generous contract arrived, they sneered at the omission of a date for production and said you would put it off as long as you could. I told them I was dealing with a Christian and they were very annoyed (being brother Semites). Frankly events have exceeded even my most sanguine expectations. I sincerely trust you will get some return for it all in *this* world if not in the other.[13]

As with most things, AH had no doubts as to her ability to assess a play's merits. In 1914, she was interviewed by the *Daily Mail* and she demonstrated her technique.

I asked Miss H if it were easy to gauge quickly the merits or demerits of a play. For answer she took out a script from an envelope that had just arrived and scanned it with what may be paradoxically called 'deliberate quickness'.

'Bad title – too indefinite' were her first remarks. 'Number of characters five. Not too many for a one-act play. Easily staged – good. Idea – good. There may be something in it. It is worth looking at again.'

The manuscript was then laid on one side. In two minutes Miss H had gauged whether it was hopeless or impossible. But this quick judgement was the result of continual practice. The experienced mind of the reader of plays could detect at once any probable chances of acceptance. Only this quick summing up could make possible the task of deciding the fate of close upon two hundred plays a month.[14]

It was this mode of selection that appeared to concern Iden Payne:

> Something else bothered me, less important but bothersome because there was always a shortage of suitable plays for our repertoire. There was one flaw in my contract with Miss Horniman, even though in accordance with Yeats's warning it had been tightly drawn up. This was that there was no proviso against Miss Horniman's reading and passing judgment on plays submitted to her directly. I was aware – indeed she told me so herself – that manuscripts were being sent to her and that she was finding great pleasure in dealing with them personally. It terrified me to think what plays meeting the standard of our avowed principles we might thus be missing.[15]

Exactly how many of the plays that came to make up the Manchester Plays were 'discovered' by AH is impossible to say. Looking at the roster of new playwrights in the first couple of years, it seems unlikely that many, if any, of them submitted work blindly. Harold Brighouse, for instance, recalls

> Miss Horniman chose the plays in agreement with her director. That may in practice have meant the director chose the plays. I sent Payne three one-act plays: *Lonesome-like*, *The Price of Coal* and *The Doorway*. 'Certainly I'll do one of them,' he told me ...[16]

At the same time, however, Brighouse was writing to AH about his plays and their progress:

> I have not heard yet from Mr Payne and I do not propose to trouble him – keen as I am to hear from him – till he sends for me. He must be burdened with business. I've just completed a 3-act play best described perhaps as a 'platform play' – which I hope you will read. Shall I send it to the Gaiety for you? Or is it heartless of me to add to the great pile of manuscripts you showed me there? With very great thanks for your interest in my work.[17]

Brighouse and Payne were old schoolfriends and met at an informal debating club called the Swan Club close by the Gaiety theatre. At least three other men whose work would appear on the Gaiety stage were also members of the club.

Others who found their plays being produced for the first time in the theatre's early years were two prominent Manchester journalists, Manchester's senior County Court judge along with two local doctors prominent in amateur dramatics. All would have had direct access to either AH or Payne without having to rely on a random selection – being plucked from the 'slush-pile' as it were.

One of the first of the new playwrights was Basil Dean, a member of the acting troupe. Dean would give a graphic description of how his first play *Marriages Are Made in Heaven* was selected:

> Inevitably, my first attempt at playwriting was set in the West Country. Typing it out on an old-fashioned Blick typewriter, letter by letter, I had no clear plan for its destiny. However, had not Miss Horniman loudly proclaimed her intention to encourage new English dramatists 'to write better than the Irish'? Indeed, we seldom saw her in the daytime without a bundle of scripts clutched defiantly under her arm as public proof of constancy, as she boarded her daily bus to the Manchester suburb where she lived in modest theatrical lodgings. So there was no harm in my trying. I sent the play to Miss Horniman.

During rehearsal a few days later I noticed her standing at the side of the stage beaming at me. My heart gave a thump. Could this really be – I had scarcely time to say good morning before she burst out:

'I feel very proud! I've just been turned out of the Octagon Court.'

'What on earth for?' I asked.

'Smoking in public,' she said proudly, waving a Turkish cigarette in its long holder in the air. She must have seen that I looked disappointed. So she added quite casually:

'Oh, by the way, I like your little play.'

'Do you really?' I said excitedly.

'H'm, h'm.' She nodded, and walked away.[18]

Notes

[1] Allan Monkhouse, *Manchester Guardian,* 25 July 1907.

[2] Annie Horniman, *Manchester Dispatch*, 26 January 1914.

[3] Iden Payne, 'Introduction', in Brighouse, *Hobson's Choice* (Doubleday, Page and Co. 1916).

[4] *Manchester Evening Chronicle*, 26 July 1907.

[5] Pogson, *op. cit.*, p36.

[6] *New Age*, August 1907).6

[7] Iden Payne, letter to *New Age* (August 1907), 286.

[8] Lewis Casson, Tributes to Annie Horniman, *Manchester Guardian*, 10 August 1937.

[9] Pogson, *op. cit.*, p37.

[10] *Manchester Guardian*, 3 October 1913.

[11] Pogson, *op. cit.*, p37.

[12] James Gregson, 'The Playwright's Progress', *Leeds Mercury*, 11 September 1926.

[13] Pogson, *op. cit.*, p38.

[14] 'A Woman's Place in the Drama', *Daily Mail*, 18 February 1914.

[15] Iden Payne, *op. cit.*, p108.

[16] Brighouse, *What I Have Had*, p52.

[17] Harold Brighouse, letter to Annie Horniman, 27 April 1908, Annie Horniman Papers, John Rylands Library.

[18] Dean, *op. cit.*, p64.

4

The Adventure Begins

Now consider what happened at the Gaiety. By stripping the gold paint and all garish appurtenances and substituting a decor of unrelieved white, the place was made as much like a schoolroom and as little like a theatre as possible.[1]

How well I remember the thrill that the white and red interior gave me. For the first time in my life I had a reserved seat! It was in the gallery and I paid sixpence for it ...[2]

THE NEW GAIETY THEATRE OPENED IN the first week of September1908. It had been an extremely rapid incarnation. Following a swift recruitment of actors during the summer of 1907, the company had put on a season of plays at the small Midland Hotel Theatre between September and November. A tour of the United Kingdom followed starting in January 1908, ending with a couple of weeks in the newly purchased old Gaiety Theatre on Peter Street prior to its refurbishment.

The original Gaiety, constructed in 1878, was said to have been the world's first theatre to use electric lights for the stage. A second incarnation, designed by Alfred Darbyshire for United Theatres Co Ltd, had been built on the same plot of land near to the corner of Peter Street and Mount Street and opened as the Comedy Theatre in 1884. Having been purchased by AH, it closed in June 1908 for a three-month reconstruction overseen by the renowned theatre architect Frank Matcham.

Reopened once again as the Gaiety on Monday 7 September 1908, it had been completely redesigned internally. Gilt had been eliminated, a thing unheard of in theatre decoration at that time, the prevailing tones being white and red. The stage had been relaid but not altered in size, and was framed by mottled marble, whilst the wall space above it had representations in white of old fashioned ships; the Gaiety having adopted a ship as its emblem. The theatrical paper, *The Era*, considered it one of the finest and most novel theatres in the kingdom.[3]

Situated where it was, AH's new venture faced stiff, if somewhat predictable competition from rival theatres no more than a short walk up or down Peter Street (or 'Theatre Street' as it was known in Manchester.) That same month, the prospective theatregoer could have chosen from a variety of popular comedians, comic operas, vaudeville acts, foreign novelties or 'hit' shows transferred from London's West End.

There was the comic opera *Tom Jones* being performed by Mr Robert Courtneidge's company at the Princes Theatre, soon to be followed by Ellaline Terris and Seymour Hicks and the original company of the *Gay Gordons*. The cockney comedian Lew Lake was at the Palace Theatre in *My Pal Jerry*. Lancashire comic George Formby (senior) was appearing twice nightly at the Empire Ardwick Green. At the Hippodrome, Oxford Street there was Madame Hanako, the famous Japanese actress starring in *Otake*, supported by L'Ingognita, the Wonderful (masked) Soprano. At the Tivoli, there was a mixed bill including a troupe of performing cats, 'Mysticus', Grant and Grant, Rita and Roma, and Ruffeil's Bioscope. At the Theatre Royal, Fred Terry was starring in *The Scarlet Pimpernel* soon to be followed by Mr George Alexander and Miss Irene Vanbrugh and the 'complete company and scenery from the

St James Theatre London' in *The Thief,* a popular melodrama.

For those unable to afford a ticket to one or any of these, times were as unsettled and uncomfortable as the wet and windy weather just then sweeping down from the surrounding Pennines. The city of Manchester and its key industries were enduring a trade slump with marches of unemployed men and women a regularly distressing event. There were reports of thousands of hungry people tramping through the city in all stages of poverty and destitution, their clothes in tatters, and watched by large crowds. There was violence: workhouses stormed by rioters, baton charges by police and accusations of police violence.

On top of this, during this month of September, a 'lock-out' occurred of cotton mills in the surrounding towns after a proposed pay cut of 5 per cent was rejected by an overwhelming majority of cotton operatives. Disastrous consequences for the cotton industry were foreseen – in fact, the strike would drag on for months causing great misery. Newspapers would be filled with pictures of idle cotton workers thronging the streets. Suicides were regularly reported amongst the unemployed.

The men and women employed by the Gaiety would not have been unaware of the conditions of the working people they were ostensibly trying to appeal to. As we shall see, many of the actors in AH's company were socialists or so inclined, and spent much of their free time campaigning and proselytising, while the Gaiety itself would become a focus for left-wing-leaning individuals.

For the first night, however, politics would be left at the theatre door, while inside there prevailed 'an excess of enthusiasm, with a section of the audience ready to cheer itself hoarse at the slightest pretext.'[4]

The Lord Mayor's of Manchester and Salford were present and the theatre, said the *Manchester Courier,* 'was filled with a fashionable audience, the beautiful dresses and jewels being shown to great advantage against the artistic decoration'.

Nor was Miss Horniman any less picturesque when she appeared on the stage at the close:

> She presented a striking figure in a handsome gown of deep geranium silk, brocaded in pale shades, girdled with jet. She also wore some fine diamonds and carried a bouquet of flowers, which was one of the many floral tributes presented to her on this occasion.[5]

The curtain rose on the debut one-act play *Marriages Are Made In Heaven* by Basil Dean. In fact, it would be the success of the evening. The critic James Agate commented:

> We very much liked a little drama by Mr Basil Dean called *Marriages Are Made in Heaven*. Briefly a young farmer falls in love with a girl, to discover that she is his father's illegitimate daughter or daughter by an earlier marriage, we did not understand which. He renounces her without explanation. The girl was splendidly played by Miss Louise Holbrook and we thought her appeal to him to go away together a piece of fine emotional acting, technically excellent. This little curtain-raiser, if it were played at a reasonable speed, would be well worth going specially to see, It is at present played much too slowly ...[6]

Other critics were not so sanguine, perhaps puzzled by the essential nature of a one-act play. Wedded to the tradition of rounding everything off and tying up all the ends, some critics found it merely an inconclusive fragment and not a play at all. 'It had arrived at its most interesting stage,' complained the *Daily Mail*, 'when it came to an end, leaving the problem unsolved.'[7]

Dean's career as a playwright would continue intermittently with more one-act plays with West Country themes. *Mother-to-be* would earn him curtain calls a year or so later: 'On the first night I was called twice before the curtain.' In her letter of congratulation Miss H wrote:

> I hope that next time you won't look so anxious when you are called so heartily as you were the other evening. You have done better

already than some who have made big names – so please go ahead bravely ...[8]

Dean's simple tale of a farmer's daughter being courted by two men, with a happy ending, was unremarkable but significant in the history of the Manchester playwrights. One critic said of it:

> It demands not merely the appraisement of the eye or of the emotions raised by superficial incident but a sense of character in the beholder and a psychological appreciation of the author's motive ... the value of the work lies underneath the incidents one sees, though the incidents are of necessity characteristic.[9]

One-act plays similar to Dean's would play a key role in the development of the new realistic drama. In fact, well over fifty one-act plays would be staged at the Gaiety in the first three seasons under Payne's direction, the majority of them by new playwrights, most of them Manchester-based.

One-act Plays are sometimes regarded as a modern product but they were written and staged throughout the 18th and 19th centuries. They were chiefly farcical and served to amuse the audience before the commencement of the actual drama as 'curtain raisers' or were staged for their amusement just after the main event had come to an end.

It was Henrik Ibsen, inevitably, who gave to the one-act play its modern touch. Before Ibsen they had been written as poetry but he made prose the medium, introducing minute stage-directions and making the drama simple and real, bringing it nearer to everyday life.

A one-act play is, in fact, a separate literary form by itself. It is not a condensed three- or five-act play, nor can it be elaborated into a three-act play. The very nature and structure of the two are entirely different. Everything superfluous is to be strictly avoided. The play must be close-knit and the greatest attention must be paid to its structure. This makes it a difficult format and much training and practice is required to master it. It is a highly artistic form and has immense possibilities for development.

Crucially for an aspiring playwright it offered itself as a simple means of perfecting his/her craftsmanship, and, probably more importantly, testing it before an audience. It is far easier to write at length than to compress. The writer who has the ability to do the latter often possesses the ability to do the former and his four-act play is likely to be well written. That some of the best of the longer plays written by the Manchester playwrights were the work of men who achieved distinction in the one-act form is no coincidence.

Just as with the development of the 'ensemble' acting, it was the Abbey Theatre and its writers that had led the way in transforming the one-act play into a serious endeavour. Synge's *Riders to the Sea*, Lady Gregory's *Spreading the News* and Yeats' *The Land of Heart's Desire* were both popular and serious. Although their work could hardly be called 'realistic', yet in terms of form and structure they set standards that those submitting work to the Gaiety would attempt to emulate.

Though none of the Irish plays would be produced at the Gaiety, it's significant that Iden Payne produced the classic one-act play *Interior* by Maeterlinck at both the Abbey and the Gaiety, and considered the latter production more of a success.

In *Interior* the audience sees a brightly lit domestic room being invaded by death. In the foreground of the stage are people who have come to tell a family of the death of the daughter. In the background are windows through which the members of the family – played by miming actors – are visible. In short, the play focuses on what can only be termed a chorus downstage, commenting on the real drama taking place on the stage-within-a-stage. The chorus, which consists of a stranger, an old man, and his two daughters, are racing against time trying to get up enough courage to tell the family of the news before the procession of villagers arrives bearing the corpse of the daughter who has drowned. The audience sees tragedy poised on the outside, waiting to descend on the people inside – the distance at which they are set from the audience in the scenic concept dispels any anticlimax.

Payne later wrote of the production:

> This was a new and exciting experience because the actors were much more responsive than those in Dublin ... For the first time I was conscious of an almost mystical sense that there was a relationship, in a creative harmony throughout the performance among all the elements involved, including even the absent author. I became aware that there was more in the direction of a play than I had ever dreamed.[10]

The first full-length play produced on that first night at the new Gaiety, however, was not by a local author, although he was relatively new to the British stage. *When The Devil Was Ill* was written by Charles McEvoy, a Londoner whose first major play, *David Ballard*, had caught the eye of Payne when staged in London. According to Payne, McEvoy

> ... effectively struck what was then a new note in the theatre – the realistic depiction of life in an average lower-middle-class family. I had seen the play with Yeats at its only previous performance, a matinee given by the Stage Society. He was as enthusiastic about it as I was.[11]

Payne considered that *David Ballard* 'fulfilled our demands for sincerity and simplicity in realistic modern drama, but also because the parts were particularly well fitted to the actors I was in the process of engaging', and he produced it at the Midland to some acclaim. McEvoy was thus asked to provide another new play for the grand opening occasion.

When the Devil was Ill, first tried out by the company at Carlisle on 29 August and received there with great enthusiasm, was apparently a satire on the 'Back to Nature' cult based, it was said, on McEvoy's rustic experiences in Wiltshire.

> McEvoy was an extraordinary character, in physical appearance more of a caricature than a normal person. His long, twisted face, with bulbous eyes and tiny chin beard, was like a note of interrogation. Possessed of a ferocious Cockney accent and a great sense of humour, he lived in a caravan and boasted his knowledge and love of the nomadic life. His appearance at rehearsal in corduroys complete with moleskin waistcoat and a red handkerchief tied round his neck was decidedly outré in those days ... [12]

Secretly, Yeats suspected that McEvoy wasn't quite as good as he was cracked up to be. He wrote to a friend: 'Miss Horniman is starting in Manchester ... with that play of Cockney life by MacEvoy the Stage Society brought out a while back. I don't know what else she has but she claims to have lots of plays – they must be pretty bad if she has.'[13]

Yeats was right. The *Daily Dispatch* thought the new play, 'thin and colourless' but the *Evening Chronicle,* on the other hand, applauded Miss Horniman 'for making good her promise not to bore us with too many serious problem plays'. The view of the *Courier* was that the dialogue, though often witty and occasionally elegant, gave 'an intolerable deal of talk to a poor penn'orth of incident' and suggested that McEvoy, like the proverbial Scotsman, joked with difficulty. Agate in the *Guardian* concluded, 'We thought the loud and prolonged applause at the end of the play intended as a sign of friendliness to Miss Horniman rather than a mark of appreciation of a tedious play.'[14]

While McEvoy's influence would be important in terms of the realism he managed in *David Ballard,* he would be a wrong turning for the Gaiety, and his plays would soon take a back seat. Writers much closer to home were now appearing on the scene and their work would soon become the staple diet of the new Gaiety.

Notes

[1]Agate, *op. cit.*

[2]Gregson, *op cit*

[3]*The Era*, 'The New Gaiety', 12 September 1908.

[4]*The Era*, 8 September 1908.

[5]Pogson, *op. cit.,* p53.

[6]*Manchester Guardian*, 8September 1908.

[7]Pogson, *op. cit.*, p53.

[8]Dean, *op. cit.*, p65.

[9]*The Era*, 7 February 1910.

[10]Iden Payne, *op. cit.*, p82.

[11]Ibid., p81.

[12]Dean, *op. cit.*, p51.

[13]W.B. Yeats, in *Florence Farr, Bernard Shaw, W.B.Yeats: Letters*, ed Clifford Bax (Home and Thal, 1946), p60.

[14]*Manchester Guardian*, 8 September 1908.

5

Judge Parry and the Swan Club

Think of the Manchester School of dramatists. When the continental countries saw plays written in time stolen from the floor of the Exchanges or from office desks they began to think about Manchester and ask what it stood for ...[1]

The idea that we are going to get a new race of playwrights is illusive – it will never happen.[2]

THE GAIETY COMPANY NOW SETTLED INTO a rhythm of rehearsing a set of plays that they would alternate weekly or even fortnightly along with the cast, and then reviving the most notable from time to time. This, combined with short tours away from Manchester, eased the burden on the actors and at the same time ensured the creation of a body of plays that could be revived at short notice. This was not exactly 'repertory' as understood in its purest form, that is, changing the 'bill' as often as two or three times a week which was considered financially impracticable.

In the first two seasons of AH's new Gaiety Theatre (1908-1911), ten new authors and fifteen new plays would be introduced. The stage-writing careers of Allan Monkhouse, Stanley Houghton, Harold Brighouse, Gertrude Robins, Harry Richardson and J. Sackville Martin would all be all launched. Others would follow in subsequent years.

That this loose collection of writers could be classified as a 'school', as such, with a common set of principles and a literary philosophy is clearly a misnomer. Harold Brighouse would write many years later, 'The "Manchester School" was never conscious of itself, as the Irish School was ... In Manchester, so far were we from any explicit ambition to create a Lancashire Drama, that we denied the fact of its creation.'[3]

It was certainly the case that the new plays appearing on the Gaiety stage were in no way revolutionary in technique or presentation. They didn't deviate greatly from accepted theatrical forms. The influences were generally realistic or poetic: Ibsen, John Galsworthy and the Irish 'School' were their models.

In 1907 the dominant theatrical form was a kind of social realism or naturalism, whether a drawing room or a scullery being the scene of the action. The flamboyant drama critic James Agate, who was drama critic at the *Manchester Guardian* during these years, described them thus: 'Time after time the curtain would go up on a Welsh dresser and a kitchen table with Sybil (Thorndike) weeping in frustration. Sometimes the dresser would be to the left, sometimes to the right. But the table and Sybil were constant.'[4]

They were certainly not representative of what was being slowly forged abroad by groups like the Ballets Russes, the Futurists in Italy and Russia, the Expressionists in Germany and the Moscow Arts Theatre. The prevailing conservation of the theatre-going public was summed up by a citizen who wrote to the *Manchester Courier* saying, 'We have no room either for post-impressionism or futurism in drama in Manchester.'[5]

Charles McEvoy, in a lecture to the Manchester Playgoers' Club, 'disclaimed the term "new" in the modern drama, and contended there might be something of a renaissance, but there was nothing of a novelty.'[6]

Iden Payne echoed those sentiments in a speech to the Liverpool Playgoers' Society in which he said he took exception to the description 'new drama', as applied to the works of promising modern playwrights. 'It was no more new than any other art which was healthy and vital and was an expression of real life, and it should be rather called 'a renascence of sincere drama'.[7]

What the new dramatists at the Gaiety did share, however, was a common background. As Laurence Du Garde Peach, a Manchester playwright himself, observed they were a mix of lawyers, doctors, commercial men in Manchester's cotton and rag-trade, academics and clerks – generally middle-class and professional.

Most had been to 'good' schools – Manchester Grammar School featured heavily and some to University. This should not be a surprise. In the first year of the 20th century working-class writers were rare. While there was certainly a growing working-class prose literature, it did not feature at all in mainstream theatre.

It's also the case that some of the 'new' dramatists were not that new. The Gaiety drew at first on a theatrical tradition that had been thriving in the decade before AH arrived, a perfect example being Edward Abbott Parry (hereafter Judge Parry).

Judge Parry was a Londoner, the son of a celebrated lawyer and educated at King's College School. He was called to the Bar by the Middle Temple at the age of 21 and after only ten years of practice was appointed County Court judge at Manchester. In the subsequent decade Judge Parry spent in the city, he would become a celebrated 'character', witty, erudite, a popular after-dinner speaker and prolific writer on the law.

Parry was a liberal and felt that justice was, above all, a public utility. He was convinced that the law was hard on the poor, imprisonment for debt being one of the favourite objects of his invective. In 1914 he published *The Law and the Poor*, a guide for 'the man in the street,' which began as a series of popular, easy-to-read newspaper articles and outlined the laws concerning insolvency, debt and poverty.

He was also a creative writer and during his Manchester period he wrote a series of children's books: *Katawampus* (1895), *Butter Scotia* (1897), *The First Book of Krab* (1897) and *Pater's Book of Rhymes* (1901).

In the theatre, too, he was very busy. A dramatic version of *Katawampus* was performed as a Christmas play at the Prince of Wales Theatre, London in 1901 and later on became popular as a Christmas play at the Gaiety in Manchester.

In 1903 he collaborated with Mr Fred Mouillot in a farcical comedy, *What the Butler Saw*, which was produced successfully at Wyndham's Theatre and which continued to be a favourite play on tour for many years.

Parry also became a leading light in Manchester's Independent Theatre Society, which between 1893 and 1898 periodically produced plays in the Gentlemen's Concert Hall before it was demolished to make way for the Midland Hotel. The Society produced three Shakespearian revivals: *Love's Labour's Lost, The Two Gentlemen of Verona*, and *Richard II*; five Ibsen plays: *A Doll's House, The Master Builder, An Enemy of the People, Rosmersholm* and *Hedda Gabler*; Shaw's *Candida*, Goethe's *Clavigo*, Browning's *Blot on the Scutcheon* and George Moore's *The Strike at Arlinford*. Apart from two of the Shakespeare plays none of these had previously been seen in Manchester.

When AH arrived, therefore, Judge Parry was one of those to welcome her and encourage her. His support, however, was heavily qualified.

Parry saw himself as one of the 'old school' and appeared scornful of anything new: In December 1907 at a meeting of the Manchester Playgoers Club in the Grand Hotel, he criticised the press, the *Manchester Guardian* in particular, for its tendency to 'sneer and

gibe at men like (Beerbohm) Tree and Bourchier and H.B. Irving
and men belonging to the mid or later Victorian day ... He would
say nothing against the 'new movement' but he didn't like it.'[8]

In 1908 at the Playgoers Club at the Grand Hotel, Manchester,
Parry debated the issue of dramatic criticism with Allan
Monkhouse, then a prominent drama critic at the *Guardian* and
a future Manchester playwright. Parry's theme was, once again,
that the *Guardian* critics didn't have a clue about plays or players:
'My quarrel with Mr Monkhouse – if it really is an argument – is
that these (dramatic) criticisms are too much written by too many
clever people who really don't know very much about the stage
and who have a thorough contempt for the acting profession
(No!)'[9]

Despite welcoming the Gaiety and Miss Horniman, Parry
seemed to resent anything that went against his own definition of
what drama should be: principally that it should never
'demoralize.' He offered little encouragement to anyone whose
opinions clashed with his own: repertory theatre, he asserted, led
audiences to feel, 'depressed with the abjectness of human nature
and with a cold feeling that the world was a drab uncomfortable
place. But the ancient dramatic stories always have a happy
ending.'

It's no surprise therefore that, apart from his very popular
children's plays and pantomimes, his attempts to deal with more
difficult themes were always laced with sugar. In 1910 he wrote a
short play for the Gaiety called *The Tallyman*, which purported to
deal with 'The nauseous and parasitic trade of the itinerant draper
... the credit business, whereby door-to-door salesmen sold goods
to unsuspecting folk, often women at home, which resulted in their
being taken to court regarding debts.'[9]

As a judge, Parry was concerned that imprisonment for debt
was a scandal and that many poor people suffered unnecessarily

due to unscrupulous 'tricksters'. He wrote:

> The tally-men, the moneylenders, the flash jewellery touts, the sellers
> of costly Bibles in series, of gramophones and other luxuries of the
> mean streets, these are the knaves the State caters for. For these
> businesses are based, and soundly and commercially based, on
> imprisonment for debt. The game is to go forth with a lot of flash
> watches, persuade a workman in a public-house or elsewhere to
> sign a paper that he has bought – one he always says, silly fellow,
> that he thought he had it on approval – and when he fails to pay his
> instalments put him in the County Court. I have known a pigeon-
> flying working man earning thirty-five shillings a week buy a watch
> priced eight pounds which had a second hand and a stop movement
> for timing that momentarily overcame his better sense of economy.
> Without imprisonment for debt it would not have paid the servant
> of the Evil One to have led him into the temptation.[11]

It seemed a fit subject for a gripping drama but the *Manchester
Guardian* critic G.H. Mair summed up *The Tallyman* thus: 'Judge
Parry, by winding up sentimentally, shrank from the full
consequences of the situation – the attack was not pressed home.
The bitter pill was coated with sugar ...'[12]

The Tallyman had a simple enough plot. Joe McIntyre, a
sturdy, honest, unimaginative engine driver worships his 'doll-
like' wife and has enthroned her as a goddess in his home. She
dresses nicely, adorns the house and so he is happy. A
washerwoman does the household chores while the wife reads
romances. But she falls victim to the Tallyman, buying dresses,
watches and fans but not having the wherewithal to pay for them.
She tries to tell the husband that she has run up considerable
debts but he doesn't believe her. The Tallyman then reappears
and tries to seduce her. The husband returns home just in time
and throws the Tallyman out ('the outburst of fury comes as a
relief') with a parting retort: 'Out you go into the gutter, that's
your place.'

The play was a popular success and well reviewed and caused sufficient outrage amongst the credit drapers of Manchester for the *Manchester City News* to run a series of letters and articles under the heading 'Is Judge Parry Right?'[13]

Various credit drapers complained that the audience had taken for granted Parry's 'unrelieved picture of cunning and cruelty', and considered the play, 'a cruel, unworthy and unjust libel'. There were, a correspondent pointed out, many honest credit drapers, 'who never see a courtroom, their businesses being proper and regular and often handed down from father to son.'[14]

Parry responded by suggesting that, 'The play is so good and so wonderfully acted that I wonder if the friendly but indignant drapers have really seen it.' Much worse happened in real life, he claimed, but, because it is a play ('and *The Tallyman* is going to be popular') 'the thing becomes really dangerous to those who wish to leave things as they are ...'[15]

The *Manchester City News* then announced it would be sending a representative out with one of the letter-writers, 'to report his experiences faithfully ... '

Another of Parry's 'realistic' plays, *Charlotte on Bigamy* dealt with 'the cheapening of divorce'. Harold Brighouse called it 'a genial piece of propaganda ... with a happy ending slightly blurring the sharpness of the moral'.

However, he added, 'We thought the preliminaries dragged a little and the arm of coincidence badly strained.'[16] Judge Parry would not have welcomed such criticism.

He most certainly would have objected to a review of his favourite children's pantomime, *Katawampus*, another popular Gaiety success, lavishly staged by Iden Payne. The reviewer was Stanley Houghton and his comments might have been taken as damning the play with faint praise:

Katawampus, Houghton wrote, was, 'full of whimsical touches and pleasant wit', although '... the clever ideas are not elaborated so ingeniously as they might be ... ' Aspects of the plot were not explained clearly enough and 'themes are started nicely but not followed through ...'

After placing the play in the same bracket as classics such as *Peter Pan* and *Alice In Wonderland*, Houghton added, 'What one does not find in *Katawampus* is any touch of real beauty or imagination.' There was 'none of the simple poetry of Hans Andersen, the deep emotion of Maeterlinck's *The Blue Bird* or the genuine if underlined sentiment of Peter Pan ... '

He concluded with this small barb: 'However, though one may not agree exactly with Judge Parry's recently published opinion that *Katawampus* is a masterpiece, one can safely say it is a very charming entertainment and a very original one.'[17]

It's probably no wonder that Parry would later attack the *Guardian* in his autobiography, asserting that,

> It was people of this type who ruined Manchester as a playgoer's centre and ultimately spoilt Miss Horniman's plucky experiment by clamouring for the drab in drama and crabbing anything with the joy of theatre in it. They were a small but sturdy clique who had a certain influence in the press. Some members of this clique were both critics and dramatists and so they could 'oil each other's little heads with mutual flattery's golden slime.[18]

Parry left Manchester in 1911 when he was transferred to Lambeth County Court. In 1917 and 1918 he served as Industrial Unrest Commissioner for the Northwestern Area and president of the Pensions Appeal Tribunal. He retired from public life in 1927, partly because of deafness, an affliction traceable to the injury he received when a man armed with a revolver in his Manchester court wounded him. On his retirement in 1927 his public services were recognised with a knighthood.

Parry was a representative of Manchester's past where drama

was concerned. A more contemporary manifestation would be a self-selected band of individuals who around 1907 came together to form the Swan Club. It would have been from the Club's ranks that some of Parry's 'small but sturdy clique' was drawn, counting as it did among its members the *Guardian* reviewers Stanley Houghton and Harold Brighouse.

The actor Basil Dean remembered the club well:

> For some time there had existed a caucus of young businessmen who used to meet informally in the lunch hour in one of the domino-infested cafes off Market Street, there to argue contumaciously about matters of public interest. As membership increased a room was reserved for regular lunchtime meetings at the Swan Inn, next door to the theatre and opposite the Theatre Royal. Thereafter, the group nicknamed themselves the Swan Club. There were no rules, no subscriptions and no credentials beyond an ability to speak one's mind and to be ready for instant contradiction; it was a catalyst of lively intelligence playing upon a variety of interests.[19]

Harold Brighouse described the Swans as

> ... a good group. From the first and by sheer chance it gathered together most of the Manchester men who, before the 1914 War, were, or were to be, creative artists.

However, while acknowledging that it had become a 'legend', Brighouse was adamant that it was no literary forcing house:

> The fabulist who printed that '*Hindle Wakes* and *Hobson's Choice* were read in manuscript by their authors' was sharply corrected by 'had anyone dared to do this he would have been pelted with dinner-rolls or had a napkin stuffed down his throat.' It was simply a luncheon club, casually but fortunately assembled, meeting first in an upstairs room of the Swan public-house in a bystreet off Market Street, later and longer in a public-house room opposite the Theatre Royal, handy for the Gaiety Theatre, from which Iden Payne, Basil Dean, and Esme Percy occasionally dropped in.[20]

Milton Rosmer and Irene Rooke, principal actors for the Gaiety,
starring in Harold Brighouse's *Dealing In Futures* (1910)
(Author's collection)

It was certainly an eclectic bunch that gathered together to discuss the latest Hallé orchestra performance, the various political issues just then thundering across the Edwardian scene, not to mention the latest pretty actress to grace the Gaiety stage.

Among the regulars was the poet and Manchester stockbroker's son C.M. Abercrombie; Haslam Mills and Herbert Sidebotham, journalists on the *Manchester Guardian*; Alfred Barker and Julius Harrison both members of the Hallé Orchestra; Walter Mudie of Mudie's Libraries; Tinsley Pratt of the Manchester Library; W.P. Price-Heywood, a bank accountant and political activist; Felix Berlyn, Harry Bamber and H.C. Hirschorn, all young businessmen dealing in cotton and tobacco.

While it's true that the Club appeared to be more of a debating society than anything else, and that classical music played a big part in drawing them together, it's significant that literature of various kinds was a principal thread binding many of them together. It's also of interest in that one can see the effect the Gaiety had on a section of Manchester's 'better-educated' youth. While Houghton and Brighouse would write plays of great significance, a number of other Swan Club members would also try their hand.

Bank clerk Charles Forrest wrote a one-act play called *The Shepherd* which Stanley Houghton persuaded the Gaiety management to mount in October 1912. It was reviewed by C.E. Montague in the *Guardian*, who detected in it a variety of influences from Synge, Hardy, Kipling and John Masefield and suggested that Forrest's writing, 'might yet acquire a fine character of its own'.[21]

Forrest, who came from East Anglia, later wrote several novels, notably *All Fools Together,* a village tale, modern or timeless, 'with a flavour of Ben Jonson'. He would also complete the novelisation of Brighouse's *Hobson's Choice.*

There was also Jack Kahane, the man most responsible for creating the 'legend' of the Swans. Brighouse, one of Kahane's best and most enduring of friends, wrote:

> At the Swan Club we watched Kahane grow unstoppably from wonderful boy into a man doing his considerable best to live, in Manchester, like a Regency buck. The American Bar at the Midland Hotel had expensive possibilities. But the Regency had virtuosity. Kahane read the old poets and kept up with the new, acclaimed Balzac and Henry James, educated himself in music, wrote two plays and persuaded Sherratt and Hughes to publish them. He was a talented salesman and lived by selling cotton velvets.[22]

Kahane would later find fame as the publisher of Henry Miller's work, not to mention James Joyce and William Burroughs.

Meanwhile, his one-act play, *The Master*, appeared on the Gaiety stage on 27 November 1913 as a curtain-raiser for Harry Richardson's *The Awakening Woman* and managed just one performance. Set in a fisherman's cottage, it was about a wife who considers leaving her husband (who is obsessed with fishing) for her old lover. However, when the husband returns home, his boat shattered, she decides to stay with him ... 'his piece has a tragic quality and imagination keeps always the better of sentiment ... '[23]

More substantial in terms of impact was businessman Michael Arabian. Born in 1876 in Crete, an Armenian who became a naturalised Englishman in 1897, he worked as a buying agent for a Romanian firm that shipped prints. He was elected to the Manchester Chamber of Commerce in 1906, the same year in which he appeared at the Midland Hotel Theatre in a French farce, *L'Héroïque Le Cadunois* by Alexandre Bisson.

His three act 'tragedy' was called *Trespassers Will Be Prosecuted* and was produced at the Gaiety on 26 April 1909. A young woman, Christophere, rushes into an ill-advised marriage with a rich man in order to escape the anguish of not being able to marry the man she actually loves, Oscar, who is already married. Christophere then elopes with a third man in order to escape from her unhappy first marriage, only to discover that Oscar's wife has died. She is about to return to her first husband, when Oscar comes to her rescue, and the play ends happily with Oscar and Christophere together.

The story, according to C.E. Montague, who reviewed it for the *Guardian*, was about the difficult choices that confront, or may confront, a woman of moral integrity and originality in a meanly imitative society, a story told 'in every mood from Boccaceio's impish glee to Mr Hardy's deep pity'.

Christophere was an intelligent woman conflicted by society's demands, and although he felt Arabian's treatment of the theme, 'a little naïve' it was deeply moving, a triumph of intelligence and one of the 'latest of a series of artistic triumphs ... ' for the Gaiety.[24]

Arabian would go on to write, novels, film-scripts and plays during the inter-war period. *Trespassers will be Prosecuted* would not be repeated, however.

Apart from Houghton and Brighouse, however, the most significant of the Swan Club members in terms of drama was probably Ernest Marriott. Brighouse considered Marriott the most talented of the group:

> He was librarian to the Portico Library, an unexacting job. He had studied under Walter Crane, and he was, perhaps, feeling his way towards something. But to what? He painted in Wales, Arran, and Italy, illustrated an edition of *Don Quixote,* got into *Punch,* wrote a monograph on the toy theatre of Jack B. Yeats, wrote verse both serious and whimsical for children. All this, if rich in promise, was the achievement of a dilettante.[25]

Marriott met Gordon Craig, the theatrical director and innovative scenic designer who was preparing an exhibition in Manchester's Art Gallery. Craig employed him as business manager at Craig's School of the Theatre in Florence. Discovering in himself a talent for stage-design, Marriott went on to plan and execute settings and lighting for exhibitions in Warsaw, Zurich, Budapest and Cologne. He would die early, however, of heart failure in 1918.

It's perhaps ironic that the individual who made no attempt to write a play was the only one closely involved with what could be termed 'advanced' theatre, something that, along with Gordon Craig himself, AH abhorred.

Caricatures by Marriott of all fourteen members of the Swan Club hung for a time on the walls of its room. He also designed a Swan emblem that was used on the title pages of a few of the Manchester playwrights' plays, but it was soon dropped.

Notes

[1] *Manchester Guardian*, 6 October 1933.

[2] *Manchester Guardian*, 23 January 1907.

[3] Harold Brighouse, 'Introduction', in *Three Lancashire Plays* (Samuel French, 1920), pp11-12.

[4] James Agate, EGO (1937).

[5] *Manchester Courier*, 10 September 1912.

[6] *Manchester Courier*, 18 March 1909.

[7] *Liverpool Post and Mercury*, 2 July 1909.

[8] *Manchester Guardian*, 5 December 1907.

[9] Ibid., 23 January 1908.

[10] Edward Parry, *The Law and the Poor* (Smith, Elder and Co., 1914).

[11] Parry, *op. cit.*

[12] *Manchester Guardian* review, 1 March 1910.

[13] *Manchester City News*, 12 and 19 March 1910.

[14] Ibid., 12 March 1910.

[15] *Manchester City News*, 19 March 1910.

[16] *Manchester Guardian*, 29 September 1914.

[17] Ibid., 26 December 1910.

[18] Edward Parry, *My Own Way* (Cassell, 1932), p235.

[19] Dean, *op. cit.*, p66.

[20] Brighouse, *op. cit.*, p40.

[21] *Manchester Guardian*, October 1912.

[22] Brighouse, *op. cit.*, p44

[23] *Manchester Guardian*, 27 August 1913.

[24] *Manchester Guardian*, 27 April 1909.

[25] Brighouse, *op. cit.*, p45.

6

Doctors in the House

I see no objection to an ash pit. An ash pit is an excellent sanitary thing, but I would not put it in front of the footlights as part of the mise en scene (Laughter) ... Equally so, the outpatients department has its excellences but personally I would not go for the themes of drama to the outpatients department ...[1]

The truth is we hardly feel that Miss Horniman and her advisers demand from our northern authors that high standard of achievement that they are as justly entitled to receive as these are competent to give ...[2]

PARRY'S COMMENTS ON SETTING DRAMA IN the 'outpatients department' were oddly prescient. The first of the genuinely 'Manchester' playwrights to be featured at the Gaiety was, in fact, a doctor, James Sackville Martin. Like Judge Parry, he was a cultured individual whose interest in drama preceded the formation of the Gaiety and who was more than ready and willing to supply it with new writing.

Martin was not, however, a Manchester man. He was the son of a popular and well-respected doctor from Sheffield, Dr John Wise Martin, lecturer in midwifery and diseases of women in the Sheffield School of Medicine. James graduated in Edinburgh in 1895, trained

SATURDAY, NOVEMBER 20, 1909.

THEATRE ROYAL, PRESTON.

RETURN VISIT TO PRESTON, COMMENCING
MONDAY, NOVEMBER 22nd, FOR SEVEN PERFORMANCES ONLY, OF

MISS HORNIMAN'S COMPANY.

UNDER THE DIRECTION OF B. IDEN PAYNE.

OF THE GAIETY THEATRE, MANCHESTER.

THE FIRST REPERTORY THEATRE IN GREAT BRITAIN.

MONDAY, TUESDAY, WEDNESDAY, THURSDAY, AND SATURDAY EVENING,
"CUPID AND THE STYX,"
By J. SACKVILLE MARTIN.

THURSDAY MATINEE AND FRIDAY EVENING,
"CANDIDA,"
By BERNARD SHAW.

"The admirable detail in the stage management and finished style of the
acting should earn a new reputation for the Company in London."—TIMES

PRICES OF ADMISSION: Ordinary Door (after 7.15)—Boxes, 15s.; Single Seats, 4s.; Dress Circle, 2/6;
Orchestra Stalls, 1/-; Balcony Gate Upper Circles, 1/0; Pit Stalls, 1/-; Pit, 6d.; Gallery, 6d.
Box Office at the Theatre, Hours 10 to 4 and 6 to 9.   Telephone 291.

(1909 Gaiety Theatre on tour)

as a doctor, worked in Sheffield and Edinburgh Royal Infirmaries,
then the Rotherham Hospital before a stint as a ship's surgeon. He
came to Leigh in 1899 and apart from his main job in industrial
general practice was soon a key member of the Leigh Literary
Society.

Founded in 1877 the Literary Society was a cultural hub: it hosted
lectures and talks on all subjects ranging from science, mechanics,
religion, travel to literature and drama. Oxford University Extension
Lectures were also held there.

Martin himself was a regular society speaker and considered an
authority on dramatic matters. In February 1905, he gave a talk to
the society on 'The Modern Stage', in which he opined that he
didn't consider modern plays and playwrights to be of the same
quality of those of the 16th century. 'He deplored the fact that a

more intellectual class of stage productions was not demanded and appreciated in the district.'[3]

He became President of the Society in 1906, and in October that year gave a talk on Robert Browning's poetry. In March 1907 he directed Shaw's *Arms and the Man* and in November 1909 gave a talk on the 'New School of Irish Comedy' combined with readings in the Irish idiom and brogue ('given with faultless diction') of Lady Gregory and John Millington Synge. In October 1911 he gave a talk on Henrik Ibsen's *Peer Gynt*.

Like Judge Parry, Martin was a liberal-minded man working in close contact with working-class folk and acutely aware of their practical dilemmas. Lecturing at Ancoats he talked of helping poor people and how difficult it was for them to pay his medical bills. (He once attended a man for six weeks who was dying of consumption and when he sent in his bill for 25s the man's wife declared she would pay him, 'if it took her 25 years ... ')[4]

But Martin chose not to write about such matters. In fact, he seemed intent on satirising movements and societies set up to alleviate those conditions.

His first play was *A Question of Property*, and was produced at Margate in 31 January 1908. It was described as a 'clever, smart skit' on socialism with a good deal of local colour.[5] A local mill-worker, Comrade Weaver is sacked because of his socialist principles. He is congratulated on his sacrifice by another 'comrade' (called Markland and presumably a Union official) but criticised by his wife ('a typical Lancashire woman, with sharp pinched nose, and her hair in curl-pins and with a shawl around her shoulders'). Weaver's Uncle John, a miner and rent-collector, arrives to tell him he's left his row of cottages to him if Weaver gets his job back. Weaver rejects the offer with scorn; the Uncle leaves to go and change his will, but is killed in an accident before he can do so. Weaver immediately repudiates his 'martyrdom' and goes off to buy special funeral clothes.

Reviewed in the *Manchester Guardian* in October 1908, James Agate commented, 'Mr Martin has dropped into Socialism from a world where it is apparently not taken seriously and he has learned it very badly ... However, it is at least an amusing travesty with some shrewd things in it.'[6]

The play was some 25 minutes long and, interestingly, written largely in Lancashire dialect which the Gaiety actors apparently couldn't handle at all well. When it was produced in Leigh in April 1909 the *Leigh Chronicle* reviewer considered it superior to when at Gaiety: 'The local amateurs had the advantage of being coached by the author and they were also able to give the Lancashire dialect in its rich purity ... that is with the correct 'burr' and breadth.' Comrade Markland had 'the lurching clumsy gait of the typical loafer' and the play appeared to have had a much better reception than when performed in Manchester.

The first of Martin's plays actually produced on the Gaiety stage was *Woman's Rights* on 21 September 1908 (and the first of the Manchester School's to be featured) it had already been given a try-out during one of the company's 'flying matinees' at Rochdale in April.

C.E. Montague thought that the ostensible subject matter of the title had hardly been considered at all. A young woman scandalises her family by causing a fuss at a public meeting, but a gallant young doctor saves her ruined marriage prospects at the last. 'Of course, in all this, the ironic possibilities of the subject are not very deeply explored but the study of one comedy-laden subject – the feeling of vulgar people that all agitation by women for women (and not merely 'ragging' at meetings) is vulgar – is quite good as far as it goes ...'[7]

Martin would follow this up with a decidedly comic piece called *Cupid and the Styx*, which would for a time be the most popular of the new School's productions. The play drew heavily upon Martin's knowledge of the intrigues and characters that populate hospitals, although without a copy of the text, it's hard to assess. It certainly became a favourite with the Gaiety audience, however, Stanley Houghton calling it a 'jolly little comedy'.

Allen Monkhouse was less appreciative, deciding that the play, 'suffers from the inevitable weakness of alternated interests which do little or nothing to support one another'. He also felt that the audience laughed when something serious was happening, in particular, a would-be suicide. Though 'most of it not intended to bite very deeply and though we might appreciate this opportunity to learn how the work of a hospital goes on, the appearance of a would-be-suicide seems to cloud the issue.'[8]

When the play was taken to London, one reviewer felt it was, 'built on hardness, even brutality':

> If it had been downright farce there would not have been a word to say; for farce is a deliberate perversion of life. Comedy is a faithful picture of it and nearly all these people are too hard for comedy – the hard scheming baggage of a hospital nurse who carries on with both the house-surgeons (good if stupid fellows both) and finally nobbles the consulting surgeon; the consulting physician (who might have been developed into a true comic figure but is left an empty jest); the porter who wants to be recommended for the vacant post of public hangman; the bank clerk with an 'artistic temperament' who takes poison just to score off the wife who laughed at his tantrums but being afraid enough to take enough for a fatal dose is restored by a stomach-pump.[9]

In fact, the characters sound as though they might have stepped out of a *Carry on Doctor* film as the play did give all three of the Gaiety's female actresses a chance to shine, Sybil Thorndike, Edyth Goodall and Miss Darragh taking it in turns to play the 'scheming baggage' of a nurse and charm every male critic.

By the time Martin's short *Purse of Gold* appeared in May 1910, however, his star was on the wane. *Purse of Gold* told of a solicitor who gets up a purse of sovereigns for a poor clerk whose ill-health has driven him from his job only to then induce the poor man to use the money to pay off a debt to the solicitor. G.H. Mair wrote, 'we feel entitled to some-thing little less trivial and more solid from his pen ...'

Mair took the opportunity in his review to bemoan the fact that plays like Martin's *Purse of Gold* along with Parry's *The Tallyman* and Arabian's *Trespassers Will Be Prosecuted* wasted the chance to utilise Lancashire and its environs. 'Round us is the throb and hum of a society ceaselessly occupied in industry and business but the rattle of the looms and the clamour of the life around them wakes no echoes or only a few in our artist's hands ...'[10]

Almost simultaneously, Mair got what he had asked for. Another doctor, also from Leigh, weighed in with a play called *Subsidence* that couldn't have been more a product of its northern environment.

Doctor Frederick Wynn was a colleague of Martin's, being the Medical Officer for the Borough of Leigh. He was older, and had also been president of the Leigh Literary Society in 1902. He'd come to Leigh some six years previously and had been struck by the contrasting views to hand from the railway carriage. In 1902 he gave a long talk to the Leigh Literary Society accompanied by slides entitled, 'The Picturesque Aspect of Leigh' in which he noted the depressing effect of squalid buildings: 'It seemed to me an endless line leading to an infinity of galling monotony sufficient to crush the souls out of a whole community.' At the same time he had glimpsed 'the essential beauty of collieries' and been 'heartened by the sight of Platt Fold Farm'. It was all about looking and seeing 'beauty in form'.[11]

Wynn's play, *Subsidence*, produced in April 1910 artfully

combined his interest in form at the same time rooting the drama in the changing landscape. In fact, the play is set in the town where he was working. (It was Dr Wynn's first attempt as a dramatist though he has been a successful novelist, having produced two striking novels, *Fortune's Fool* and *Faith Unfaithful*.)

Reviewing it in the *Guardian* G.H. Mair (April 1910) wrote:

> It was only a week or so that we were complaining that Miss Horniman's venture had failed to provide us with anything that could be called local drama, a literature of play-writing that is, drawing its inspiration right up from the soil of the strongly-marked individual and racial peculiarities which give its fertility to the life of the North. *Subsidence* goes far to make up this defect.[12]

Wynn set his play on a local Leigh feature, the Plank Lane Flash. Oddly enough, it was described in the *Guardian* a couple of years later when flooding was causing a problem:

> One of the large sheets of standing water, known in the dialect as 'flashes', which gather in the neighbourhood of old colliery workings where the land has subsided enough to leave the area undrained and incapable of natural drainage. The Plank Lane Flash lies on either side of the London and North-Western Railway line, which runs over it as though crossing a lake. On the south side it extends well over a mile and almost to the next station at Pennington, and it is quite half a mile broad[13]

Reviewing the play in the *Leigh Chronicle*, the reviewer commented:

> The plot has a substantial substratum of truth, for everybody in this district knows that owing to the extension of the Plank Lane Collieries the land towards Lowton has gradually subsided, and what was a few years ago dry land is now submerged to a considerable depth, several farmhouses having also disappeared or been reduced to ruin.[14]

The first scene of the play makes it clear that the Flash was going to play a prominent part in the action:

It is now a wild waste of waters which during a gale threaten the railway embankment on the one side and to stretch further on the Lowton side. The first act takes place outside Lythgoe's farm, on the borders of Plank Lane Flash. The curtain rises and discloses an old tumble down farmhouse, bearing date AD 1658 with an irregular crack seaming the walls. In front is a little garden, and just beyond is the Flash. A few rushes peep up here and there from the water, but for the most part it is an unbroken sheet of water stretching away in the distance, with the chimneys and head-gears of Plank Lane Collieries rising up in the background beyond the railway embankment.[15]

The story line was somewhat melodramatic.

Act I is set on a farm where an old farmer, Adam Lythgoe, is refusing to take money from the local colliery to move out so that they can take up the coal beneath. He doesn't trust the colliery nor the warning that his farmhouse might sink due to the burrowing beneath: 'I don't howd wi' these few fangled notions abeaut subsidence ...' His family had been on the land for 200 years and will remain there.

At the same time, his daughter, Jane, wants to marry a man that her father doesn't approve of. She wants to marry a bank clerk called Walter Travers. He is planning to rob the bank where he works as he feels the money stored there 'is no good to anybody. There must be thousands like ourselves shut out of the world and what it means for the want of a hundred pounds.' Jane urges him to go ahead with his plan. Walter borrows a boat from the old farmer in order, he says, to go shooting ducks on the Flash. The other suitor, James Bent, tries to persuade the old man to sell, but he won't. Travers and Jane plan to run off together but are stopped by Adam and Bent.

Adam orders his daughter to go home and bring the boat back across the Flash. The third act opens in the Lythgoe household with a storm brewing outside and the walls of the old farmhouse creaking. It transpires that Adam has been found drowned by the Flash although Jane has survived unhurt. The suspicion is that she has drowned him but nothing can be proved. The funeral has already taken place. Walter then appears saying he has robbed the bank and they must go and get the money where he has hidden it. That moment Bent arrives with the police and Travers is arrested. Jane tries to throw herself into the Flash but Bent restrains her. Just then a servant rushes in screaming that the Flash has burst its banks and they must run for their lives. Jane refuses and Bent stays with her as the house is engulfed.[16]

The Gaiety was packed with people from Leigh: 'We have seldom seen an author at the Gaiety 'called' with such enthusiasm as fell to Dr Wynne's lot last night.' For Mair, in the *Guardian*, although he felt the plot somewhat 'over weighted' the play was not simply about an old man refusing to leave his farm. It was a 'critique of the ever advancing forces of commercial progress'[17]

> On the old fields and farmland creep the slag and cinder heaps of advancing industry, marching grimly on all sides forward, a plague of dust and darkness and blotting out in its on-come not only the green of the fields and the blue of the sky but habits of mind and knotted growths of character rooted deep down in the soil of older and cleaner days. 'Subsidence' is not only the settling of one farm or another down on the honey-combed borings of the coal-pits, it is the subsidence of an old order of things, the foundations of whose thought and belief have been undermined by new and different ideals and the irresistible forces of 'progress'. The waters of destruction are out for a crumbling civilisation.[18]

For the *Leigh Chronicle*, it was the sight of recognisable local people (one character 'bore a strong resemblance to a well-known official at Plank Lane Collieries ...') plus dialogue of a high standard and 'Northern humour that will appeal strongly to Lancashire audiences ... ' that made it such a success. 'Leigh people can understand the local colour and allusions better than Manchester folks,' the reviewer commented.[19]

Rex Pogson noted: 'An amusing aftermath of the play was a controversy on the pronunciation of the play's title, Lancashire people preferring the long 'i' against that used in the play.'[20]

One imagines this fine detail was lost on the Gaiety's principal actress. Mair wrote in the *Guardian* of the performance of Miss Darragh in the part of Jane Lythgoe: 'Her quick and suppressed intensity of emotion is the creation of a much more sophisticated walk of life than Lancashire farmyards can show ... ' while 'the Lancashire dialect was beyond her ... '[21]

Notes

[1] *Manchester Guardian*, 5 December 1907.

[2] G.H. Mair, *Manchester Guardian*, 1 May 1910.

[3] *Leigh Chronicle* (February 1905).

[4] Ibid. (November 1909).

[5] *Manchester Guardian*, 31 January 1908.

[6] Ibid., 6 October 1908.

[7] Ibid., 22 September 1908.

[8] Ibid., 9 February 1909)

[9] iReview, ibid.,15 May 1912.

[10] Ibid., 1 May 1910.

[11] 'The Picturesque Aspects of Leigh', *Leigh Chronicle*, 15 December 1902.

[12] *Manchester Guardian*, 12 April 1910.

[13] *Manchester Guardian*, 28 August 1912.

[14] *Leigh Chronicle*, 12 April 1910.

[15] Ibid.

[16] Ibid.

[17] *Manchester Guardian*, 12 April 1910.

[18] Ibid.

[19] Ibid.

[20] *Leigh Chronicle*, 12 April 1910.

[20] Pogson, *op. cit.*, p89.

[21] *Manchester Guardian*, 12 April 1910.

7

A Singular Woman:
Gertrude Robins

It is almost impossible for example to find any play on the subject of Women's Suffrage, surely the single most important social issue of the period, in the repertoire of the repertory theatres, an omission all the more surprising, since Miss Horniman and some of her actresses were keen suffragettes.[1]

'If women are not taking a more prominent place as dramatists,' said Miss H, 'it is because they are suffering from centuries of inferior education. They have been kept back from self-development and as yet have not risen to their proper position.'[2]

IN RECENT YEARS IT HAS BECOME clear that women were writing for the theatre in the early 20th century in considerable numbers, but that their work rarely made it onto the stage. That the majority of theatre-owners, not to mention theatre critics as well as academics who wrote about the theatre, were men may be part of the explanation.

Brander Matthews, for instance, one of the most influential American sponsors of the new drama, in his 1916 book about the Theatre posed the question as to why women, successful as actors and as novelists, had apparently failed to become as popular or as prolific as their male playwriting colleagues.

Women, he concluded, knew less about life than men, and had succeeded as novelists 'in the narrow realm of domestic fiction, where they need not 'explore deeply ... the great passionate crises of existence'.

Where the writing of a play was concerned, he discerned another problem: the 'relative incapacity of women to build a plan, to make a single whole compounded of many parts, and yet dominated in every detail by but one purpose'.

Thus, he concluded, 'we find in the works of female storytellers not only a lack of largeness in topic but also a lack of strictness in treatment'.

A couple of years earlier, AH had been asked by a *Daily Mail* reporter to account for the relative absence of female playwrights featuring at the Gaiety. Her reasons were rather more prosaic than Matthews'. She pointed firstly to the social mores concerning the theatre and women that lingered on from Victorian times:

> As a matter of history it is only since the days of Macready that a respectable woman could go alone to a theatre without masculine protection. How then could she expect to take her proper place in an art whose representation she was not allowed to witness at her convenience?[3]

Here she was drawing on her own experience, of course, having taken it upon herself to visit continental theatres such as the Théâtre Français or the Burgtheater Vienne against a backdrop of parental and societal disapproval.

'If women are not taking a more prominent place as dramatists,' said Miss H, 'it is because they are suffering from centuries of inferior education. They have been kept back from self-development and as yet have not risen to their proper position.'[4]

There was also a wider point that appeared to include both men and women: 'If there is no great woman dramatist in the English theatre today Miss H feels inclined to attribute it to the fact that the dramatic art in this country is not taken so seriously as it is on the Continent.' 'In France, Germany and Austria there are great theatres where classic plays are performed. We have no theatre in England resembling them ... '[5]

At the same time AH typically insisted: ' ... as a matter of fact, I can truly say that of all the plays I have ever read by women dramatists not one has ever reached the level of "howling idiocy" that has sometimes distinguished the plays sent in by incompetent men writers!' adding, 'And one of the best one-act plays that was performed at my theatre was by a woman writer and I can see no reason why women should not make their names as dramatists.'[6]

Her advice to women was the same as one might give anyone, male or female, aspiring to write:

> Let them read the best plays by foreign dramatists – French, German and Italian. Let them study the technique of Ibsen. Take a play like *Hedda Gabler*, for instance. Go through it with a pencil and mark any line that might be thought superfluous. This is an impossibility as there is absolutely nothing that could be cut without loss to the construction of the play. But it is in this way that technique can be learned.[7]

She continued, 'The best advice I can give to women dramatists is, 'Open your eyes and notice ... Technique can be learned and many women have the gift of writing dialogue. But the most important thing of all is the right treatment of the idea. It is not sufficient to have the idea alone for it is of little use without the treatment.'[8]

Finally she encouraged women to do as men had done: 'Some men dramatists have gone on the stage merely to learn the art of construction and technique. And if any woman thinks that course would be helpful to her as a dramatist there is no reason why she should not also follow it.'[9]

It was typical of AH that she would keep the twin issues if

technical competence and political content of drama well apart. She was a suffragist, but not a militant one. She frequently addressed meetings of The Actresses' Franchise League and had spoken out at the Queen's Hall London and the Free Trade Hall Manchester on the suffrage issue. Mrs Pankhurst sent her letters of congratulation to her now and then.

In typically droll fashion she told the *Daily Mail* that she had promised to speak for the Suffrage at the Queen's Hall the next month. 'I expect a first class reception for I shall speak for just three minutes. They will find that refreshing.'

However, the Gaiety was a business. It had to be profitable at some level in order to survive. It was not an experimental theatre and certainly not one with a 'political axe to grind'. It was enough, AH thought, that she was setting an example as a theatre owner, a shining example of what women could do if they put their minds (and obviously their money if they had some) to it.

> Miss H instanced other women managers and lessees beside herself. Her own place in the drama of today may be cited as an incentive to the woman who feels that she has the priceless gifts of initiative, perseverance and ceaseless hard work as well as the genius for supervision and the real love for the best interests of the theatre. What one woman has accomplished as a pioneer in presenting the best plays in her own theatre perhaps other women may achieve through the same means of thoroughness and the qualifications only gained by incessant study and perseverance in the face of almost insuperable obstacles ... [10]

It's certainly true that AH did not give women any preferential treatment, no matter how prominent and possibly even lucrative their work might prove. The bestselling woman author, Victoria Cross, was tactless enough to send Miss Horniman an anti-suffrage play which was rejected, not because of its content but because, Miss Horniman said, 'it contained language such as I would not permit in my theatre.'[11] 'I need hardly say that Victoria Cross's play was more impossible than even her unspeakable novels.' She also apparently rejected a play from Marie Stopes.[12]

On the question of politics, however, and the Suffrage cause, it's not quite true to say that she and the Gaiety ignored the issue. While plays written by women writers might have been few and far between, their content was frequently concerned with the plight of women in a man's world, in particular, the economic imbalances that condemned many women to wretched lives and sometimes desperate straits. Most of the women writers featured were radicals of some form or another.

In 1907, at the Midland Theatre, Antonia Williams's *The Street* was one of the first Gaiety productions. Next (January 1908-August 1908) came Cheshire-born Mrs Havelock Ellis' (Edith Mary Oldham Ellis) *The Subjection of Kezia*. In 1909 Fabian writer Margaret Mack (later Macnamara) had her short play *Unemployed* produced. Her subsequent three-act play *Our Little Fancies* – influenced by Beatrice Webb's desire to reform the system of workhouses – was premiered at the Gaiety after Mack's friend and mentor George Bernard Shaw thought it 'unlikely to be commercially successful'.

In 1911, Elizabeth Baker's celebrated play *Chains* was mounted. Two more of Baker's plays were staged at the Gaiety in 1913: *Miss Tassey* and *The Price of Thomas Scott*. *The Searchlight*, by Mrs W.K. Clifford (Lucy Lane), a novelist and journalist, a friend of Henry James and part of a wide metropolitan intellectual circle was a study of the entrapment of women in marriages with dominating, even brutal men set in the milieu of the comfortable middle and upper classes (1910). Finally, another Fabian writer, Githa Sowerby, had her breakthrough play *Rutherford and Son* produced by AH, as well as her next play, *A Man and Some Women*, this when Sowerby could not convince a single London theatre to take it.

None of the above writers could be considered 'Manchester' playwrights, not least because the majority of their plays were often set in London and were premiered in London, generally for the Stage Society. Only Elizabeth Baker's *The Price of Thomas Scott* and Githa Sowerby's *A Man and Some Women* received first outings at the Gaiety. But it isn't stretching things too far to say they set a tone of seriousness that pervaded AH's theatre.

The only female playwright one might consider a 'Manchester' product would be Gertrude Robins whose debut one-act play *Makeshifts* appeared on the fourth Gaiety bill in October 1908 and would be repeated regularly over the next few years. As AH said, it was 'one of the best one-act plays ... performed at my theatre ... ' and Harold Brighouse agreed.

Unfortunately for Gertrude, although she was to write half a dozen more plays, the majority being produced at the Gaiety, none quite matched *Makeshifts*.

Born on 5 February 1880 in Chigwell, Essex, of a German mother and an Irish merchant father, Robins was a woman of many parts. She claimed to have achieved an Honours degree in Modern Languages at Oxford University when still in her teens and had considered becoming an academic, 'but I discovered that for a woman to follow such a career the drawbacks of sex are strongly defined. I ultimately decided that the theatrical profession offered a wider and fairer scope for a woman's activities.' [13]

Married to the artist Charles Edwin Dawson in 1906, she enjoyed a reasonably successful stage career in the West End, partly due to her friendship with Lillah McCarthy, the wife of Harvey Granville Barker. She appeared in plays at Wyndham's Theatre and the Little Theatre, and had a successful run in a 'merry and clever farce', *Officer 666*, at the Globe.

In 1910 in an interview for the *Daily News* beneath the headline 'An Actress Farmer' she recounted her recent purchase of a farm

Gertrude Robins, actress, farmer and the only female Manchester
Playwright (*National Portrait Gallery*)

at Naphill, four miles from High Wycombe, Bucks where she and her husband kept cows, calves and pigs as well as chickens and pheasants. 'In the intervals between golf and gardening, acting and my varied literary work, I contribute to a certain London Daily articles chiefly relative to Country Life.' She and her husband were also keen aviators, building and flying bi-plane gliders.[14]

Makeshifts was reviewed by James Agate in the *Manchester Guardian* on 6 October 1908 and considered, 'a grand little comedy, dealing with the lives of two unattractive middle-class girls living at home with a sick mother, and no "prospects". "What chance have we got to know fellows?" says Dolly. 'Authentic, convincing and sincere. Splendid ... ' [15]

In fact, it was slightly less humorous than Agate suggested. The two women, Caroline and Dolly, are spending an evening at home together waiting for a young office clerk called Smythe to visit.

Dolly, a teacher, opines:

> Fat lot of men wanting to marry a schoolteacher! Bless'm – they'd be afraid they'd get Euclid instead of eggs and bacon for breakfast, and that their buttons would never be sewn on. Oh, no. Men fight shy of girls like me. They think we're too clever; they like nice, domesticated, homely girls. (Pause) Besides, what chance do we have of ever getting to know fellows? We've no father and no brothers. How should I get to know men at a girls' school, or you sticking at home all day? Why, we don't see a man to speak to from one week's end to another, except Mr Thompson. And there's precious little romance about our lodger as far as I am concerned, even though he is a chemist's assistant.

When Smythe appears, he is a smug little bore who plays the two girls along, teasing and suggesting so that both girls come to feel he's about to propose matrimony to one or other of them. Ultimately, however, he announces that he's getting married to someone else entirely. Both girls are acutely embarrassed as well as

stricken. One secretly sheds tears and the other is left at the end of
the play with her head in her hands – hardly a happy ending.

Without delving too far into what was a one-act play that
contained a great deal of sly humour, the plight of the two girls
(and many young unattached girls like them in Edwardian London)
is brought home quite starkly:

> Dolly: (Throwing book on floor and gazing into fire) 'It's all so
> hopeless, because neither of us can do anything different. With the
> skimpy, rotten education we got when we were kids, and no training
> to do anything in particular, we are expected to earn our own living
> — you as genteel general servant, and I as an assistant teacher of
> infants. And so here we are, hopeless and helpless, and we might as
> well be on a desert island.'[16]

T.S. Eliot would paint a similar picture of genteel female
desperation being taken advantage of by 'a young man carbuncular'
in 1922 in *The Waste Land*. 'When lovely woman stoops to folly
and/Paces about her room again, alone ... ' [17]

So popular was *Makeshifts* that it featured regularly on the Gaiety
bill for the next couple of years. In book form it went into several
editions and was played over a thousand times in Great Britain,
Australia and Canada. It also featured on the Gaiety's American
tour.

Nothing else Robins wrote matched *Makeshift*'s popularity,
however. In 1909 she published five plays, generally light-hearted
pieces such as *The Point of View*, 'a modern comedy with a
somewhat cynical estimate of soldiers' (1910 at the Gaiety) plus
Launcelot and the Leading Lady – described as 'a theatrical comedy'.

In 1911 came *Realities* also produced at the Gaiety, a sequel to
Makeshifts with similar characters, only this time the girls were
married. ('Sequels are proverbially inferior and we are afraid Miss
Robins's refuses to prove the rule ... ')[18]

In 19 March 1912 came *Old Jan*, 'a study of peasant life in

Volendam.' James Agate's summary was typically unsparing:

> A centenarian who recovers his speech to utter a warning about a little boy being in a burning mill. The boy turns out not to be in the mill at all but the old man dies and it is understood that had he lived he would have been better treated. Life may be pointless, but pointless plays are pushing realism too far. This little play was rather a mistake.[19]

1914 she produced *Loving As We Do* and *The Plaything* a three-act play that featured Gertrude as the leading actress. Harold Brighouse considered it 'a brutal assault on the feelings', or rather a melodramatic rewriting of *A Doll's House*. 'An unhappy married woman runs off with another man who is a villain and who deserts her. She tries to kill him, then herself, before settling down to do good works ... '

'WBC' in the *Manchester Courier* wrote:

> Miss Robins is a sound suffragist and an outspoken feminist on orthodox lines. Judged as an exposition of the tenets of those schools, *The Plaything* will pass muster; it certainly appealed last night to a considerable section of the audience. But that which was most loudly applauded was embedded in dramatically arid wastes.[20]

An attractive, unpretentious, enthusiastic character, Gertrude passed away aged just 37 on 24 December, 1917 in Shotter Mill, Surrey.

Notes

1 Alasdair F. Cameron, *The Repertory Theatre Movement, 1907-1917* (University of Warwick Ph.D, thesis, October 1983).

2 *Daily Mail*, 18 February 1914.

3 Ibid.

4 Ibid.

5 Ibid.

6 Ibid.

[7] Ibid.

[8] Ibid.

[9] Ibid.

[10] Ibid.

[11] *Manchester Courier*, 27 November 1913.

[12] Pogson, *op. cit.*, p37.

[13] *The Era*, 1 February1913.

[14] *Daily News*, 29 December 1910.

[15] *Manchester Guardian*, 6 October 1908.

[16] *Makeshifts* play text

[17] T.S. Eliot, 'The Fire Sermon', in *The Waste Land* (Faber, 1922).

[18] *Manchester Guardian*, 24 October 1911.

[19] Ibid., 19 March 1912.

[20] *Manchester Courier*, 9 November 1914.

8

The Press Bites Back

Why can't we (The Press) be true about it and tell the public what liars we are.[1]

It is an interesting comment on the basic solidarity of the Victorian system and the English temperament that [repertory theatre was] not inspired to copy (Bernard) Shaw and write Socialist propaganda drama.[2]

A H HAD FROM THE VERY FIRST set her face against 'politics' in drama, and by that she probably meant overt proselytising of the kind that had characterised the Abbey Theatre, if not through the actual productions then via the pervading ethos.

However, this did not result – as far as one can tell – in a policy of censorship. The criteria for acceptance of a new play always remained that vague, subjective notion of 'quality'. Pogson has said,

> Her love of drama, like her love of music and painting, was strong and genuine, but she was never a member of any particular camp nor restricted to any theory ... She saw the theatre in the broadest possible outline – what was needed was good drama, what was to be avoided was bad drama; it was as simple as that.[3]

Her antipathy to 'politics' certainly had no bearing on whom she employed. Many of the actors working at the Gaiety held

left-wing opinions and were active in political movements beyond
the theatre. In 1912, one such radical – Gaiety's director of plays
Iden Payne – was replaced by another – Lewis Casson – who was if
anything even more to the left in politics.

Many of the local writers who came forward with new drama in
the early Gaiety years also held strong left-wing opinions. Two in
particular – Harry Richardson and Frank Rose – were also well
established as professional journalists in Manchester as well as being
prominent Union officials at the critical time for the labour
movement. Their work at the Gaiety would, in widely differing
ways, reflect their deeply held convictions.

Harry Richardson, the younger of the two by a decade, was first
into the fray. He was born in Bolton in 1876 where his grandfather
was a prominent solicitor. He was educated in a private school and
by 1894 was working as a journalist on the *Staffordshire Sentinal*
in Hanley. He spent four years on the *Birmingham Gazette* before
coming to Manchester to work on various Edward Hulton
newspapers. He was assistant editor and leader writer for the *Daily
Dispatch* (1903-4) and Literary Editor for the *Manchester Evening
Chronicle* until 1909. He also spent nine years as a freelance on the
Sunday Chronicle writing as 'Dux'. Along with Frank Rose, who
also wrote for Hulton's *Dispatch* and *Evening News*, he was a firm
Union man and was instrumental in establishing the National
Union of Journalists in Manchester in 1907. He helped set up the
NUJ Journal, edited it for a decade, became the Union's first paid
General Secretary in 1918 and would remain so until his death
aged 60 in 1936. He was also on the executive council of the Printed
and Kindred Trades Federation and on the Joint Industrial Council
and helped found the International Federation of Journalists –
indeed was chosen as its second President in 1931-2.

Despite this apparently conventional and impressive career,
Richardson was highly eccentric in many ways, his maverick

personality often seemingly at odds with the demands of holding responsible posts.

> The main criticism in Richardson of his Union career was that he was a 'left-winger'. The membership on the right, a large but often inactive body so far as attendance at meetings was concerned, called' him a 'Red,' a revolutionary, a 'Bolshie'. Everyone knew, of course, that he was a Socialist, and he was popular in the ranks of the left not perhaps a very large section, though at some conferences they became vocal in debate and had their fling afterwards at midnight, when the strains of the Red Flag might be heard from an effervescent little group.[4]

Richardson also possessed a biting sense of humour, sometimes regarded as cynicism that often went unappreciated in official union circles. As with many satirists, it was difficult at times for his more conventional colleagues to discern whether he was being wholly serious.

A good example would be his decision in 1910 to found, along with a colleague, an illustrated satirical venture called *Laughter*. With its subtitle, 'Grim and Gay', it was intended as a rival to *Punch*. Ernest Marriot of the Swan Club provided almost all the illustrations and caricatures. Judge Parry wrote humorous pieces for it. Its editorial office was a socialist meeting place, the Clarion Café at 50a Market Street in Manchester where The Fellowship Press printed *Laughter*. It ran for a year before running out of money and folding.

The paper was full of jokes and light-hearted comment mixed with somewhat serious pieces that revealed Richardson's bitter outlook on the world in general. For instance, Richardson brought together a jumble of 'news' events in a remarkable cut-up collage piece called 'The Laughing World'.

Apparently seating comfortably in an idyllic garden in summer where the world seemed to be laughing in joy, the writer refers to the imminent football Cup Final, the pioneering flyer Grahame White's attempt to fly from Manchester to London, a speech by American President Roosevelt on eugenics and the extravagant wedding of a New York socialite:

> Then the laughter of the world about me suddenly becomes harsh and sardonic, the noise of the gibbering apes behind bars, the discordant shrill laugh I once heard in the grounds of a lunatic asylum. For while the eyes of the world were on the football, or following the flight of Mr White or gloating at the trousseau of the newly wedded heiress and the ears of the world were open for the wisdom of Mr Roosevelt on the duty of perpetuating the race, an unemployed London car man, once a soldier of the King, was cutting the throats of his three babes so that he could no longer hear them crying for the food he could not earn ... The laughing lunatic world that forces fathers to murder their children because the timid and trembling world is taught to believe a Socialist State would tear away babes from their mothers; the gaping giggling world that starves children so that it may see 2,000 arum lilies adorning the altar of a bride and bridegroom; the insensate world that forces sane men and women to sterilise their unions so that they may never hear the horror of babes crying fro bread! ... The laughing world grows dark ... [5]

This sense of outrage at the injustices of the world would find a partial outlet in his drama where he would attempt to bring his anger and resentment at the world alive.

His first foray came during the opening weeks of the Gaiety, in May 1908, a one-act piece called *The Few and the Many*. Its subject was prostitution, allied with the hypocrisy of a middle-class that in Richardson's eyes was as as much responsible for the problem as those individuals who controlled the women.

He'd written an article in 1910 called 'The Outcasts' for the National Union of Women's Suffrage Societies in which he asserted: 'Employers of female labour don't pay their hands sufficient to enable them to live without prostitution. Such employers were morally in the same category as the "bully" who lives on the earnings of a woman's immorality ... society, in getting cheap commodities, is actually parasitic upon these women.'

His one-act play illustrated this by situating the action in a, 'superfine drawing room' where a Mrs Ebdon-Smith, president of the Refuge for Fallen Sisters, finds herself confronted with a young woman who has been made pregnant by her daughter's prospective husband. Ebdon-Smith, ('empanelled before the tribunal of her own conscience' according to the *Manchester Courier* reviewer) offers the woman £20 to disappear.

'If there were more like you there would be more like us,' the young woman says, taking the cash. It was 'realism without one glint of relief,' and 'even if it is suggestive of morbidity and – and some would say – unfitted for the stage, [it] cannot but appeal to the deeper feelings of human nature.'[6]

It was successful enough for Richardson to be asked for a second play, *Bringing It Home* (5 October 1908), a one-act 'thriller' in which a callous magistrate (what the socialist orator would call the 'plutocratic' motorist ... commented James Agate) accidentally runs over his own son ... ('people who ride in swift motor cars should not throw sneers ... 'Agate quipped)[7]

Having vented his spleen on the greed and callous nature of the middle-classes, Richardson's next play *Going On Parade* (15 March 1909) was set in Slopers Court, which according to the *Manchester Courier* reviewer resembled a Hulme or Ancoats slum: all too common in Northern towns.

'We know the dirty lime-wash, economically used, and only in part disguising the clammy bricks and outward hideousness. We know the festoons of washing, the rickety spouts, the oozy flags and miasmic air ...'[8]

The name Sloper would have been immediately recognisable to his working-class audience. Aly Sloper was an early, very famous comic strip character, a red-nosed, blustery, archetypal lazy schemer who was often found 'sloping' though alleyways to avoid his landlord and creditors. Richardson would have been a fan of Sloper as a boy, reading his nefarious exploits in the *Judy* magazine, a rival to *Punch*.

His play contained just such a character who shares the lodgings with his wife, plus another woman (a 'voluble Irishwoman') and a Mr Richards, an out-of-work cobbler and ex-soldier who, facing a notice to quit from the landlord, chooses to kill himself rather than go to the workhouse.

James Agate thought it 'not quite worthy of some fine things that are in it'. The old man, 'recounts the bodies he has seen brought into the court, of men killed at work and of men murdered and talks of lives he has known and little children who have died ... '

The title is in fact a military euphemism for suicide – an act that re-appears in Richardson's next and most significant play, *Gentlemen of the Press.*[9]

It was perhaps inevitable that Richardson would ultimately bring onto the stage some references to his own profession. Devoted as he was to the press world and to those who laboured in it, he was under no illusions as to the nature of the job itself as a socialist working for a 'popular', primarily right-wing, newspaper. What is intriguing about the subsequent reception of the play was the clash between the *Manchester Guardian* journalists, and men like Richardson, labouring in less salubrious environs.

The play itself, which sadly has not survived, centred on the love of Harry Blake, a pressman, for the wife of Dale, a fellow pressman. When Mrs Dale returns Blake's affections, he pleads with her to give up her husband and leave. When the latter discovers the liaison, he too thinks his wife should leave him – and then kills himself, ostensibly to facilitate the divorce.

The plot itself, however, seemed less significant to those reviewing it than the fact that Richardson had written a play that called into question the morals of those who wrote for newspapers. The *Daily News* reviewer (13 September 1910) commented that 'one cannot help feeling a little sorry that he has portrayed journalism in a somewhat unpleasant light. In fact, the impression left upon one's mind by the play is that it is impossible for anyone with a conscience to take up work on a newspaper, and that does not give a true picture of Press life.'

Richardson had asserted that leader writers who worked for papers whose policies they disagreed with still produced copy intended to persuade people to think in ways contrary to their own. The *Daily News* reviewer refuted the 'accusation' that 'journalism is a profession which demands its members to sacrifice conscience for their bread and butter ...'[10]

The *Guardian* was equally scathing. G.H. Mair took Richardson to task, devoting the majority of his review of the play to the question of journalists and their morals. He identified Richardson as 'plainly interested in the propagation of socialism', but felt he was wrong to apply such words as 'cant', 'hypocrisy' and 'lying' 'to the occupation of thousands of his fellows.'

'To attack bad journalism is one thing; to assume that not a single redeeming feature exists in the whole of journalism is another.' Mair went on to say that the 'horror' of the Yellow Press (a pejorative term used to decry any journalism that treats news in an unprofessional or unethical fashion) wasn't that its writers did not believe what they said, but that they did.'

Regarding the play itself: 'Only, if our authors would let the play be the thing; the stage is not a pulpit or a platform ... ' He wanted, 'no more of the propagandist play which takes a short cut to our sympathies and makes its people speak at the audience instead of at each other ... ' [11]

Whether it was a deliberate decision on Richardson's part or sheer chance, it so happened that at the moment when his play was opening in Manchester, down in London the Institute of Journalists – a body Richardson would struggle against and ultimately reject when setting up the National Union of Journalists – was holding its annual conference in London. Not only that, but it was discussing ways 'to bring the Press and the stage into closer communion'!

'AFR' in the *Pall Mall Gazette had* noticed and he dismissed Richardson's play, bemoaning the fact that 'no dramatist had managed to present anything approaching a likeness to a working journalist of the period with which they dealt.'[12]

That wasn't quite true as Richardson certainly wasn't the first playwright to utilise newspapers and those who work in them for dramatic purposes: The German writer Otto Ernst had written a popular comedy in 1903 suggesting that most newspapermen were corrupt and base. Georges Thurner in *Le Passe Partout* (1908) had depicted the interior of a great daily newspaper in Paris as being a 'sink of moral and financial corruption'.

In Britain, the contemporary concerns with monopolist newspaper proprietorship had already received West End treatment in James Fagan's *The Earth* and Arnold Bennett's *What the Public Wants* (both appearing in 1909 while Bennett's play would be staged at the Gaiety in 1911). These latter productions had been concerned with the newly acquired power of those who owned the papers and the dangers to democracy they presented – clearly inspired by the activities of Edward Hulton.

Even closer to home, however, a novel appeared earlier that year (1910) written by the prominent Guardian journalist and leader-writer C.E. Montague. Called *A Hind Let Loose*, it told the tale of a working journalist who produces reviews and leaders for two competing newspapers of utterly opposing political outlooks. So skilled was he that the owners of the respective papers never spotted the fact that he was hardly altering a word of each piece. Though essentially a comedy, the novel – soon turned into play – called into question the very nature of journalism as a craft. Full of sardonic wit it was accepted by many as a satire on modern political journalism.

Montague had dedicated his book to his father-in-law, the *Manchester Guardian*'s editor and future owner, C.P. Scott, whose paper, Montague declared rather pompously, was, 'clear of these stains'. Montague's dedication placed the *Guardian* on a pedestal, high above the common herd.

Arnold Bennett reviewed the book for the *Guardian* and remarked,

> The more one reflects on this singular novel, the more deeply destructive it seems. Not journalism only, but the whole use of words is its theme ... The one moral generalisation that can be drawn ... is that practically all journalism says the same thing and in practically the same words, and that what it says equals practically nothing.[13]

Bennett, however, disagreed with the sentiment, feeling that where the press was concerned, 'I am utterly convinced one side is, upon the whole, appreciably less base than the other.' That side, of course, would feature the *Manchester Guardian* ...

What is interesting about the debate is that Montague's book was treated by Bennett, and by extension the *Guardian*, as an intriguing piece of literature that explored issues concerning the nature of words and their meaning, with a central (Irish) character who delighted, almost revelled, in the duplicity of his craft. It wasn't simply a satire on journalism in general.

What irked Mair was that Richardson was making no distinction at all between different papers. He was making a statement about the plight of every working journalist, many of whom were struggling to make ends meet, who were obliged to write things they did not agree with.

Richardson responded to Mair with a letter to the *Guardian* denying that socialism was mentioned in the play and that 'it was not fair to the management [of the Gaiety] that your critic should paint the theatre red simply because he has heard that the author is interested in socialism.' He then denied that he had denounced *all* journalists. Lastly, interestingly, he had a dig at the *Guardian* and those who wrote for it, clearly referencing Montague's dedication: 'What should the stainless know of the lost and lapsed? What does the white press know of the yellow? What does he know of journalism who only the *Manchester Guardian* knows?'[14]

He then took Mair to task, suggesting that he knew of many journalists who were opposed to their papers' stands on issues like the Boer War and Tariff Reform yet who were 'driven by their families' needs to write against their convictions'. The *Manchester Guardian* editor retorted that he felt, 'yellow' journalists were, 'in the main sincere', that is that no-one forces them to write what they do.

The problem where Richardson's denials were concerned was that he had expressed the opinion that all journalists were little more than paid 'hacks' on more than one occasion elsewhere. In May 1910, in his satirical magazine *Laughter*, he'd commented, 'Journalists are so busy forming other people's opinions that they haven't time to form any of their own – on public questions. They have private opinions about their employers which are never printed and are frequently unprintable.'[15]

As late as 1925 when asked by the editor of the *Journalist* magazine to contribute a piece on 'The Art of Leader Writing', Richardson, 'mixed a deal of cynicism with his pleasantries and advices'. Arthur J. Cummings (a future President of the Institute of Journalists) declared that any applicant for the job of leader writing who professed Richardson's, 'cynical, and contradictory, negatives would go away empty, for the writer would have no use for that particular brand of moral imbecile'.

Another leader writer regarded the article as lamentable: 'If the leading official of the Union can give no better counsel to young journalists than to sell their souls for their mess of pottage with a grin, and make the best of it, then we shall all do better to go potato-hoeing.'[16]

Richardson once told a colleague, 'Provocation is my favourite pastime at least that's what a lot of people seem to think altho' I hate provoking people.' Yet his dedication to the truth, despite his reservations concerning the integrity of the hack journalist's calling, was absolute.[17]

His work with the Fédération Internationale des Journalistes in striving to establish a code of conduct for journalists speaks for itself. The Court of Honour formed by the IFJ to restrain offences against journalistic ethics which endangered international good will – stopping the dangerous falsification of international news – Richardson considered, 'a first move towards making journalists realise that it is as immoral to 'frame up' a case against a foreign country as it is to tell lies about one's townsmen'.[18]

In 1930, H.G, Wells, who had been a member of the NUJ for ten years, sent his warmest congratulations to Richardson on the latter's election to the Presidency of the IFJ:

> We journalistic writers can do immeasurable service to mankind by pitting the full weight of our influence against those delusions of nationalism that are not simply threatening the world with open war, but also strangling day by day the economic life of our species, through outrageous tariffs and the new strategy of banking patriotism. The world is one in its prosperity and in its needs. It is for the journalist to keep that truth alive.[19]

Gentlemen of the Press wasn't Richardson's last theatrical foray. In November 1913 came *The Awakening Woman* – a family saga with a bullying husband and a put-upon wife plus a daughter trying to break away. Later that year *In The Black Forest* was produced by Stockport Garrick Society and reviewed by

Harold Brighouse – but neither play was successful.

Immediately after the First World War Richardson became the first salaried General Secretary of the NUJ and dedicated the rest of his life to that organisation although he did find time to produce a couple of novels, *The Temple Murder* and *The Rock of Justice.*

Whether or not he might have developed into a substantial writer for the stage is debateable. It was clear that for fledgling writers like him, the 'repertory' system employed by the Gaiety meant that new plays had little chance of enduring success. He wrote to the *Guardian* in December 1913 that the process of running a play for a week, then taking it off before its reputation was built up, meant that there was no time for publicity to work in its favour: 'Many a good play which fails in a week would pay if it were played for three weeks continuously, because three weeks is sufficient to allow news of a good thing to go round.'

He cited *Hindle Wakes,* which had been produced first in London before opening in the Gaiety:

> ... had it been produced first at the Gaiety it would have run for a week, to nightly increasing 'business', until on the Saturday the theatre would have been full. Then it would have been taken off and 'put up' again, perhaps *six* months later, by which time many would have forgotten it, and the same process of building up the business would have had to be repeated. That is the weakness of the repertory theatre.[20]

Richardson died in December 1936 but his memory lives on wherever journalists foregather: In the 1990s organisers of the NUJ Conference discovered the music and libretto to 'The Song of the NUJ', written in the 1930s by Richardson and composer Herbert Caesari, Professor of Singing at The Trinity College of Music, and the man apparently responsible for the great revival of the Old Italian School of Singing.

The chorus goes:

> Come Ev'ry Fellow
> Of Blue Press or Yellow,
> Of press that is humdrum or gay,
> Come list to my praise
> Of the Union ways,
> The song of the NUJ ...

Notes

[1] *Gentlemen of the Press*, play text.

[2] Lynton Hudson, *Twentieth Century Drama* (Harrap, 1946), pp. 46–7.

[3] Pogson, *op. cit.,* p. 20.

[4] F.J. Mansfield, *'Gentlemen, The Press!' Chronicles of a Crusade* (Official History of the NUJ, 1943).

[5] *Laughter*, 7th May 1910, p126.

[6] *Manchester Courier*, 5 May 1908.

[7] *Manchester Guardian*, 6 October 1908.

[8] *Manchester Courier*, 16th March 1909.

[9] *Manchester Guardian*, 13 September 1910.

[10] *Daily News*, 13 September 1910.

[11] *Manchester Guardian*, 13 September 1910.

[12] *Pall Mall Gazette*, 'Journalists on the Stage', 17 September 1910.

[13] *Manchester Guardian*, 3 March 1910.

[14] Ibid., 19 March 1910.

[15] *Laughter*, 13 April 1910, p. 102.

[16] Mansfield, *op. cit.*

[17] Ibid.

[18] Ibid.

[19] Ibid.

[20] *Manchester Guardian* (15 December 1913)

9

A Lancashire Fairy Tale

Industrial Lancashire had previously been treated realistically and didactically but this was the first attempt to make the area a subject for imaginative treatment while at the same time preserving the dialect.[1]

Before the coming of the spindle I fear the boggarts fled. There would scarce be room in the narrow valleys for both the spirit of enterprise and imagination. So most of Lancashire people forgot how the gnomes, the elves, and even the 'goblins damned' once chirruped where the looms now moan ... [2]

ON 6 DECEMBER 1912, CECIL CHISHOLM in the *Manchester Courier*, writing about what he termed the decline of the pantomime, bemoaned the lack of what he termed 'local legendary':

It is very well to interest city children in the far-off fairylands of Maeterlinck or Barrie. But why not bring the fairy folk to their own doors? Why not rekindle the still smouldering flames of the childish imagination that have been stifled in our smoke-laden atmosphere? In the hum of machinery and the roar of looms the sense of Nature's presence has been lost. But it should not be to difficult to recapture.[3]

In March the following year, Chisholm had his wish granted.

Frank Rose, an engineer by trade but also a regular columnist in Manchester's daily and evening newspapers writing on industrial and union affairs, surprised his friends and colleagues by producing a play called *The Whispering Well*. Lewis Casson, an admirer of Rose and his socialist-inclined newspaper columns, having taken over from Iden Payne as director of plays, decided to produce it at the Gaiety. It created something of a sensation.

Rose was a Londoner, born in Lambeth in July 1857, and educated at the British School, George Street. He studied at evening classes at Westminster to become an operative engineer, and early in his career began his trade union activities. Joining the Amalgamated Society of Engineers when he was twenty-two, he was a union organiser for seven years, finally becoming organising delegate for Lancashire and Ireland living and working in Manchester. He would serve the Union for over fifty years.

In 1900 he joined the staff of the Manchester *Daily Dispatch* as a freelance journalist and became a recognised authority on Labour history and statistics, contributing regular articles on Labour topics and industrial life to publications such as *The Morning Leader*, the *Manchester Evening News*, the *Manchester Courier* and others.

He was described in the latter in 1914 as 'A middle-aged man of fine physique, his hair tinged with grey, with hands that seem more suited to wield a sledgehammer than a quill. Unbending in his convictions, one moment as fierce as a lion, the next as meek as a kitten, with a humour which is often mistaken for cynicism ... '[4]

Rose was a similar character to Harry Richardson in that neither could be safely bracketed: both were dedicated Union men and members of the fledgling Independent Labour Party, but neither stuck to the accepted party line.

'From his early engineering days, Rose was a strong Socialist of the William Morris school. He joined the Labour party, but speedily fell foul of some of its leading lights, whose Socialism smelled too

Frank Rose, political rebel and writer; Harry Richardson, dedicated
Pressman and satirist (*Author's collection*)

strongly of State Socialism, which Rose detested. He had a horror
of bureaucracy and based his opposition to nationalisation schemes
on the ground that they would create an array of officials.'[5]

Given his day jobs, one might reasonably have expected Rose to
pen a play with an industrial background, perhaps, or dealing with
Union affairs. Instead, he was the only Manchester School writer
to look backwards in time and draw upon Lancashire folk-legend,
albeit in order to make a broad political point.

The Whispering Well was described as 'a modern morality play
concerned with the degrading results of monetary greed for wealth
in the place of the passion of life'. It was a Lancashire fairy tale, but
the fairies are not creatures of light and fancy, 'but ugly boggarts
equipped with an armoury of moral whips'.[6]

Set in the Lancashire district of Ashton in the early eighteenth
century, it concerns a home weaver, Robin O'Tums, and his wife
Malkin, who work hard all day, save a little and are happy in the
possession of two children, a loom, an acre of land, a cow and each
other's love. Robin has to go into Manchester to sell his cloth, and
during one such trip he meets up with merchants living in great

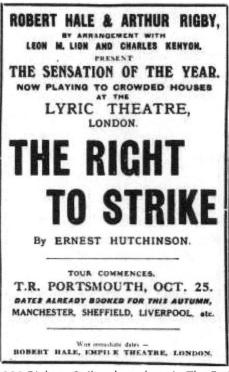

ROBERT HALE & ARTHUR RIGBY,
BY ARRANGEMENT WITH
LEON M. LION AND CHARLES KENYON.
PRESENT
THE SENSATION OF THE YEAR.
NOW PLAYING TO CROWDED HOUSES
AT THE
LYRIC THEATRE,
LONDON.

THE RIGHT TO STRIKE

By ERNEST HUTCHINSON.

TOUR COMMENCES.
T.R. PORTSMOUTH, OCT. 25.
DATES ALREADY BOOKED FOR THIS AUTUMN,
MANCHESTER, SHEFFIELD, LIVERPOOL, etc.

Wire immediate dates —
ROBERT HALE, EMPIRE THEATRE, LONDON.

(1920 Right to Strike play advert in The Era)

prosperity. The contrast with his own simple life makes him discontented and on his return he listens to his wife telling the children the story of the 'whispering well' close by in which those who have evil desires can hear the voices of 'boggarts'.

He quarrels with his wife, after which she goes off to bed unhappily. As he sits alone by the fire in his chair he falls asleep, whereupon the 'Spirit of Desire' appears and offers to take him to the well where he can obtain riches in proportion to the value of his sacrifices.

The bargain is made with his plough. As the tale progresses, Robin gains more and more power but in doing so sacrifices almost everything he loves, thus becoming more and more unhappy and discontented. His happy home is denuded and his wife becomes a slattern. She joins with him in his greedy endeavours and sacrifices their children for a mansion and servants. However, she is ultimately saved from permanent perdition by her love for the children. Robin, however, can't give up his money and he is tossed down the Whispering Well into a hellish torment – but then wakes up. He realises his folly, happiness is restored and the play ends.

Rose had used a legend that had acquired some significance for northern dialect writers, particularly those from Lancashire, during the previous fifty years or more. 'Boggarts' were supernatural creatures frequently described as 'fairies', sometimes as 'ghosts'. There were plenty of literary examples to draw upon: *The Hazel Clough Boggart* (1860) by Benjamin Brierley, who was born in Failsworth in Lancashire and was sub-editor for the *Oldham Times*. *'Th' Boggart Blacksmith! Or the return of the Boggart Bridge Ghost* (1863) by Edward Slater, a cotton worker from Burnley who wrote plays employing the Burnley dialect. *The Boggart of Orton Clough* (1870) by W.E.A. Axon ('the intellectual of the Lancashire dialect movement') who wrote dialect poems and songs. 'The Haunted Man' (1897) by 'John Ackworth' (Frederick Robert Smith), a Methodist minister. In 1909 there was even a Boggart Sketch advertised as part of a music-hall show at Manchester's Tivoli Theatre.

Boggarts were not treated as terrifying supernatural entities as tradition demanded, however. Rather, they had gradually become a source of comedy because boggart tales were usually based on misunderstandings, and boggarts ultimately had prosaic explanations. A wizard lays a 'boggart' in the local woods, only to discover that a 'ghostly' sound heard by locals was actually the wind blowing through two branches. A man on the Isle of Man sees a *buggane* (actually a drunkard giving a woman a piggy-back). A child in Wales sees a fairy that turns out to be a turkey. A man captures a leprechaun only to find that he has jumped on a travelling pipe-player of diminutive size. Similarly, in Rose's play, the boggarts are merely the stuff of a bad dream.

However, it was clear to those reviewing *The Whispering Well* that Rose was trying to make a deeper, almost a romantic point. The *Manchester Guardian* critic wrote:

> The dominant impression of the author that one gets from his play is that of a keen moralist seeking to inculcate his philosophy of life. The subject of the play is the discontent which is not divine; its philosophy is that what a man has may be his worst enemy, that greed which Mr Rose would define as the desire to get without giving anything in return, is the root of evil and the destroyer of love and happiness; that nothing is to be had in this world without sacrifice, and that if the sacrifice be not of work and of the means of life it will be of something far more precious, of the ends that make life worth living.[7]

Chisholm in the *Manchester Courier* felt it was more than a 'Lancashire Fairy Play': 'It is a folk play, a social satire, a study in Lancashire life and a modern Morality – among many other things ... '[8]

Chisholm felt that Rose was giving the public his

> ... vision of a Lancashire wealth corroded and luxury-tainted through its success in the industrial struggle. Whether the awakening of Robin points to a return of the cotter artisan population as the only remedy for civilisation's ills is another question. Suffice to say that caustic criticism today is writ large over this loom legend of yesterday. Robin o' Tums at least stands for more than an outgrown economic type; he is the Lancashire man of today.[9]

It must have been a difficult play for the Gaiety to mount, given that the second and third acts involved complicated scene changes. 'We fear that it is impossible to praise the boggart scenes. Both in the second and the third act the stage was too dark to see and one could not hear very well either for the noise.'[10]

The *Manchester Guardian* critic wrote:

> He increases the difficulty of his task by making the whole of the
> rest of the play a dream which Robin is supposed to have on the
> night of his dinner at the Seven Stars, and from the beginning of the
> second *act* to the last scene of the third of the Play is a phantasmagoria
> of the unrealities such as dreams are made of – a procession of
> pictures and scenes and symbols.
>
> It is sustained by the imaginative power of much of the writing, by
> grim, racy humour – the scene at the well, when Robin throws down
> his plough as the first sacrifice is a good example – and by subtle
> observation, which redeem the dream unrealities from losing touch
> with our interest. In the second act the whispering well has to fade
> into Robin's kitchen, and in the third act there is a still more difficult
> transition of scene from the palace to the kitchen by way of the well.[11]

Nevertheless, the stage managers coped although almost every
critic thought the play too long:

> It has other faults, but they are on the surface and can be removed
> without serious operation. But the stuff of the play seems to us
> extremely fine, and with care and good fortune it may come to be
> acknowledged as one of the most remarkable stage pieces of our
> time.[12]

The play was rapturously received, and Rose was forced onto
the stage to make a speech. Reactions got progressively less ecstatic
the further one got from Manchester, however. The *London Globe*
critic wrote: 'It cannot be suggested that this Lancashire "Dream
Play" possesses any excessive merits, or that in writing or
construction it reveals anything but the very 'prentice hand. Both
author and composer are, we understand, Manchester men, but
their "goods" while serviceable in a way are not of first quality ... '
It added, 'It would have been better if their realism had not often
carried them to the point of an inarticulate Lancashire accent.'

Sybil Thorndike was the star, however, playing the mother with
'tenderness and charm, and her accent was a joy.'[13]

Interestingly, the following year Iden Payne would prune it and produce it in the USA where it was a great success, considered by the *Chicago Evening Post* as 'an ideal holiday offering' ('even if you do not like the Lancashire dialect in which so much of it was spoken'.)[14]

Rose would write just two more plays, both of one-act. *The Second Mrs Banks* (October 1913) was a knockabout tragi-comedy in which 'a decent girl marries a drunken brute in order to take care of his child.' When the drunk tries to exact his filial dues (and take her money) she rebuffs him.

This was followed by *The Hanging of Hey-go-Mad Jack* (1914) written in Lancashire 'dialect'. Jack is under sentence of death in Preston Gaol and his mates, drinking in a pub called 'The Clucking Hen', are debating who is likely to perform the hanging as no one has volunteered. A mysterious stranger then arrives carrying rope and, thinking he is the hangman, Jack's friends hatch a plot to kill him. It turns out, however, that he's merely a farmer holding a tether for an errant ox.

In similar fashion to Harry Richardson, Rose would move on to bigger things in 1918 when he was elected Labour MP for North Aberdeen. Although he was reported to have written a play about profiteering in the munitions industry (reported on in May 1919) and to have collaborated with James Sexton, fellow socialist MP (and author of the acclaimed play *The Riot Act*) on a piece called 'The Quality of Mercy' nothing came of them. Rose henceforth concentrated on his political and journalistic career.

Typically, he was a controversial politician, forever at loggerheads with his constituency party due to his anti-Soviet views and his opposition to industrial action. In one speech in 1924 he advocated compulsory industrial arbitration as a substitute for strikes and lockouts, claiming that not 2 per cent of strikes in the last forty years had been wholly successful, with 70 per cent ending in compromise or total defeat for workers. 'Until the strike and the lock-out were made impossible there was going to be no social advance and no industrial betterment.'[15]

An article opposing the coalmine nationalisation scheme caused demands from the Scottish Independent Labour Party that he should leave the Labour Party and 'join some bosses' party'. But Rose was not to be silenced:

'I am going to do my duty by the big working class electorate I represent.' His vigorous criticism of the 1926 General Strike (Those who promoted the Strike he described in Parliament as 'silly devils')[16] resulted in the Independent Labour Party deciding to oppose him at the next election, but he died in July 1928 before they had their wish.

It's ironic, however, that at the same time as Frank Rose was forsaking the stage for Parliament, one of the last of the Manchester Playwrights, Ernest Hutchinson, would produce one of the only industrial-themed plays the Gaiety ever mounted and dealing directly with Rose's principal bugbear: the industrial strike.

Notes

[1] Pogson, *op. cit.*, p140.

[2] *Manchester* Courier, 21 March 1911.

[3] *Manchester Courier*, 6 December 1912.

[4] Ibid., 24 March 1913.

[5] *Manchester Guardian*, 11 July 1928.

[6] Pogson, *op. cit.*, p140.

[7] *Manchester Guardian*, 24 March 1913.

[8] *Manchester Courier*, 24 March 1913.

[9] Ibid.

[10] Ibid.

[11] *Manchester Guardian*, 24 March 1913.

[12] Ibid.

[13] *The Globe*, 16 May 1913.

[14] *Chicago Evening Post*, 10 January 1914.

[15] *Manchester Guardian*, 9 April 1924.

[16] Ibid., 11 June 1928.

10

The Doctors' Dilemma

The practice of medicine stands apart from any other calling and those who seek to instill into it the methods of the office and the shop, or to associate it in any way with such an act as a strike, only reveal their own sad lack of the spirit which the public are entitled to expect to animate their doctors.[1]

AH'S PRINCIPLED STAND AGAINST OVERT POLITICS was probably unnecessary during the Gaiety's heyday in the years prior to the First World War as there were few, if any, plays being written that challenged the political status quo in the UK. By 1920 when the national political scene became more challenging and the Gaiety was on the verge of closing, a Manchester playwright did produce a piece of work that caused a stir, although not from the political left.

Ernest Hutchinson was born in 1885 near Manchester and educated at Dover College and Manchester Technical School. His father, Major Hutchinson, lived in Prestwich and was in business in Bury as a mill owner where the Hutchinsons were a well-established and wealthy family. In the eighteenth century they had been the wool merchants who built Daisyfield Mill, a cotton-spinning mill at Elton, Bury.

Ernest Hutchinson author of *The Right To Strike*
(Bury Archives Library)

Following school, Hutchinson returned to Prestwich and worked at the cotton-spinning works for some eight years, but he wasn't happy. He travelled, living in Russia for a while before returning in 1910 to become secretary to Sir Montagu Barlow, an English barrister and Conservative Party politician who between 1910 and 1923 represented Salford South in the House of Commons.

An original member of the Manchester Playgoers Club, Hutchinson was friendly with Stanley Houghton and, according to the *Manchester Guardian*, it was 'partly through the success of *Hindle Wakes* that he was induced to try his hand at playwriting.'

He wasn't particularly prolific at first. *Votes for Children* was produced at the Little Theatre in London in November 1911. His next play, the one-act, *Complaints*, was produced at the Gaiety Theatre on 24 October 1914 on the same bill as *A Man and Some Women* by Githa Sowerby. Considered 'a clever little comedy' by the *Manchester Courier*, it dealt with 'the egoism of the Lancashire cotton worker and the technical ignorance of the mill director. It is rather burdened with too much technique of the cotton mill even for Manchester but apart from this it is a bright little thing ... '[2]

The *Manchester Guardian* reviewer wrote:

> It brought back the hearty Lancashire atmosphere to the Gaiety stage. Both atmosphere and accent are, indeed, so extremely local that much of the spinning-mill detail would probably be better understood in Oldham than in Manchester, and – we put it purely as a question – does the nickname 'Maggie o'Sams' survive, particularly in a place that boasts a town council? The scene is a minutely conscientious reproduction of a mill-office and the fable is of the efforts of an amateur director, otherwise a valetudinarian restaurant proprietor, to trace the culprit in the matter of a stained warp. Warper, winder, ring-over-looker, carder, and cotton mixer all were interrogated in turn; then the manager returns and that warp, of course, is of someone else's spinning ... [3]

Although considered, thoroughly amusing it was felt to be too long, 'as if Mr Hutchinson intended to spin us his yarn in 32s and spun it out to 46s ... '

It was repeated on 7 November, after which Hutchinson joined the army and spent the next four years in the Royal Horse Artillery. Invalided out with rheumatic fever, he served in the War Contract Office (having to deal, inevitably, with cotton). Once demobbed, he found himself disillusioned with the state of England, riven by what he called 'class war', and so immediately began to write his major work, *The Right to Strike*. He was quoted as saying that he wrote the play, 'because he was so disgusted to find on returning from the war that there was so much class war in England'.[4]

It was certainly a turbulent period in British labour history. 1919 witnessed the broadest and most serious wave of strikes yet seen in the country. Thirty five million working days were lost in strike action – six times as many as in the previous year. This included strikes of the police and the armed forces while miners, transport workers and printers joined those who had been taking industrial action throughout the war.

The Clyde Workers' Committee organised a mass strike in January 1919. In Belfast a huge wave of strikes paralysed the city. More disturbing still, the threat that Britain might actually declare war against the Soviet Republic (the Bolshevik Revolution had taken place in 1917) resulted, in August 1920, in the formation of over 350 Councils of Action largely based on trades councils which pledged, with the support of the TUC and the Labour Party, to mobilise mass strikes should the threat prove real. In 1920 London dock workers refused to load arms onto a ship destined to supply the anti-communist forces in Russia, while the first intimations of a possible national strike were being mooted and agonised over.

The Right to Strike was immediately secured by Major Frank Vernon – a producer, author, and translator – who'd collaborated with theatre manager Vedrenne before the war at the Royalty

Theatre, producing Arnold Bennett's plays. It was mounted at the Garrick Theatre, opening on 28 September 1920, and would appear on the Gaiety stage in November that same year, the last Manchester playwright production to do so.

An idealistic and principled young doctor, Eric Miller, returns with his bride from their honeymoon abroad to Valleyhead, an industrial town in Lancashire served by a small railway branch line. Dr Miller's father and Dr Wrigley and Dr Donald, surgeons and physicians at the local infirmary, receive the homecomers with joy, but when Eric begins to ask questions as to how things are in Valleyhead he learns that England is threatened with class war and that a railway strike on the local railway, stirred up by outside agitators (led by a union official called Montague) is threatened. What's more, the strikers' leader is an old friend of Miller's.

The strike takes place and Valleyhead is completely cut off from the outside world, the strikers even refusing to allow goods through for the hospital's patients. Eric and other doctors try to beat the strike by organising lifts in cars, but a wire stretched across the road by the strikers kills Eric accidentally. Dr Miller is completely overwhelmed by his loss and the other doctors are furious and resolve to go on strike in retaliation.

They refuse to treat railway workers or members of their families and as a result Ben – a local union leader seeking only 'fair play' and the 'land fit for heroes' which he has been promised in return for fighting in the war – watches helplessly as his beloved wife struggles with a difficult confinement which the physician in attendance (who has declined to side with his professional colleagues) is unable to handle.

Ben is summoned to his wife's bedside and, afraid she will die, he appeals to the doctors for help. The younger physicians refuse to go saying that Ben 'has asked for a fight and shall have it', but his suffering has added to the natural and professional pity of old

Dr Miller, who breaks the doctors' strike by returning to help his patient. Simultaneously, the railway strike is called off.

The play thus ends with remorse on all sides and the suggestion that only by living in harmony and avoiding conflict can mutual suffering be avoided. Specifically, Eric's widow explains to Ben the need to return to a life lived through the peaceful principles of Christianity:

'Haven't we all rather lost sight of something this past fortnight – these past six years? Haven't we all rather forgotten that we're only God's children? We've been so busy fighting each other – fighting each other to kill, and fighting each other for our own selfish ends ... Wasn't it shown us in Galilee two thousand years ago!'[4]

The actor Leon Lion, who played Montague 'the Bolshevist' in the original production, described his character prior to the play's opening as 'a zealous young social worker of the Ruskin College type'.[5] Later, he added, 'In the play he was embodied somewhat as the mouthpiece of evil in contrast to the gallant young Lancashire doctor, emblematic of courage and toughness.'[6]

Montague, however, is no outright villain. There is no doubting either his sincerity or the fact that he expresses and organises the genuine thoughts and wishes of many local workers:

> MELLOR: It's no good tilting at the whole economic system of the country, Mr Montague. It's the law of nature, and a hard law I admit, but a law parliament can't alter for you.
> MONTAGUE: That's where you're wrong. You say it's the law of nature that the few should have everything and the rest of us work for them. We say nature gave to all men equally – not that one man should be born with a hundred thousand pounds and another with nothing at all....
> SIR ROGER: In fact, you're a Bolshevist.
> MONTAGUE: Yes, if you like – call me a Bolshevist ... if that's the only way left to us, we'll turn Bolshevist tomorrow.

JOHN: And shoot down anyone who opposes you?
MONTAGUE: Why not? The end justifies the means.
JOHN: Start Russia in Lancashire?
MONTAGUE: You may joke about it, but every thinking man knows
we're nearer to it than you care to admit.[7]

The Lord Chamberlain at first banning the use of the word
'bloody' and then changing his mind did not hinder the play's
reception. *The Right to Strike* immediately provoked considerable
public reaction both inside and outside the theatre, Leon Lion
subsequently recalling that performances were regularly punctuated
by outbursts from different sections of the audience: 'Calls of
"Cads!" and "Profiteers tricks!" were heard from the gallery and
there were cat-calls at certain moments. The line "You bloody
murderer," spoken by Dr Wrigley to Ben Ormerod on hearing of
the death of his friend was greeted by boos and hisses.'[8]

The Spectator reviewer was not amused by the angry passions
aroused in the audience:

> One would have thought that the vast European upheaval and the
> death of millions would have satisfied any appetite for combat; but
> no, it was quite obvious that the audience, whether pro- or anti-
> proletarian, were all most cheerfully, most joyfully, out to hit
> somebody and were revelling in this spectacle of a 'scrap'. Let the
> pacifist with his theory of millions of obedient working men driven
> unwillingly to slaughter observe the curious phenomenon which
> takes place at the Garrick Theatre ...[9]

Lion himself claimed he was later required to answer questions
about the play from King George V who'd been anxious to see it
but somehow missed it.

The play was the talk of the political salons and the London clubs,
of all, in fact, who would today be dubbed 'intelligentsia', notable among
them being Winston Churchill, John Simon, Keir Hardie, J.H. Thomas
and many other prominent politicians and Labour figures.

Press reviews following a tumultuous first night were full of praise for the way the debate concerning the ethics of doctors striking was presented, although the quality of Hutchinson's writing left much to be desired. *The Spectator* critic considered the play was, 'Ill-put together', that it suffered from 'extraordinary bad dialogue' and 'inexpensive sentiment'.

'The author's knowledge of strikes appears to have greatly surpassed his knowledge of plays,' while, 'his dramatic expression was so completely old-fashioned, so – we must say it – provincial.' The audience, however, was certainly 'revelling in this spectacle of a 'scrap' and the whole evening was 'very enjoyable ... '[10]

The *Daily Mail* felt the playwright was 'playing with fire to treat this question just now', and that the play lacked the 'tremendous grip of Galsworthy's *Strife*' although containing some 'excellent comic character studies' [11]

The Times opined that the play would be bad propaganda because it was impossible to discover the author's own views. It, 'discussed much and achieved nothing', and that 'the problem became too big for Mr Hutchinson in the last act.' It was still, however, a 'courageous production with lots of good performances'.[12]

The *Guardian* reviewer concentrated on the 'really detestable' Montague ('The paid middle-class agitator who is shown to be clearly responsible for the worst phases of the labour troubles ... '). He was necessary because otherwise all would have been settled amicably, 'So we readily forgive Mr Hutchinson his agitator on whom so much that is interesting hangs, though we refuse to believe that those hard-headed Lancashire men would have been taken in by him for a minute ... ' 'There were, 'over-generous chunks of sentiment and melodrama,' loading the play but 'as a whole it was stimulating and well put together.'[13]

The *Daily Mirror* seized the moment. It arranged a special

matinee performance and posed the question: 'Should the professional class "counter-strike"? The matinee will endeavour to obtain a consensus of opinion on this point.'[14]

Invitations were sent out to Medical Officers of Health from around London and the regions, along with several hundred doctors, MPs, various mayors, prominent academics, society do-gooders and suffragists. Playwrights and writers such as Stephen McKenna, Hugh Walpole, Max Pemberton were also invited. Each guest was given a voting slip and asked to vote on the following questions:

Is the strike an antiquated weapon?
Is it, in certain circumstances, a crime against the community?
Are the sufferers justified in undertaking reprisals?

In the event, 1,400 people attended and voted 58 per cent for and 42 per cent against doctors being allowed to counter-strike. 41 per cent were for and 53 per cent against 'reprisal strikes'.

The furore, quite understandably, disturbed the medical profession. The *Daily Mail* carried a piece by a 'medical correspondent' entitled 'As Others See Us'. Doctors had a special role and they did not go on strike, the writer insisted, and while exasperated at the play's inaccuracies (no doctor could be struck off in just 10 minutes, for instance) yet, 'Perhaps for the first real time in his life he [the doctor] will see himself as the world sees him ... '[15]

Medical Journals carried letters discussing the issue. Dr Arthur Cox, medical secretary of the British Medical Association, wrote in the *Lancet*:

'I have always held that in this country a real strike by doctors is almost unthinkable. The idea of withholding service from one's own patients – people you may possibly have known since birth – revolts every professional instinct.' Nevertheless, he added, 'But I do not say that a refusal to serve would in any circumstances be wrong. If I were practising in a country cursed with a set of bloodthirsty scoundrels who had temporarily got the upper hand and who declared their intention of wiping out the "bourgeois" class to which I belong, I should think it quite right to decline to give my services to anybody expressing that intention. In the words of Clough, 'Thou shalt not kill, but needst not strive officiously to keep alive.'" ... [16]

Ernest Hutchinson himself steadfastly refused to take sides. On the first night he'd taken to the stage to deny that the play was propaganda. Interviewed in the *Daily Mirror* he insisted:

> The mutual suspicion between the two parties in the dispute is surely at the root of half the trouble (in Valleyhead). It is precisely the existence of this dormant suspicion among all classes and my post-war observation of its workings that I have tried to express in dramatic form ... Far from writing a propaganda play I have tried to paint (as I believe it is the duty of the dramatist) an impartial picture. I can scarcely be blamed if this picture of our country seems rather less bright than that idealised memory we carried with us overseas.[17]

It wasn't, he declared, the dramatist's job to provide solutions to the problems he had portrayed: 'That surely, in a case like this, is the business of the sociologist; not of the dramatist who has performed his part when he suggests the atmosphere in which human catastrophe is bred.'[18]

Hutchinson talked of his intimate knowledge of the 'working man'. Ben Ormerod, he felt, was the 'typical British worker': 'Loyal-hearted and with a deep sense of right, he is perhaps the most unready fellow in the world when it comes to talk. That is the type of man whom I met during the eight years I worked among the Lancashire cotton mills.'[19]

When pressed for a solution, however, he suggested it might come from Dr Miller – 'a conciliator or rather a spectator who sees the big common human interests standing out above any sectional claim'. A strike was a three-sided issue: 'with some woman or some child (or merely a hard-working "consumer") as the forgotten and neglected factor'.[20]

He ended by quoting one of the female characters (Mary Miller) at the end of the play when she talked of God and Galilee.

Leon Lion felt that Hutchinson, although hoping and believing he was being equally fair to each, could not avoid 'being a Lancashire professional man himself – an unconscious, astigmatic squint when stating, or overstating, the case for Labour ... ' [21]

Nevertheless, it was clear that *The Right to Strike* was not really concerned with workers' rights as such. It was very much about how the middle class might respond, and whether they ought to strike back against the insurgent forces gathering all around.

The experience of the war just finished ran though the play as well as the subsequent novelised version. The room in which the strike-breakers plan their campaign is described as, 'busy as an orderly room'; a strike-breaker, warned of the cold night, laughs that, 'It won't be half as bad as Belgium in January'; one of the helpers organising convoys whistles 'Mademoiselle from Armentières' and asks, rather contentedly, 'Isn't it like being back at the war again?'

The strikers, on the other hand, are compared to those ever-unpopular villains of Twenties texts, the wartime profiteers: 'Though they dealt in pounds and even shillings, were they not equally guilty with those magnates who were even now holding up commodities in order to extort a larger profit later?'

The main representative of the workers, Ben Ormerod, who during the war had been, 'a strapping sergeant of the Lancashire Fusiliers', is portrayed as a thoughtful man, a good husband and a natural leader – but led astray by the rhetoric of a socialist agitator. His instincts are humane and practical but the 'extremist ideology' leads him into a position where he is unable to control the violence of the men that he is leading in the strike. Where the officer-led strike-breakers are efficient, organised and controlled, the strikers are represented as volatile, violent and chaotic.

Despite this (unconscious?) imbalance, the play did allow a real debate to take place at the time of great uncertainty, and hence its success. The Chairman of the Railway Company promises that 'the capitalist has still a good deal of kick left in him', and that he will fight if the workers 'push matters to extremes', while the local Labour MP insists that Parliament is the only effective way to improve society. Agitator Montague argues that such promises are simply, 'the drug to keep the working man quiet', and when the MP complains that the workers' behaviour is 'not English', Montague points out that 'It's as English as starving the strikers' women and children to death, as capital has claimed the right to do in the past', and insists that workers must strike effectively. Trapped in the middle is Ben, who seeks no more than the opportunity to live a decent life, and for wartime promises to be fulfilled.

Steve Nicholson in his article 'Bolshevism in Lancashire: British Strike Plays of the 1920s' makes the point that it would have been extremely difficult for any play that attacked the status quo or advocated the end of capitalism or the need for violent revolution at such a point in history to have been granted a licence. Playwrights

> ... could go no further than calling for greater mutual understanding and a willingness for the different classes to be reasonable, to understand each other, to compromise, and to work together in harmony rather than confrontation. Fundamental change was not an option worthy of serious consideration, and though the economic system could be tinkered with, there was no question of revolution. Strikes were inevitably and entirely destructive. In the years just before and after the General Strike, that was, of course, a highly political stance to adopt.[22]

Whether Hutchinson's play was being 'used as a vehicle for an overt defence of capitalist principles' is debatable although Hutchinson's politics were clearly not of the left.

The Right to Strike ran for 82 performances at the Garrick, Lyric, and Queen's Theatres, London, between September and December 1920. Although it did not make a great deal of money, offers for the rights poured in from every part of the world, the lending libraries made large 'deals' and Hutchinson was urged to start another play.

A bright future beckoned for him. He quickly wrote a novel based on the play; the play itself went on tour, was taken to the USA and opened (and quickly closed) on Broadway. In Europe it was translated into a number of languages.

Within six months Hutchinson was contributing sketches and lyrics to a frothy André Charlot revue called *Puss! Puss!* at the Vaudeville Theatre, London. He appeared to be moving in all the right circles. In his heyday Charlot, or 'Guv', as he became known, was rivalled only by that other great showman, Charles B. Cochran: he would launch the careers of theatrical stars Beatrice Lillie, Gertrude Lawrence and Jack Buchanan, Jack Hulbert and Binnie Hale; Noël Coward made his first appearance in a Charlot revue in 1923 co-starring with Gertrude Lawrence in *London Calling,* the same year that the silent film version of *The Right To Strike* appeared starring silent film star Lillian Hall-Davis.

Hutchinson, however, didn't live to savour the success. On 5 November 1921, following a 'slight operation', he suffered a heart attack and died aged 36.

There would be only one other Manchester School writer who would tackle such a theme, and his play would appear some years after the Gaiety had closed. Allan Monkhouse's *First Blood* is again set against the backdrop of a Lancashire strike, and takes place in, 'the uncertain future'. The two central characters, Lionel the son of a millowner and Phyllis, the daughter of a working family, are ultimately shot while trying to prevent an attack on the millowner's house by striking workers.

'The play proposes no neat resolution to the conflict between management and workers on which it focuses, but again its unquestioned and unargued assumption is the familiar one that 'at all costs class war must be avoided.'[23]

Monkhouse's play, however, received little attention and no more than a handful of performances. His major achievements would be elsewhere, as we shall see.

Notes

[1] W.A. Stokes, *British Medical Journal* (1920), 609.

[2] *Manchester Courier*, November 1914.

[3] *Manchester Guardian*, 27 October 1914.

[4] *The Right To Strike* play text

[5] *The Times*, 11 September 1914.

[6] Leon Lion, *The Surprise of My Life* (Hutchinson, 1948), p88.

[7] *The Right To Strike* play text.

[8] Lion, *op. cit.,* pp86, 87.

[9] *The Spectator*, 16 October 1920.

[10] Ibid.

[11] *Daily Mail*, 29 September 1920.

[12] *The Times*, 29 September 1920.

[13] *Manchester Guardian*, 2 November 1920.

[14] *Daily Mirror*, 30 September 1920.

[15] *Daily Mail*, 30 September 1920.

[16] Quoted in the *AMA Journal*, 4 December 1920, pp1571–2.

[17] *Daily Mirror*, 1 October 1920.

[18] Ibid.

[19] Ibid.

[20] Ibid.

[21] Lion, *op. cit.,* p88.

[22] Steve Nicholson, 'Bolshevism in Lancashire: British Strike Plays of the 1920s', *New Theatre Quarterly*, 30 (1992), 8/2.

[23] Ibid.

11

Allan Monkhouse:
A Manchester Novelist

> The number of good novelists at work is disconcerting to any one
> who looks for eminence in that line, but the play-writers that the
> ardent young man thinks worth consideration may almost be told
> on the fingers of one hand ... Was this sham world his real one?[1]

Thus far, the roll-call of Manchester playwrights has included
newspaper journalists, union officials, actresses, doctors,
barristers and Manchester businessmen. All had been encouraged
to write plays and some had seen them put on with success – but
none of them considered themselves professional dramatists. They
had their day-jobs, so to speak. With Allan Monkhouse, however,
things were very different.

Already 50 years old in 1908, a novelist and one of the *Manchester
Guardian*'s most prominent theatre critics, his influence on the
establishment of the Gaiety would be significant and his
participation in Miss Horniman's enterprise from the very start
was a message that the city's intellectual community was solidly
behind her.

As early as July 1907, with the prospect of AH setting up a theatre
in Manchester a real one, he wrote: 'Who knows whether we may
not even develop our own school of dramatists? We must not imitate
the Celtic temper nor Mr Shaw's paradoxes, but tragedy and comedy

may be found in Lancashire life ... and we have men here who can observe it and might dramatize it.'[2]

Monkhouse was quite correct: and his would be the second play by a 'local' playwright to be produced on the Gaiety stage.

Monkhouse never wrote an autobiography although pressed to do so many times. Fortunately, his novels often feature a character clearly based on himself and one or two pertinent facts can be gleaned from them. The opening chapter of the novel *Men and Ghosts* (1918) is even considered to be straight autobiography, with only the names changed:

> I was born – let us get to the beginning – at Balliol [actually Barnard Castle] in 1858 on the 7 May – the fine, windy old town that stands just on the Durham side of the Tees and stretches downward and across the river into Yorkshire. It was in a little unobtrusive semi-detached house ... [3]
>
> My mother was a Londoner and my father met her when he was employed in the London warehouse of a then comparatively prosperous carpet factory. I was born when my father was running the factory and about a year after my birth it was abandoned. I think that for years it had been a decaying industry and that other members of his family who had managed to escape to more profitable occupations had left my father in it as a kind of scapegoat. So, with the four children, as we were then, he and my mother had to seek their fortunes elsewhere and they came to Manchester where my father became a salesman and traveller with a firm of carpet merchants to which he formerly used to sell goods.[4]
>
> When we first came to Manchester we lived in a very little house at the end of a row in Bury New Road and, though for long afterwards I had no standard of comparison, we must have been very poor. We had no garden but there was a kind of neglected field behind called 'the hill' where we played and made some sort of intimacies with other children.[5]

When the real Monkhouse was six, his mother died of a neo-natal infection after giving birth to her seventh child. Two of her children died in infancy, leaving Allan with a brother and three sisters. He told the Town and Counties Club in 1932, 'One of my earliest recollections is of the cotton famine in Lancashire which was a real famine and a real crisis ... ' He remembered being given as a child a soup ticket to hand to an unemployed man sitting on a bench where now is the Cromwell Monument: 'Why a soup ticket delivered by a toddler should have been more acceptable in those days he was unable to determine. 'We were sentimentalists then ... '[6]

What Monkhouse didn't tell the audience was that his godfather Matthew Noble was responsible for Cromwell's statue. Sculptors ran in the Monkhouse family on his mother's side. Noble's works include Prince Albert in Manchester's Albert Square.

Allan was educated at private schools, was a good athlete, a keen walker, climber, cricketer and golfer. Leaving school, he went straight into the cotton business as a yarn agent on the floor of Manchester's Royal Exchange where he worked for some twenty years. He recalled on radio in the 1930s, 'I was a Manchester businessman dallying a little with literature. Sometimes now I lure a companion down certain streets and, pointing to a fairly imposing block, I say casually, "I used to be manager there".'[7]

In 1893 he married an artist Lucy Dowie, but she died of tuberculosis a year later. It was while he was married to Lucy that he was approached by W.T. Arnold, the first leader writer of *Manchester Guardian*, to write 'occasional dramatic criticisms'. He seemed rather doubtful at first, feeling that he wasn't equipped educationally but it turned out to be the start of a new career.

Occasional work for the *Guardian* continued until he joined the staff in 1902, the same year that he married his second wife, Dorothy. He was taken on as an all-rounder, writing reports on the cotton exchange by day (when part of his duty was to announce that the demand for shirtings was slow or that there had been 'a little more activity' in the China market) and dramatic criticism by night. His industrial expertise was such that he contributed to the seventh edition of *Encyclopaedia Britannica* on the British home and export trade in cotton goods and yarn. He also contributed golf notes, a first for a daily newspaper.

His role on the literary side of the newspaper gradually grew until he was widely recognised as the literary editor although he himself disliked the title ('There's no such thing,' he once claimed). Such self-effacing replies suggest that he felt ill-at-ease working alongside men who had been to University and had a classical education.

In his novel *True Love*, the *Guardian*'s (re-named The 'Herald') recruitment policy was described thus: 'When Lindsay wanted a new man on the staff he wrote to some bigwig at Oxford and asked for a list of the best young men about. Brilliant young double firsts tumbled over one another to get on the *Herald*, but they had to be something better than double firsts to stay there. Yes, the pace was hot ... '[8]

In the same novel, a journalist called Geoffrey Arden (based upon Monkhouse himself) reflects:

> [He] had been pitchforked into journalism ill equipped without adequate training in economics or history or anything else. His schooling had been cut short early; he had pursued 'business' half-heartedly while casual, copious reading tended to a sort of culture. And, really, he was finding the pace too hot. He hadn't the boundless energy to overhaul the others.[9]

The only truly fictional part of that quote relates to Arden (Monkhouse) not having the 'energy' to succeed. Monkhouse would work harder than anyone else for the next thirty years, his output being prodigious. His first published work was a collection of critical literary essays *Books & Plays* (1894) when aged 36. He then began his long career as a prose fiction writer. Beginning with *A Deliverance* (1898) he would write another nine novels plus numerous short stories until his last, aptly titled *Farewell Manchester* (1931). All were situated in Manchester and its surroundings and drew their characters from the life that Monkhouse knew best, that of newspaper offices and of business, the theatre, the profession of letters, and the social contacts and humours and aspirations of the suburbs.

A Deliverance (1898) was somewhat original for the times, presented a dying lover as setting up platonic house with a young woman (who just happens to review books in the *Guardian*) who turns out to possess such a fastidious and demanding temper that he has had to resort to a warm-blooded adulteress.'

In *Love in a Life* (1903) John Axon, a working-class young man employed in a Manchester warehouse and a Socialist by conviction, goes to live for a time in a middle-class suburb, falls in love. He then struggles between his conviction that he should go back to live with the people in whose midst he was born and the longing to marry his love. He chooses to leave the woman (who marries Axon's middle-class, cultured friend) rather than be a traitor to his own class. One reviewer considered 'the realism of [Elizabeth Gaskell's] *Mary Barton* is wanting ... ' but that it 'showed promise'.

Nine years later came *Dying Fires* (1912), involving another love-triangle, this time set in upper-middle-class Manchester. A married couple finds their union disintegrating following the death of their infant child. The couple's closest friend loves the wife and the novel tracks the gradual, painful decision she ultimately makes: not to leave her husband for the friend.

Early in the novel, Monkhouse gives a pen-picture of the Manchester Exchange, where he had once worked buying and selling cloth. The friend meets the wife there:

> Her glance roamed over the whole vast assembly; her heart lifted, but the concentration upon groups of little shabby men and their obscure chafferings depressed her.

'I see they are ill-dressed little men with bowler hats, but, together, what a shout they could raise.'

'There' s a big thing behind them. All the mills and spindles and looms and the operatives. Manchester's only the bargaining centre. You get to the heart of it at Oldham or Burnley. They're the tragic places. Of course they don't know it, and there's a queer little fringe of philanthropy with parks and things and arid religious sects for those who like them, and great, queer interests in betting and football. And you mustn't judge the operatives when you meet thousands of them – eager little men and boys in caps – going to a football match. They're not lovable so. Don't judge any class by its crowds. Mighty, blind powers.'[10]

Men and Ghosts (1918) featured two young men, 'sedulous sceptics', who both fall in love with a gracious but implacably Christian girl. One of the young men impregnates a village girl, has a fatal fall in the Lake District, and is nursed by the girl but dies, after which the girl adopts the child.

My Daughter Helen (1922) portrayed a father through the eyes of his daughter. Considered at the time a 'psychological, experimental' novel, one reviewer noted that Monkhouse 'does not shrink from illuminating the inability of one generation fully to understand the attitudes of another'. A central character in the book was based on the future novelist Christoper Isherwood who had befriended Monkhouse's daughter.

Alfred the Great (1927) was the psychological study of a thwarted man, a successful novelist for a short time, whose public ultimately tire of him until a convenient operation gives him the opportunity of retiring to his bed where he remains, surrounded by his admiring family.

Farewell Manchester (1931) was also set in Manchester and the suburbs and is about Walter, Jack and Laura, the children of cotton manufacturer John Henry Tunstall, a self-made man who's married slightly above himself. It takes the story from immediate post-World

War when Jack returns, won't talk about his experiences, and his brother becomes a priest ...

Reviewing his novels in 1958, the critic Anne Duchene summarized them:

> His heroes bear a striking resemblance to one another: They are all Manchester men or Derbyshire dwellers given to holidays in the Lake District. They are middle-class and suburban with jobs – not over-specified – in cotton or the law, save for a few who are writers or 'Herald' (*Guardian*) men; they have gardens and tennis clubs. In love they choose clever cryptic women. They are rigorous with themselves demanding wit, impeccable exactness of expression and impeccable reticence; they want to be able to 'perfectly trust themselves' and they question themselves until 'every action becomes a kind of moral adjustment.' Monkhouse's method is to push them to the uttermost limits their intelligence and passion can sustain, in some big challenge, a moral and emotional convulsion ... [11]

Unfortunately for Monkhouse, though admired and well reviewed, his novels had little general appeal. His friend and protégé Frank Swinnerton wrote that they 'were fine, rarefied and unpopular (another friend once said to me of *Men and Ghosts* 'What was the title of that awfully good book I couldn't read?') and he suffered from the consciousness that while they were all greatly admired by the percipient among his fellow craftsmen 'they never, if they were novels, sold more than fifteen hundred copies ... ' [12]

Swinnerton felt that the treatment of his characters

> ... is at all times full of charm, wit, wisdom ... If they failed to arouse popular enthusiasm it was because they were too 'literary', and because the small, the fine, the delicate, while they have their delicious joys for those of like mind, do lack robustness, power, and the colour and movement of irresistible life ... [13]
>
> But though grieved and puzzled by a public indifference he did not repine and he was incapable of envy – even of that almost vicarious envy which regrets the success of unworthy people in any

profession. Subtle and repressed, he laughed to himself and went again to his desk, working in miniature but with his eye forever upon greater horizons ... [14]

Harold Brighouse, who wrote in his autobiography that he 'revered' Monkhouse, recounted how the latter had written to him expressing bemusement at how a particular novelist was able to sell 40,000 copies before publication. 'I had just heard that Pinker (his agent) can't place *Alfred* in New York and my sales before publication here were 384. Not that I'm embittered.'[15]

Reviewing Monkhouse's 1920 novel *True Love*, Katherine Mansfield probably summed the problem up succinctly:

> Mr Monkhouse is an author who drives a pen well under control. He is a professional novelist quietly confident, carefully ironical and choosing always at a crisis to underrate the seriousness of the situation rather than to stress it unduly. Admirable as this temper undoubtedly is, it nevertheless leaves the reader a great deal cooler than he would wish.
>
> The 'false' writer begins as an experimentalist; the true artist ends as one; but between these two there are a small number of writers of unquestionable honesty and sincerity who do not feel the impulsion toward unknown issues. It follows that in novels of this kind there is room for most delicate distinctions, but high excitements are out of place; all is, as it were, at second-hand, and while we are not expected to share the experience with the author, he would seem, by the care he takes never to make an unguarded statement, to expect of us a kind of intellectual running commentary. *True Love* is an extremely good example of this peculiar kind of novel.[16]

Peculiar novelist though he might have been, however, in 1907 AH had fired in him the desire to broaden his appeal. It is to his plays that we must now turn.

Notes

[1] Allan Monkhouse, *True Love* (Henry Holt, 1920).

[2] *Manchester Guardian*, 25 July 1907.

[3] Allan Monkhouse, *Men and Ghosts* (William Collins, 1918).

[4] Ibid.

[5] Ibid.

[6] *Manchester Guardian*, 17 June 1932.

[7] BBC Radio North Region 1930s, 'The 90s and Now'.

[8] Monkhouse, *True Love*.

[9] Ibid.

[10] *Dying Fires* (Duckworth, 1912).

[11] *Manchester Guardian*, 3 May 1958.

[12] Frank Swinnerton *An Autobiography* (Hutchinson, 1937) p259

[13] Frank Swinnerton *The Georgian Literary Scene, 1910–1935* (Hutchinson, 1935), p179.

[14] Swinnerton *Autobiography op cit* p259

[15] Brighouse, *What I Have Had*, p171.

[16] *The Athenaeum*, 28 November 1919.

12

Proud Mary

It was one of those half-baked plays by amateurs in ideas that the repertory theatres have loosed on us.[1]

I had out of *Mary Broome* one of the finest and most stimulating entertainments ... that I ever remember having. It was Montague, I think, who called it 'one of the Gaiety's happiest adventures.'[2]

Monkhouse's playwriting career began on 28 September 1908 in the third week of AH's first new Gaiety season. His one-act *Reaping the Whirlwind* opened a double bill alongside Charles McEvoy's *David Ballard* and was well received, although curiosity concerning the identity of playwright must have surpassed any interest in the play itself.

It was quite a courageous act when one considers Monkhouse's position. He was by then one of the *Guardian*'s most prominent literary critics, was already an established novelist, had published two volumes of criticism and his judgements on other people's work appeared each week. He was setting himself up to be shot at. Then again, it could be said, he was amongst friends – a critique regularly aimed at the *Manchester Guardian* and its 'coterie' of playwriting critics.

Frank Swinnerton wrote of the 'literary' *Guardian* staff:

They all, or nearly all, wrote plays to fill its repertory; and when they did not write such plays they made a point of going to see what their comrades had written, and of criticizing it as they would have done if they had been still in the literary set at Oxford. They made a family, and a happy one. And the family had the feeling that its affairs were of supreme importance to modern literature.[3]

It was, in fact, James Agate, a protégé and subsequent close friend of Monkhouse's, who reviewed his first effort in the *Guardian*. The plot was straightforward: 'A wife, neglected by a husband preoccupied with his work, seeks distraction elsewhere. Her passion that sweeps her off her feet fails her, an attempt at running away ends dismally, she goes back to her husband and the lover shoots himself on their doorstep.' Monkhouse, according to Agate, 'makes a simple net statement of an event, leaving us to size it up, to make if it what we can ... This little piece is sane and real and full of our irrepressible helplessness in the face of terrible happening.'[4]

His second play, another one-act piece, came almost two years later on 6 June 1910. *The Choice* was loosely called a 'War' play when published in 1916 and will be looked at a little later. 9 October 1911, however, saw the unveiling of what was to be considered by many at the time and since as his finest achievement: his first major three-act play, *Mary Broome*.

The action of the play is set in a solidly middle-class, prosperous household. Mary ('the best housemaid I ever had,' according to Mrs Timbrell, the household's doyenne) has had a moment of weakness with the household's younger son, Leonard, and is pregnant. Leonard is a wastrel, sponging off his very proper father for funds and fancying himself a writer, but also (conveniently for him) possessing very freethinking views when it comes to issues of sex and class, views much too advanced for his staid relatives and to a certain extent for Mary as well.

Allan Monkouse. Novelist, critic and playwright.
(*Permission Harriet Monkhouse*)

Mr Timbrell Snr, thundering with righteous wrath, insists that his son does the right thing and marry the girl or be banished from the family. They marry under duress, they have a child, but the child dies – partly due to Leonard's feckless behaviour. No longer desirous of coping with Leonard's capricious behaviour, Mary decides to leave him and start a new life in Canada with an old flame, a milkman, to the astonishment of the Timbrells, Leonard included.

Like almost all of Monkhouse's fiction, either prose or drama, it is a story of middle-class angst, with working-class characters somewhat on the periphery. Mary herself, possibly his strongest female character, was said to have been developed by Monkhouse from a waitress who had once served him in a teashop.

Irene Rooke the actress who first played Mary wrote to Monkhouse, 'I tried to bring to bear maids I have known. One I once had was in somewhat the same position and what struck me forcibly was her detachment from the matter, she stated startling facts quite unemotionally and then waited patiently for something to happen.' She added that she'd struggled with the role at first and kept getting it wrong. The audience apparently laughed in the wrong places, particularly when she said, 'Well, I shall be a mother soon.' She changed her interpretation: 'I have tried each night since to be more normal, brighter, not the dumb thing that that class of girl usually is with her "masters".' [5]

Frank Swinnerton agreed with some critics who felt Mary's calmness and dignity made it 'difficult to imagine so discreet a young woman yielding to passion or the importunities of an egoist like Leonard.' He went on:

> But the author was more concerned with the effect upon others of Mary's conduct than with the consistency of Mary herself; and the point of *Mary Broome* to which I direct attention is that the young and talkative seducer addressed his parents in these terms:

LEONARD: You parents are in a middle stage. Once you'd just have been brutal to the girl. I don't mean you, but parents generally. Presently we may have more sense. I'm a selfish brute but I've got some sense. But I'm powerless. (*To his father*): Haven't you any imagination? It's all very fine to make a scene here and put down your foot and coerce me into your beastly righteousness, but think of the years to come. Do you see us married? Do you see our married life?

That, according to Swinnerton, was the 'voice of self-conscious thought in 1911'.[6]

In fact, much of the drive and energy of the play stems from Leonard whose outrageous diatribes and posturing have led some modern critics to dub him an Edwardian 'Jimmy Porter'. At one point he taunts his family with this Porter-ish put-down:

(To Mary): I've wronged you, as the saying goes, but I don't wrong you with every instinct, at every hour of the day. After all, I'm the only member of this family that's achieved any kind of human relationship with you.[7]

On that first night, the Manchester audience was divided: some were unhappy about the play's morality and that it had at its centre an, 'unmitigated cad'. Harold Brighouse felt that the actor Milton Rosmer as Leonard played the part badly, 'shouting and acting like a "bounder" all night. He shouted his speech to make an affect.' All the same, 'All the people in my lot have been discussing and wrangling about it.'[8]

Stanley Houghton sensed that some of the audience, 'seemed to be a little uncertain whether they ought to be shocked, and ... undoubtedly suppressed their pleasurable emotions lest their friends should have disturbing ideas. After the first act I heard a worthy lady behind me remark, "It's a good thing we didn't bring Phyllis".'

In the same letter he commented:

... the general impression one gets is that you have a burning scorn for most of the persons you have chosen to put on the stage, and that is why the stalls and the circle are uncomfortable; they feel that they would have acted like the people you laugh at and that therefore you are laughing at them.[9]

Edward Garnett, a great supporter of Monkhouse's, enjoyed the way that Monkhouse had 'ripped open most dexterously the stuffing of the bourgeois ideal and contrasted it with the simpler, more direct working-class ethic'. Garnett could easily see, 'how the Manchester audience appreciated his putting "that section" of the middle class into the dock ... '[10]

The *Manchester Courier* reviewer agreed, seeing the play as an example of what the newer school of dramatists were after: 'The mean little pretentiousness of the Timbrell household, their false geniality, their bogus tolerance, are all shown up,' although he noted that even the working-class characters were not spared. Mary's parents, especially her redundant cab-driver father, who are prepared to see Mary married off are not depicted with much sympathy. The reviewer concluded, however, that Monkhouse 'might give us a little more broad humour and less subtlety'.[11]

The Gaiety Company took the play to London for a season at the Coronet theatre in Notting Hill in May and June 1912. There, the reception was somewhat different. *The Times* reviewer saw nothing but, superficial cleverness, 'the whole affair being absolutely insincere and derivative' with the only good thing about the play being Irene Rooke's playing of Mary.[12]

The *Evening Standard* thought it, 'a shallowly clever play, well worth seeing as a freak specimen of so-called advanced drama', while the *Observer* felt it was merely imitating Shaw and Barker. The *New Statesman* lauded the first act as a 'masterpiece of pointed compression', but as for the whole play, 'psychologically, nothing happened.'[13]

It seemed that the apparent absence of a clear didactic message caused some confusion amongst the critics who couldn't place it in any particular dramatic bracket.

Mary Broome, despite its prominence in the Manchester playwrights' canon, would not be seen again on a professional stage (or any stage for that matter) until early in the 20th century when it was successfully revived both in London and New York.

Monkhouse's reaction to the apparent failure of *Mary Broome* is made clear in his novel *True Love*, in which Monkhouse becomes a journalist called Geoffrey and the play is renamed *Alice Dean*:

> Geoffrey soon discovered that Alice Dean had not advanced him far in what some of his friends would call his practical career. It had not made a profound impression on the general consciousness but when people met him they inquired encouragingly whether he had got 'anything on the stocks?' It was not a very difficult question to parry, and he found himself extremely unwilling to discuss his work with genial people who had no interest in it.[14]

Leaving aside the fact that critics and audience might find a play like *Mary Broome* problematical for social reasons (although hardly original where its basic plot was concerned) there was clearly something about Monkhouse's method that made him a difficult writer for audiences to warm to.

Friends and colleagues regularly offered him advice, sometimes wrapped in praise. John Galsworthy wrote to him of *Mary Broome*: 'In many ways so admirably, I felt that a fantasist by nature was struggling too hard with a deliberately chosen naturalistic technique ... I felt that your characters stated themselves too much, were too conscious of themselves. "Art demands indirect evidence before it can convince." But when carping is all over they remain stimulating and genuine work.'[5]

His admirer and protégé Stanley Houghton wrote:

> It struck me that you were not concerned so much with the outsides as the insides of your people – a pretty obvious thing to say of novelists now – but not yet actually, of dramatists, although Ibsen

has been dead a long while. And I thought you were so keen on tearing out the insides that you left the outsides to take care of themselves, rather. I don't know quite what I mean, unless it is that you tried to reveal the people by what they said more than by what they did ... The natural result of your method is that you make your comedy astonishingly deep and brilliant, and just a little inhuman ... The wit of your dialogue is perfectly astonishing.[16]

The novelist Charles Morgan, writing in 1933 and comparing Monkhouse's work with that of Eugene O'Neill thought Monkhouse spoilt his play with a 'too-rigid devotion to the principles of dramatic economy. So determined had he been to make every word of his dialogue perform a precise purpose that the dialogue considered as a whole lacks pliancy and freedom.'[17]

Edward Garnett suggested that there was a certain 'dryness' about his characterisation, that his work, 'is always rarefied, appealing by its high dry atmosphere ... but that it lacked "real women" ... I feel that you have not lived these experiences ... they are brainwork chiefly ... '[18]

It would be his other great friend and fellow Manchester playwright, Harold Brighouse who would analyse what he saw as Monkhouse's main problem. Brighouse, an expert technician where plays were concerned, had proffered some advice to Monkhouse that the latter had felt useful. Monkhouse joked that Brighouse deserved the commissions that he paid to his own agent, Pinker, who Monkhouse felt failed to promote his work sufficiently. Brighouse continued:

The fault was not in J.B. Pinker, but in the plays of Monkhouse, whose comment on Shakespeare is relevant:

'I've seen little indeed of modern production of Shakespeare, but I don't think it would move me far from my moorings if I had seen it all. Shakespeare's plot, construction, balance, appeal to me very little. It's as a dramatic poet he does appeal to me. He

sticks his people on rather childishly, but they say such splendid
and moving things. They say them as well – or better – to me
when I read them as when a competent actor recites them. A
man of genius like Irving does help, but my appreciation of
Shakespeare must at best be at least nine parts reading to one
acting.'

That is Shakespeare for closet reading. But Shakespeare, supreme in
all, was supremely a dramatic technician: Shakespeare the playwright
is the playwright's Shakespeare. The constructive weakness of
Monkhouse's plays was deliberate, defiant, and suicidal.[19]

Monkhouse would remain unmoved by any suggestions and
criticisms and consistently rejected any attempts to alter even so
much as a line in any of his plays.

In an essay entitled 'The Words and the Play' written in 1925,
while conceding that authors cannot demand there be no changes
at all to their text, he nevertheless confessed how he could not
understand how the author of a play, 'unless he be beaten to his
knees, can give a general consent to managers and producers to fit
it to their needs and *the supposed desires of the audience* ... We
must all try to be reasonable but I think we must stick to our words
until it is clear to us that change would be improvement.'[20]

He wasn't above teasing himself where this tendency was
concerned and even satirised himself later on in a small one-act
play called *Nothing Like Leather* that spoofed the both himself and
the Gaiety in general. In fact, *Nothing Like Leather* would be the
last of his dramatic pieces mounted by the Gaiety Theatre, although
his output of drama would remain extraordinary – as many as 16
more one-act and three-act plays written between 1912 and 1932.

Once again, his novel *True Love* gives a glimpse of how he would
sum up his Gaiety experience:

It chanced that he passed the Playgoers' Theatre, a commonplace
enough structure but with associations, speaking to him already of

memories. It had a disused, irrelevant look in the daylight, and even at night its brilliances were rather dingy. He stood looking at it ... Was this his life? This sort of thing? This provincial inconsiderable temple of the mediocrities? He could idealize it but was it *good enough* on any terms?[21]

Nevertheless, Monkhouse's tenacity, his tendency to stick to his dramatic guns, would ultimately, belatedly, bring him his reward.

Notes

[1] Allan Monkhouse, *True Love*.

[2] Stanley Houghton, letter to Monkhouse (15 October 1911), Rylands Library (ANM12).

[3] Swinnerton *Georgian Literary Scene*, p173.

[4] *Manchester Guardian*, 29th September 1908.

[5] Letter to Monkhouse, Rylands Library (ANM/1/6/29).

[6] Swinnerton, *Georgian Literary* Scene, p175.

[7] *Mary Broome*, play text

[8] Letter to Brighouse, Rylands Library

[9] Houghton, letter to Monkhouse, 15 October 1911.

[10] Edward Garnett, letter to Monkhouse, 23 February 1912, Rylands Library.

[11] *Manchester Courier*, 10 October 1911.

[12] *The Times*, 25 May 1912.

[13] *New Statesman*, 24 May 1912.

[14] Monkhouse, *True Love* (1920).

[15] Galsworthy, letter to Monkhouse, 12 April 1914, Rylands Library.

[16] Houghton letter to Monkhouse, 15 October 1911.

[17] *New York Times*, 9 April 1933.

[18] Garnett letter to Monkouse, 12 March 1912, Rylands Library.

[19] Harold Brighouse, *op. cit.*, p172.

[20] *Allan Monkhouse*. Essays and Studies by Members of the English Association, vol. XI, ed. Oliver Elton (Clarendon Press, 1925).

[21] Monkhouse, *True Love* (1920).

13

The Pity of War

The Conquering Hero is not a play that will set the common people talking. It is not a play for aesthetic snobs. It is a play for people who are not afraid to think, who dare to face a truth even though it be terrifying.[1]

THE THEME OF WAR, AND THE use of wartime situations to intensify an individual conflict, entered Monkhouse's work early on in his playwriting career. In 1910, following his debut with *Reaping The Whirlwind*, he wrote *The Choice*, which opened at the Gaiety in June 1910 and reappeared in March 1912 on the same bill as Stanley Houghton's *The Dear Departed*.

The Choice utilises a situation from the Boer War but could easily be transferred to any wartime situation. It concerns Ella, a girl whose fiancé has been killed in South Africa in unknown circumstances. She discovers that it was her present suitor, a Major Greig, who shot her fiancé when he was paralysed by fear during an enemy attack. Greig tries to persuade her to marry him and live with the truth. (She feels guilty because she pushed the fiancé to go to war knowing he was weak.) She ultimately refuses and he leaves.

Monkhouse, as usual, is interested solely in an individual's conflict of conscience. Other playwrights would later develop this fairly simplistic situation to greater theatrical effect.

In 1916, Monkhouse wrote two more plays, *Night Watches* and *Shamed Life*, both clearly motivated by the major conflict at that moment engulfing the world. They are much less melodramatic, as well as being rare examples of Monkhouse setting the action outside the middle-class milieu.

Shamed Life takes place in a country cottage. A mother and son are listening as a military band passes under the window. They are, according to stage directions, 'like tormented creatures hiding their agitation from one another'. The mother refuses to allow her son, Claude, to join up. He appears to agree with her, considering the war a distant, pointless event. Two women arrive to buy eggs, one the mother of a young man already in the army, the other the young man's fiancée. The fiancée and Claude discuss Claude's situation. He tells her: 'You're a high and mighty person with a lover at the war. You're hard. You're like steel. Jim Bowes is a hero, of course. You're all for heroes.'[2]

His own position he considers philosophically: 'It's such a narrow line that divides. Go or stay. Hero or coward. Such a little step. One might be either. Skulking behind the hens or running to meet danger.' After some heated discussion, during which Claude admits that although his mother insists on keeping him away from the conflict, in her heart of hearts she wants him to go, news comes that Isabel's fiancé has been killed. Claude then hurries off to enlist. The development – the rather sudden 'reversal' – of this one-act play is similar in many ways to Monkhouse's *The Conquering Hero*, as we will see.

Night Watches is a one-act 'comedy' set in a military hospital, the tale of two soldiers and an orderly looking after them. One of the men is deaf and dumb – apparently shell-shocked. The second soldier suspects him of malingering. After some amusing verbal interplay with the orderly, the second soldier succeeds in getting the first solder to hear. They become friends, the nurse arrives to pack them off to bed and the play ends. 'We're groping among strange things, nurse,' the orderly says.

It's a surprisingly modern piece with short, sharp dialogue and sudden switches of emotion. However, with its indirect discussion of shell shock and 'malingerers', it could never have been produced when it was written. It bears the hallmark of reality, however, and no doubt relies on Monkhouse's correspondence with friends at the front such as C.E. Montague and James Agate.

Agate volunteered in May 1915 at the age of thirty-seven for the Army Service Corps, and was posted to France. He had an arrangement to supply a series of open letters about his wartime experiences to Monkhouse at the *Guardian* which were published in Agate's first book, *L. of C.* (Lines of Communication).

Monkhouse himself was too old to join up and, in the event, underwent an abdominal operation around 1916 that rendered him more or less immobile for the rest of his life. His concern with the war and the many questions it raised prior to its commencement, during and after it, would be reflected in his subsequent work.

First came the novel, *True Love*. This would be followed three years afterwards by the play *The Conquering Hero*. Both would try and grapple in broadly psychological terms with the consequences of the conflict.

As we have seen, *True Love* began with a look back at the Gaiety years. It continued with a depiction of the effect the war had on the *Manchester Guardian* (renamed *The Herald*).

In August 1914, the paper moved from strong advocacy of peace attempts to a measured support for the conflict. ('England declared war on Germany at eleven o'clock last night. All controversy is now at an end. Our front is united,' the paper announced on 5 August.)[3]

Despite this change in attitude, the *Guardian* continued to be the target for 'patriots' accusing it of a lack of patriotism, and even of treason. Monkhouse would include a scene in his novel showing Manchester businessmen in a club berating the 'radical rag', one asking whether a majority of the paper's shares were not held by Germans, and whether the leaders were not written by men of German extraction.

> *The Herald* strove yet against the stream, and its final, impassioned protests roused some childish displays of popular fury. Charges of German influence, of mere treachery, were less to bear than the reproaches of those ungenerous opponents who professed to find nothing but perverseness and sentimentality in a great and courageous policy with hard thinking behind its idealism.[4]

Monkhouse's *alter ego* in the book, Geoffrey Arden, suffers, 'the unhappiness of perpetual and alternative opposition'. For him, 'it seemed that the world was divided into the warlike and the pacific, and there was no room for those of the middle way. They seemed to be weak even while they held strongly to what they could perceive of reason and justice.'[5]

Just like his character in *Shamed Life*, after some heart-searching, Geoffrey ultimately decides to join up, seeing his decision as not simply jingoistic but something principled, with high ideals.

Monkhouse had more axes to grind, however. In 1914, Manchester boasted a large and culturally significant German population. Many of the latter suffered persecution, some hounded from the city, others interned. Monkhouse dealt with this distressing situation by making Geoffrey's love-interest in the book – the actress Sybil – a German. She reveals this to him after he has joined up. She agrees that Britain is in the right but she cannot disown her German heritage; he feels it a duty to fight against the German army but insists that he will not be fighting against the German people (a typically fine and precarious Monkhouse distinction).

During their honeymoon, the news comes of the sinking of the *Lusitania*, an atrocity that puts more strain on their relationship:

> She read, and looked blankly at Geoffrey over the top of the paper, read again and laid it down.
>
>   'Perhaps it is not true,' she said.
>
>   'Let us hope so.'
>
>   'Geoffrey, do you feel any resentment towards me?'
>
>   'You?' he cried.
>
>   'That's what I think of first. It isn't all these poor people children, babies. That's far away. I only feel it bluntly yet. It's you and me. Have we made an awful mistake? Are you thinking she's a German? Because I am. It's my people who have done this. Tell me what you feel. No, don't come near me just yet.'[6]

Their anguished relationship continues by letter when he is posted to France. He is upset to learn, not from her, that her German origins are causing her to be badly treated back in England. The ending of the book can be summed up in Katherine Mansfield's droll fashion:

> This, then, is the task they set themselves – to love and to be loyal. But Geoffrey goes to the war and is killed while they are still trying, and she, left in England, dies in childbed, hunted to death by the anti-Germans. There is nothing left of them but – two men talking their tragedy over in a teashop ...[7]

The novel made no declarations of right and wrong: it simply placed the uncomfortable, perhaps irreconcilable, facts before the reader and left him/her to come to a conclusion. Nevertheless, it was in tune with the uncertain, desperately unhappy post-war mood that pervaded a nation racked with internal dissention, labour disputes and despair at where the country was heading.

Monkhouse's *The Conquering Hero* would take this sense of unease and soul-searching and turn it into the first truly serious play about the First World War to reach London's West End.

It arrived there via a somewhat circuitous route, however.

With the decline of the repertory companies during the war – including the Gaiety, which closed its doors in 1920 – the chances of a relatively unknown dramatist getting his or her work onto a West End stage were minimal. However, small play-producing societies had sprung up to try and fill the gap. Half a dozen enthusiastic playgoers with a set of rules had formed one of these, the Play Actors, in 1914:

> 1. To discover clever comedies and dramas and to produce them on the London stage.
> 2. To discover clever actresses and actors and launch them onto the London stage.
> 3. To produce in London translations of classic plays previously performed in GB.

Another, the Stage Society which operated out of the Court Theatre, was a prominent play-producing organisation formed in 1910 and composed of members of the Actors' Association. A third was the Repertory Players.

These quasi-amateur companies relied on existing West End theatre managements allowing them to mount plays in their theatres, usually for a single Sunday performance for members who paid a small subscription. If popular, the run might be extended to Monday afternoon when the general public would be admitted. It was a means by which commercial theatre managers might 'discover' a good play. Elizabeth Baker's *Chains* had been one such notable success while work by both Harold Chapin and Manchester playwright Harold Brighouse had also transferred successfully to West End theatres after an initial 'amateur' performance.

It was the Repertory Players that had already broken something of a taboo concerning 'war plays' where the West End was concerned. In the years immediately following the Armistice, there seemed no way to present the conflict, that had devastated so many lives, suitably on the stage. According to one critic, there existed a prejudice by theatre managements against war plays, something unhesitatingly accepted by the public.

That changed in November 1923 when the Repertory Players put on *Havoc* at the Regent Theatre. The author, Harry Wall, was a Yorkshire solicitor and amateur playwright with a handful of local productions to his same. After badgering a score of London managers, however, he had succeeded in getting his 'war' play produced.

It was a melodramatic piece in which a girl is caught between two soldier suitors. Although Violet is engaged to Roddy, she decides she prefers his comrade in arms, Dick. Dick brings the news to Roddy at the front and the hurt, furious Roddy falsifies orders that will probably send his rival to his death. Dick isn't killed but is blinded, and the guilt-ridden Roddy commits suicide. When Dick returns to Violet, the fickle girl tells him she has found another love. She tells a woman who protests at her double-dealing: 'Dear, you're dreadfully pre-war.' Happily for Dick, Roddy's sister Tessie is there to care for and love him.

Leaving aside the simplistic plot, it was the scenes set in a Flanders dugout that stirred London audiences, one in particular drawing 35 curtain calls. Transferred to the Haymarket in January 1924, it was still running in March.

It was at this point that old Gaiety Theatre connections enter the picture. One of AH's finest actors, Milton Rosmer, who had played Leonard in Monkhouse's *Mary Broome*, had taken over as Vice-Chair of the Play Actors in 1923. Rosmer decided to produce *The Conquering Hero*. It opened with an amateur cast in Leeds on 23 February 1924, was well received, and then was transferred to the Aldwych Theatre on 23 March.

By chance, across town a couple of days later, Sybil Thorndike –

possibly the Gaiety's finest actress who had starred in *Hindle Wakes*, *The Whispering Well, Cupid and the Styx, Trespassers Will be Prosecuted*, as well as playing Miss Stormit in Monkhouse's own *Nothing Like Leather* – made her leading debut in Bernard Shaw's play *St Joan*, a part that would establish her as one of the country's leading actresses. Her husband, Lewis Casson, once director of the Gaiety, was also in *St Joan* – indeed was producing it. Rosmer, too, had a part in it. It proved a good omen for Monkhouse.

As it transpired, the single matinee performance of *The Conquering Hero* caught the imagination of critics. This in turn alerted yet another Gaiety veteran, Basil Dean, to the play's commercial possibilities.

Basil Dean was just then making his way in the West End play-producing scene, having joined forces with the theatre mogul Alfred Butt. Butt controlled many of the leading theatres and music halls in London and it was Dean's role to find him profitable plays. Having just taken over the Queen's Theatre, they were looking for a hit play and chose an Edward Knoblock comedy called *Conchita*.

Dean had persuaded a young ingénue called Tallulah Bankhead to star in *Conchita*, but the play was a terrible flop with Bankhead playing a Spanish dancer wearing a black wig and mixed up with a murderous American sailor. One act involved a live monkey who decided to steal the scene on opening night when he removed Tallulah's wig and waved it at the audience. Tallulah, not to be outdone, did a cartwheel. Critics panned *Conchita*, and Dean decided to take a gamble on his one-time Gaiety colleague. *The Conquering Hero* was swiftly moved to the Queen's on 3 April and Monkhouse had his first West End production.

Monkhouse had dedicated the play, 'To those who hate war and went to the war'. At its centre is Christopher Rokeby, who could well have been Geoffrey from *True Love* or Claude from *Shamed Life*, and who initially refuses to succumb to the prevailing war hysteria. As a creative artist – a writer – he believes himself capable of taking an objective stance while most of the middle-class Rokeby family, particularly the women, consider the outbreak of war as cause for celebration and a chance to bandy about patriotic and apocalyptic sentiments.

Christopher and his clergyman brother Stephen are less than convinced by the prospect of adventure and heroism, and Christopher spends the first two acts of the play agonising over whether he should enlist, arguing with his sister Margaret, his fiancée Helen and other family members, although his father, a colonel who has never seen action, takes a more conciliatory line.[8]

Christopher always considered his creative work as too important to sacrifice:

> CHRIS: Self-sacrifice! The only sort worth having is when you won't sacrifice yourself. Anything but that. When you've let the baser parts go there's nothing so austere. You ask me to give it all up, as though I were a child with a toy

For Stephen, who partially agrees with his brother, his faith is the problem:

> STEPHEN: I've felt something of what you say. I'm not bloodless. And yet I've wanted to serve Christ. I wish I could talk to you, Chris. I haven't a friend. Not one but Him. And now they want to take Him from me. He was a man, you know; saying things clearly and meaning them. Now, Christianity has to conform to common sense. It's rational and liberal, and there's quite a nice infusion of Christ in it ... Am I running away like a coward? Ought I to stay?

Christopher adopts some of the attitudes of Geoffrey in *True Love*:

> CHRIS: You want me to look at these Germans as a patriot. I don't know how. I can only look at them as a man. You say they're savages, and if it is so it's extremely interesting. Of course as a man I'm

horrified when I hear of their atrocities – that is, when I believe in them.

He also makes what could be considered a pacifist's case for not resisting:

CHRIS: If that ghastly accident comes – if they invade us and subdue us and govern us – d'you think I and my kind will be conquered? It would all be a hideous irrelevance. They may trample on us or kill us, but they can't enslave our minds. We'll go on living – some of us. I've my faith too, and it isn't just in guns – England! I can think of England too. Humiliation and defeat may be our salvation ... Those that we call traitors may be the heroes – the men of conscience and ideals. It's my work to look into men's souls. It's truth I want, not this blatant simplicity. We are to be all one way now. What a time! The day of the cheap patriot has come.

Their dogmatic sister Margaret conducts the bullying and accusations of cowardice:

CHRIS: You think I'm negligible, but I'm not.
MARGARET: You think yourself too good to be shot.
CHRIS: *(After a pause)* Yes, Margaret. It's true. I do feel that.
MARGARET: Too clever, too important, too superior.
CHRIS: Yes, I suppose that's true. And we've no quarrel with these people.
MARGARET: We? Who are we?
CHRIS: Oh! – the artists, first and last. English or German, they're my comrades.

Margaret demands that all young men follow her already-enlisted husband Frank's example, while their aunt and uncle wholeheartedly agree. Christopher's fiancée Helen threatens to jilt him as soon this difference of opinion arises. Eventually, Chris's brother Stephen joins up as a Red Cross orderly,

STEPHEN: Here am I pretending that it's a call to me as a Christian, and now I know that I want to be in the battle, I want the excitement of it. I'm not thinking of Christ at all. Yes, sometimes, but I cheat myself.

Chris, too, then succumbs to the pressure although his 'conversion' is rather sudden and his explanation intriguing as it involves the faithful family servant Dakin:

> CHRIS: Dakin! Dakin a soldier! Why! He's footman incarnate. He's got his vocation. This war will pass over Dakin like vapours over a rock. He can't be moved, can't be touched. Thank Heaven for Dakin. He makes one feel safer. He's an institution.

Chris rushes out to enlist, but only as a foot soldier rather than using his family's influence to enter at officer level:

> CHRIS: I was extremely curious about Dakin. You'll hardly believe it, but I followed him. I wanted to see him enlist. I hadn't made up my mind about anything. And then – yonder – I came on those fellows waiting their turn. They were standing in a queue – Dobson, Pettigrew, that sturdy little fellow at the forge, some I didn't know. They were not very formidable to look at. The might of Germany wouldn't think much of them. Dakin fell in at the back, and that somehow – affected me. They all looked so humble and faithful. They seemed to be gazing at something a long way off and not thinking of themselves at all. And then it came upon me that there had never been anything in the world like this, that in all my life nothing had ever mattered so much, that I should never be happy again if I held back now ...

The third act takes us into battle where a captured Chris finds himself threatened by a German officer with death – unless he gives vital information about his regiment. Chris is humiliated but ultimately saved when the Germans retreat.

On his return home in Act IV he is welcomed as a 'conquering hero' but finds the reception utterly 'indecent', especially as Stephen, along with his brother-in-law and the family butler, have been killed. He tells his father,

CHRIS: Father, I think on the whole I came out pretty well. Of course I had my moments of funk like most people. I was complimented once or twice. I ought to have got my commission, but I was in hospital so long. Nerves, breakdown – that sort of thing. Quite common. It doesn't always mean funk. I got lost and had a horrible time wandering about. Don't ask me to talk about that. Not that. May I blot out a few hours, a few minutes? I was very low. To become a sergeant isn't so bad. No, I haven't disgraced you.

As for explaining what happened to him:

CHRIS: How could I tell you? It's what a man carries in his heart. The Germans? I had impulses of affection for them. Decent folk. But it's no use charging with the bayonet unless you become a wild beast. I like the way they write about it in the newspapers. Nice, hearty sport. Oh, hell! Oh, hell!

His return is celebrated locally with a hero's welcome, but he resents it and manages to miss the event.

CHRIS: My skin's whole, and it's the skin that counts. You treat us all alike. The world's justice. Of course a few poor devils are cashiered and publicly disgraced. They may be no worse than the rest. But we come home to brass bands, and there are secrets in our hearts. We're different; every man is different, but you give us the same tune. The brass band is ridiculous now. It was right when we went out. We were heroes then; we'd taken the plunge and we were all alike. I think I was never so happy as when I first marched to it.
HELEN: You are a hero now.
CHRIS: That's my business.
CHRIS: You mustn't judge things by their results. It was right to go. I have no regrets. How could I stay while Frank and Stephen and all the rest were dying there? How could I see my father every day? And deep down in me – yes, deep – I'm an Englishman – all the old voices and the old tunes were calling.

CHRIS: We've both done our best, Daddy.

He begins to cry, and his father leads him to the armchair.
COLONEL: You want rest, my boy – rest.
Chris sinks into the chair and lies back in it, staring before him. His father hesitates and then goes quietly out.

END

Notes
[1] *Western Daily Press*, 5 January 1924.
[2] Allan Monkhohouse, *Shamed Life*, play text.
[3] *Manchester Guardian*, 5 August 1913.
[4] Allan Monkhouse, *True Love,* novel text.
[5] Ibid.
[6] Ibid.
[7] *Athenaeum*, 28 November 1919.
[8] All subsequent quotations are from *The Conquering Hero* text.

14

A Conquering Hero

I do not hesitate to say that his is one of the finest pieces for the stage written by an Englishman since the war and the product of one of the most delicately-conditioned and percipient minds which have ever ennobled the English theatre.[1]

The greatest treatment of war that has been seen in London.[2]

THE RESPONSE OF CRITICS TO THE single performance of *The Conquering Hero* at the Aldwych was overwhelmingly positive. The *Evening Standard* thought it a 'moving play' even though it felt Monkhouse was, 'profoundly wrong about the circumstances of active service and the mental consequences of it on those who for our protection took part in it'. Still, 'Last night nobody coughed without a low but unmistakeable rebuke from the rest of the audience ... '[3]

The *Sunday Times* reviewer thought that the war scene in the play 'turned out to be so *moving* as to dwarf the individual'. The *Daily Express* review appeared beneath a headline, 'Haters of War In a Play'. 'Conscientious Objectors' Ethics', and began, 'It could not have been produced in London eight years ago, but it is better late then never.'[4]

The *Daily Telegraph* felt 'Mr Monkhouse has tackled a great theme gallantly; the exquisite quality of his workmanship and the depth of sympathy and understanding in the drawing of his characters make this a play quite head and shoulders above the average even of serious contemporary plays.'[5]

Ivor Brown compared Monkhouse favourably to the Bernard Shaw play: 'There is none of the direct speechifying with which Mr Shaw permits himself to drive a general argument home ... Mr Monkhouse keeps to the plain prose of realism as he keeps to the careful portraiture of individualism ... thus the universal truth glides in unforced as beauty may glide on to paper with two or three plain strokes of a pencil.'[6]

The *Daily Express* critic, by contrast, felt it was Galsworthy who came off worse: 'Like Mr Galsworthy, Mr Monkhouse gives fairly the viewpoint of his characters. Unlike Mr Galsworthy, his characters are human beings rather than ideas ... '[7]

The Times by contrast felt the dialogue 'is too often repetitive' and felt the 'turns in the action and in the characterisation which are here and there taken with a suddenness threatens the play's truth'. Nevertheless, Monkhouse 'has written a closely observed and deeply moving play.'[8]

The *Observer* critic pointed to a characteristic of the main character, Christopher, that appeared to fascinate the average playgoer: 'We seem actually to see into the mind of this cultured youth who starts by aiming at a million and only realises his utter desolation when he misses a unit.' Christopher was not 'a typical Englishman but he is a typical example of a large class of Englishmen and although it is to be doubted that any Englishman would talk quite so much as he does throughout the play yet there is never a moment when either the hand of the author or the voice of the actor loses its cunning.'[9]

'There were as many curtain calls as those latterly reserved mainly for the popular musical comedy stars and revue comedians.'[10] Sadly, with so much by way of thoughtful praise coming his way, Monkhouse was too physically incapacitated to make the journey to London to take the plaudits. It was Basil Dean who, heeding the urging of the majority of critics to give the play a proper run, transferred it to the Queens Theatre – where it continued to garner praise – and stood up on stage to thank the audience for its enthusiastic reception. It was noted, however, by the *Stage* reviewer that some subtle alterations had been made. There was the omission in the programme of Monkhouse's significant dedication. Also missing from the programme notes was the cutting description of Margaret Iredale as a cheap patriot – 'for fear of ordinary playgoers reactions?'[11]

So much a topic of general conversation was the play that an open debate was arranged – a clever publicity ploy by Arthur Butt – at the Queen's Theatre on 10 April between performances. The subject was 'Does the play tell the truth about the war?' and was attended by various writers and commentators, as well as some military folk. It was the second time in a couple of years that a play by a Manchester writer had attracted such publicity, the first being Hutchinson's *The Right To Strike*.

This was a more low-key affair. The novelist Gilbert Frankau paid tribute to the play's impressive 'reality' but thought the women in the play might give foreign countries 'the wrong idea of British women'. Julian Grenfall's poem 'Into Action' was cited and it was suggested Grenfall might have written the play had he lived. There was the inevitable mention of war profiteering, and while Alfred Butt thought that, although the play was only partially successful, every potential statesman 'irrespective of nationality' ought to witness it.[12]

Allan Monkhouse's achievement was to bring into open debate ideas that had been suppressed for some years, sentiments that were as painful as any of the heart-searching that accompanied and followed the Vietnam War and its denouement.

Monkhouse's great friend and workmate ('My oldest living comrade at this game') C.E. Montague, had already written a book, *Disenchantment*, published in 1922, that had begun a period of introspection concerning the First World War, its original aims and its ultimate achievements.

Montague documented the disillusionment and death of the dreams of those men who, like himself, had joined up in 1914 after going through an initial period of painful doubt. *Disenchantment* was a book of despair written by a man who found the world he was fighting to save was not worth saving: 'At the heart of the magical rose was seated an earwig' (p.227). The war – so full of hope at the start – had produced none of the benefits for which the man in the street had volunteered. The lies of wartime propaganda had been carried over into the new world – 'that new lie-infested and infected world of peace' (p.127). Even victory had been ruined by a 'shabby epidemic of spite' (p.185), the rush of politicians to coin votes for themselves, and a worthless peace which did nothing but drive starving Germans ever more to hatred: 'So we had failed – had won the fight and lost the prize' (p 189).[13]

The Conquering Hero seemed like a logical follow-on from Montague's book in its fearless questioning of terrible choices, seen post-war to be somewhat less than clear-cut.

C.E. Montague went to see it in April 1924 and wrote to Monkhouse:

> What rejoiced me was to see the big audience of ordinary people ... following it all most absorbedly and just making little quick noises – chuckles or grumbles – at everybody's points alike, apparently without the slightest prejudice against or for pacifism or militarism. It's an amazing change since five years ago and I can't make out this post-war generation with its apparent mixture of intelligence, liberality and raffishness.[14]

As a drama, *The Conquering Hero* has its flaws. Christopher's sudden decision to join up rather than press on with his conscientious objections appears inexplicable. It's like two plays bolted together, the first two acts a thoughtful discussion of moral choices, the second two a rather more straightforward depiction of the dilemmas facing men returning to cheering crowds while harbouring darker secrets.

Kosok has written of it:

> The outcome is strangely inconclusive as is the whole play: it never becomes clear where the author's sympathies lie because he evades the question whether the War, and Chris's involvement in it is absolutely necessary. Quite different from his 1916 play *Shamed Life*, where Monkhouse seemed to think that it was mandatory for a young man to enlist, he here leaves the decision in the balance. Chris, a reluctant pacifist, a reluctant soldier and finally a reluctant hero does not come over as a representative of a whole generation, however much the author may have wished to see him in such light.[15]

Horace Shipp felt Monkhouse had failed in creating a consistent and universal character; instead, the play was merely 'the study of an intelligent coward'. '(Christopher) should have been prepared to 'go to the stake if need be for humanity's sake'. Only then would he have 'influenced humanity'.[16]

Perhaps Monkhouse had felt the need to break a policy of a lifetime and try and depict action in his work rather than just words. Harold Brighouse certainly felt that it was his strongest play, 'both constructively and cerebrally'. He added that, as a consequence, Monkhouse almost succeeded in breaking the mould completely: 'and thereby almost happened one of the strangest associations in stage history. Not once, but again on second thoughts, did David Belasco consider producing *The Conquering Hero*. Belasco and Monkhouse! Belasco, playmaker, Broadway showman, and Monkhouse, of the *M.G.!* It did not happen, but I have in

Monkhouse's letters evidence of that grotesquely incongruous might-have-been.'[17]

The *Brooklyn Daily Eagle* announced on 8 June, 1924 that the Theatre Guild in New York was planning to present *The Conquering Hero* sometime during its 1924-25 season, but it never happened. After just 60 performances and a transfer from the Queens Theatre to St Martin's, *The Conquering Hero* ended its run. 'I do not recommend it to the London commercial managers. It is not, in their sense of the word, a winner,' Agate had written perceptively.

The Conquering Hero was Monkhouse's last and biggest success on the stage. Later that year Lewis Casson and Milton Rosmer would produce his play *The Hayling Family* for the Play Actors at the Aldwych, again hoping a West End company would take it up, but its one performance failed to convince anyone beyond the critics. It would reappear many years later, however.

Monkhouse continued writing for the stage. Prior to *The Conquering Hero* he'd written another one-act piece called *The Grand Cham's Diamond* (in 1918), a farce parodying the sensational thrillers of the day. Then came *The Stricklands* in 1920 (never produced in the UK). After *The Hayling Family* there followed *First Blood* (1925), *Sons and Fathers* (1926), *O Death Where Is Thy Sting?* (1928), *The Rag* (1928), *The Wiley One* (1929), *The King of Barvender* (1930), *Paul Felice* (1930) and, finally, *Cecilia* in 1932.

Only *Sons and Fathers* was produced in London, a single performance by the RADA players in which a young John Gielgud played Dick Southern, a virtuous family man and businessman who at every crossroad surrenders his high standards rather than cause suffering for his family.

Despite his failure to become a nationally recognised playwright on a par with Galsworthy and Shaw, Monkhouse was for many years an extremely powerful and influential figure in the literary world. He organised the Book Reviews section in the *Guardian* that in the days before radio and television was an essential element of the literary world. Novelists and publishers relied heavily on the printed press to publicise and sell their wares. Adverts and reviews were crucial. Newspapers *were* the mass media and the *Guardian* was one of the most prestigious of outlets.

Anne Duchene explained in 1958:

> To organise (the reviewing of novels) is one of the hardest things in literary editorship. From five to ten times as many new novels are sent by their publishers to a newspaper as it is possible to review. Many of them are first books by unknown authors. Every one of them – except the few that are by authors of established quality – must be carefully considered and for that purpose at least partly read lest anything of merit by an obscure writer escape notice.[18]

For decades Monkhouse spent great effort and patience on this heavy and – more often than not – unrewarding labour of critical justice, and the two columns of novel reviews appearing once a week in the paper represented far more than most of its readers can have suspected of critical toil and discrimination.

The collection of his letters in the Rylands Library is testament to his ubiquity and familiarity with the great and the good in the British literary world. Joseph Conrad, John Galsworthy, Thomas Hardy, David Garnett, Katherine Mansfield were on first-name terms. Galsworthy, Garnett and Bennett would meet and dine with him in his home in Disley or in Manchester (Bennett wrote that they should meet at the Midland, 'where the nuts have tea with the flappers' in 1915).

On his 70th birthday, his many friends and admirers penned a letter to the *Guardian* expressing their admiration and affection for him, both as a writer and as a man. The signatures included Bennett, Galsworthy, Harley Granville-Barker, Gordon Craig, John

Drinkwater, Laurence Houseman, John Masefield, H.G. Wells and many more.

He was for a time the most prominent of the 'Manchester playwrights' and the only one who could have persuaded AH to tread the boards. When rehearsing *Nothing Like Leather*, his satire on the Gaiety produced in 1913, Monkhouse had at first hinted that one of his rash ideas had been to persuade AH to appear on stage but felt he had little hope of doing so. It was intended that a member of the cast would be made up to look like her, but producer Lewis Casson telegraphed AH in London suggesting she might like to appear in person. She later said that it was one of the greatest moments in her life. When Monkhouse sent her a signed copy of the play in December 1930, she wrote back, 'I appeared at every performance, matinees, as well, and was told once how "perfectly made up was the actress who appeared in the part". It was *me*, myself of course! What a long time ago it seems. The dear old Gaiety a "movie" house and the then owner an old woman now ... '[19]

Notes

[1] *Western Daily Press*, 5 January 1924.

[2] *The Era*, 26 March 1924.

[3] *London Evening Standard*, 24 March 1924.

[4] *The Sunday Times*, 30 March 1924.

[5] *Daily Telegraph*, 24 March 1924.

[6] *Manchester Guardian*, 24 March 1924.

[7] *Daily Express*, 24 March 1924.

[8] *The Times*, 24 March 1924.

[9] *The Observer*, 30 March 1924.

[10] *The Stage*, 10 April 1924.

[11] Ibid.

[12] *Manchester Guardian*, 10 April 1924.

[13] *Disenchantment* (Brentano's 1922), pp227, 127, 189.

[14]C.E. Montague, letter to Monkhouse, April 1924, Rylands Library

[15]Heinz Kosok. *The Theatre of War: The First World War in British and Irish Drama* (Palgrave Macmillan 2007).

[16]'History in the Theatre', *The English Review* (May 1924).

[17]Brighouse, *Autobiography*, p172.

[18]Anne Duchene, 'Allan Monkhouse, a Manchester Man of Letters', *Manchester Guardian*, 3 May 1958.

[19]Annie Horniman, letter to Monkhouse, December 1913, Rylands Library.

15

Houghton's Apprenticeship

When Miss Horniman started her company at the Manchester Gaiety I saw there was a chance of such work as I cared to write being produced.[1]

I can never thank you enough for the chance you have given me of getting a footing, and the encouragement and experience your production of my plays have given me. I started to write expressly and absolutely for you; had the Gaiety not been there I wouldn't have written a line.[2]

STANLEY HOUGHTON STANDS OUT FROM THE Manchester playwrights as the potential 'star' writer, the man who might, had he not died at the age of 32 in 1913, have gone to the become a match for Galsworthy and Shaw, perhaps even Bennett and Wells. His good friend and colleague Harold Brighouse revealed that in the period just before his death Houghton had been working on a novel about Manchester: 'He had, beyond doubt, an unexpressed desire to do for Manchester what Mr Arnold Bennett had done for the Potteries ... He would, of a certainty, have done better than that.'[3]

Like many of the 'Manchester School', Houghton was initially both a journalist and a businessman. He was born in Altrincham,

Stanley Houghton
(*National Portrait Gallery*)

(Cartoon *Author's collection*)

his father then a cotton cloth merchant in Manchester, partner in a small firm and a registered member of the Cotton Exchange where Stanley would also work. His was a happy, comfortable, lower-middle-class family existence.

He was a fee-paying pupil at Manchester Grammar School where James Agate, Harold Brighouse, Gilbert Cannan, Iden Payne among others involved in Manchester dramatic scene also studied but, like most of them, he eschewed university. On leaving the Grammar School in 1897, Houghton commenced work in his father's office in Meal Street, Manchester and according to Brighouse, wasn't happy with the idea of a remaining a businessman for the rest of his life:

> Asked to choose between entering his father's business, which naturally, in Manchester, is connected with the cotton trade, and the selection of a profession, he decided without hesitation upon business, with the intention, even at that time fully formed, of regarding the cotton trade as a mere stop-gap till he had perfected himself in the profession of letters.
>
> The work itself – his position was that of a salesman – was neither arduous nor unpleasant, and had the immense advantage of bringing him, through his calls on shipping merchants and his membership of the Cotton Exchange, into intimate contact with men and affairs.[4]

Thus, between the years 1897 and 1912 he was, whatever his other activities and with the exception of a business man's holidays, in daily attendance at his father's office between the hours of 9 a.m. and 5 p.m.

Brighouse would attribute Houghton's eventual success to hard work rather than natural-born ability:

> The word 'genius' was freely used of Houghton even in organs of opinions so opposite as the *Times* and the *English Review*. Let it be here admitted that genius is of two kinds. There is the heaven-born genius, leaping almost at once to full maturity, finding its commonest

expression in lyric poetry; and the self-made genius, for whom was invented the tag about ' an infinite capacity for taking pains'.[5]

Gerald Cumberland, in his memoir puts it less generously:

> Genius is one of the wombs of vanity, but Houghton had no genius; there was not a trace of magic in him; he was merely extraordinarily clever, closely observant and possessed of an instinctive sense of form and of literary values.[6]

Houghton could have become a full-time journalist. The *Manchester City News* invited him to be an unpaid critic and between March 1905 and September 1906 he contributed some sixty short reviews, mostly on music hall shows and suburban theatre productions. He then graduated to the *Manchester Guardian* and from 1907 to 1912 wrote drama and book reviews as well as occasional sketches.

However, according to Brighouse, 'he possessed a combination of innate Lancashire shrewdness which made him hesitate to leave security for hazard.' Nevertheless, Houghton felt that it would be through drama that he would make his name in the world.[7]

He certainly worked hard at developing his dramatic skills: between 1901 and 1912 as a member of the Manchester Athenaeum Dramatic Club he appeared in over seventy parts as well as producing, an invaluable education for his future trade as a writer.

> One remembered the confident figure of the young man weary if just trifling with letters in minor theatre criticisms and 'back page articles' ... and always very properly (if inconveniently) more resentful of sub-editing than rejection. And always Houghton's confidence that he would and could write something that should force the elder generation to admit that he was no vain trifler.[8]

Physical descriptions of him tend to emphasise his slightness, a certain frailty: 'The tall, spare figure, parading certain pleasant signs of dandyism, seemed always too fragile for the harsh conflict of life. The boyish face, with its aquiline nose something too delicately chiselled, the mobile lips a thought too sensitive and the far-seeing, eloquent eyes of the born master of words'...'[9]

As a person, there was something indefinable about him, a reserve that kept him aloof, almost. Brighouse described him as 'A quiet somewhat self-effacing man, at times, almost morbidly shy, expressing opinions only after pressure, and then with diffidence ... Socially, Houghton was widely popular, but he was at his best in the fewer intimate friendships he made than in a large gathering. In a crowded room he sought a chair upon the fringe of things, and sat alert, observing silently. He played bridge well. But, in general, he was reserved to the point of secretion.'[10]

Gerald Cumberland sensed something else about him: 'There was something forbidding in Houghton's nature – a barricade of reserve that he himself had not wilfully erected, but which had been placed there by Nature. It was impossible for people who met him casually a few times to form a high opinion either of his intellect or of his personality.'[11]

Brighouse concluded that it was Manchester that had 'stunted him'. 'It was only when one knew him very well, and then only for a few, that the habitual reserve fell from him, and one discovered what a conversationalist he could be,' and only when he achieved success in London did he open up: 'Successful, he became a comrade, a talker, giving out from himself where before he was too often, through sheer shyness, contented only to receive.'[12]

The truth is that Houghton was highly ambitious and it would be his desire to be recognised and his shrewdness where seizing an opportunity was concerned that would mark him out from most of the rest of the Manchester playwrights. In fact, he would progress so swiftly that he felt obliged at one point to apologise to Allan Monkhouse, whose career resolutely refused to take off no matter how hard he worked.

In December 1912 the playwright and critic Hamilton Fyfe contributed a lengthy article headed 'The New Dramatist – Mr Stanley Houghton', based on a meeting he'd with Houghton at a party. The article assessed some of Houghton's plays including *Hindle Wakes* and described Houghton as the 'leader' of the Manchester dramatists with Monkhouse and Brighouse following on.[13]

Houghton was furious and on the same day wrote to Monkhouse:

> In today's *Daily Mail* you will find a leader – about me & a column by Hamilton Fyfe about you, me & Brighouse. I hope you'll believe I never said such foolish things as he reports. I never saw a column fuller of inaccuracies. And that stupid passage about you & Brighouse, 'following' me. I lead only in one sense; the sense that John the Baptist led Christ; by going in front & announcing the advent of a greater than myself.[14]

Significantly, it had been a Houghton play that had first caused Monkhouse to muse on the possibility of Manchester producing its own playwrights. Prior to the Gaiety arriving, Houghton had collaborated with a fellow worker on the Manchester Cotton Exchange – a part-time *Guardian* journalist Frank G. Nasmith – to produce a number of plays, among them *The Reckoning* which had been presented at the Queen's Theatre, Manchester in July 1907.

Monkhouse had reviewed it and criticised its construction but had commended the dramatists, seeing their work as, 'experimental, and suggestive' and indeed 'worth doing'. He added: 'one feels that better things are to come.'[15]

Whether the two men knew one another at that point is unknown, although it's the year Houghton began writing for the *Guardian*. It was an auspicious beginning and one Houghton swiftly built upon. Cumberland had noticed that Houghton never rested on his laurels for long: 'With Houghton, when a play was completed his interest in it immediately intensified. He sent his plays everywhere: to the provinces, to London, to America, to agents. As soon as a play came back, "returned with thanks", out it went again by the next post. And he pulled strings – oh ! ever so gently, but he pulled them.'[16]

Acquainted with Iden Payne as a Swan Club member and an ex-Manchester Grammar School boy, noticed by Monkhouse the *Guardian*'s leading critic as well as a working colleague, it was hardly a surprise when a Houghton play appeared on the Gaiety programme.

The Dear Departed was selected for production and appeared on the 2 November 1908 as a curtain raiser to Bernard Shaw's *Widowers' Houses*. The programme note for the first production attributed the play's basic storyline to that of a de Maupassant story entitled 'En Famille'. Houghton later admitted that when he read the tale 'it immediately occurred to me that here was an idea that might very well be exploited on the stage. So I used the idea creating my own set of characters and of course writing my own dialogue. I called it *The Dear Departed*.'[17]

Houghton never worried too much about plot ideas and where they might come from. In a piece he wrote for the *Daily Mail* in 1912 discussing new trends in drama he asserted that currently popular plays that presented a picture of a group or family intimately observed 'depended for their interest and variety upon subtleties and differentiation of character rather than upon the incidents of a cunningly-devised plot ... '

In the past, he suggested, characters in plays were 'rather generalised, drawn according to broad types and more attention was paid to the construction of an elaborate plot and to the march of the scene', which led to 'utter sterility and drabness'.

However, 'I am convinced that provided the proper attention is paid to character one plot may even last a man for several plays all of which shall be different.'[18]

Even so, Houghton's first effort had initially proved to be too long for a curtain-raiser and needed re-shaping according to Brighouse, 'under strong managerial guidance'.[19]

The Dear Departed is a simple but compelling tale concerning a family dispute over the goods of a deceased relative, Old Abel Merryweather, who lives with his married daughter and is discovered by her in a state of unconsciousness which she imagines to be death.

Before communicating with her other relatives, her first care is to secure for herself as many of his effects as she can, removing various articles of furniture from his room and depositing them in her own. Her sister duly arrives with her husband and a wrangle soon arises over the distribution of Abel's effects.

Recriminations are indulged in but are speedily ended by the entrance of the supposed dead Abel who has simply been in a drunken stupor and, so far as giving up the ghost, eats a hearty meal, in the course of which he announces his forthcoming marriage to the keeper of a neighbouring public house.

Despite being somewhat overshadowed on the night by Shaw's play, *The Dear Departed* was an immediate popular success, mainly for its humour and its authentic representation of Lancashire life by the 'well-nigh perfect cast' of the first Gaiety production. It was also the first new play at the Gaiety to draw directly upon Lancashire working-class life.

It was taken to London the following summer as part of a Gaiety season at the Coronet Theatre, Notting Hill, where it once again opened with Shaw's play and ran for three weeks. The opening night in London was a sell-out with distinguished guests in the audience: Shaw, apparently, 'beamed approval upon a curtain-raiser entitled *The Dear Departed* and at a later showing the celebrated actress Ellen Terry 'was deeply interested in the presentation of ... *The Dear Departed*'.[20]

The prominent critic William Archer noted that Houghton's play was a rather cynical but remarkably well written 'low-life comedy (with) two rapacious sisters, a Goneril and Regan of the Slums'. He added: 'This Manchester movement is the most important fact in our theatrical history since the opening of the Vedrenne-Barker campaign at the Court Theatre.'[21.]

Allan Monkhouse, despite being happy for his younger friend, must have privately been gnashing his teeth as the play attracted overseas interest and led to Houghton's first-ever contract outside the United Kingdom.

Houghton's career now proceeded apace, but with his next play he suffered what might be termed 'second play syndrome'. *Independent Means* opened on 30 August 1909, 'a neatly constructed comedy of contemporary manners, whose non-didactic and "somewhat shallow" characterizations suited the public taste but disappointed the critics'.[22]

Houghton later conceded, ' I don't mind at all telling you that I regard this as the weakest play I have ever written.'[23]

Reviewed in the *Manchester Chronicle* in July 1914, a year after his death, it was considered to be a piece that 'voices the new spirit that is "in the air" ... ardent, clear-eyed, sane, courageous' – but also, impatient, somewhat intolerant, a little hard'.[24]

Brighouse suggested that the play was 'a work not wholly satisfying, a reliance upon technique to pull matters through, showing Houghton expressing in drama the results of his inspired observation of suburban life ... '[25]

For the next six months Houghton stopped writing but the lapse of time was not wasted. He apparently liked to 'incubate' his ideas. He also wanted to repeat the success he'd achieved in London with *The Dear Departed* because by now he had developed a taste for London – a tough market which, having succeeded in once, he was determined to do so again.

The three-act *Younger Generation* was written between November and December 1909 and sent off to the Gaiety not long afterwards where it was produced on 21 November 1910 alongside his Manchester Grammar School friend Gilbert Cannan's play, *Miles Dixon*.

Houghton, writing in the *Observer* in November 1912, described it simply as:

> ... just a study of a middle-class family living in the suburbs of Manchester. It is a conflict between children who are growing up and parents who wish to restrain them. One has seen this sort of conflict in many families including one's own. The parents do not make sufficient allowance for the intelligence of the children and hold them too tightly in leading strings. There is no attempt, however, to preach in the play. It is merely a study and I leave it to the audience to draw whatever conclusions they like. Some possibly will approve the parents. Others may like the spirit of the children. There is even the attitude of the grandmother, of a third generation, to choose from.[26]

It is, in fact, a gentle comedy portraying generational conflict in a pious, supposedly teetotal, middle-class family in Salchester (a Manchester suburb derived from combining Salford and Manchester). The three children of the Kennion family are young adults in their late teens and early twenties: the eldest, Grace has found the man she wishes to marry, Clifford, and they frequently spend time together alone, in secret; Arthur works in a bank but longs for a more interesting and exciting life; and the youngest is Reggie, who dreams of giving up the secretaryship of the Sunday School and emigrating to Canada to live 'a man's life'.

William Archer wrote in 1910, 'Quite admirable are the technical ease and finish which he displays in this very entertaining and apposite study of middle-class life in Lancashire.' Archer continued,

> How is it, I often ask myself with astonishment, that so many young men in the provinces have suddenly awakened, as it were, to find

themselves workmanlike, and even accomplished, playwrights? The reason is partly, no doubt, that the new generation has learnt what not to do; but it nevertheless remains astonishing that so many of them should have mastered, seemingly without effort, the difficult art of compressing their observations of life into the narrow dimensions of the theatre.[27]

Four years later (July 1914) the *TLS* reviewer thought the play, 'a true picture of the suburb of Manchester where Houghton himself dwelled – a comfortable middle-class neighbourhood, dominated by a widely-known Nonconformist chapel and a tower of strength to the Radical Party at election times. In this comfortable region of semi-detached villas and tree-lined roads paved with macadam, the Kennion family can be matched in scores. Manchester ... invariably puts into office men like Mr Kennion who bully and lecture the lower classes as they domineer over their children, 'for their own good' and are convinced, as was the old Manchester School, that poverty and failure must be the result of moral defects ... '[28]

The play's comic potential lies in the concentration on all three young adults deciding, independently, to break out from their parents' strict grip at the same time. Quite suddenly they gain the confidence to say what has hitherto been the unspeakable and demand the unthinkable, leaving their parents baffled, alarmed and reactionary.

Writing in the *Daily Mail* ('Family Plays The New Taste', September 1912), Houghton concluded:

> The most interesting advantage of the substitution of character for plot is the consequent widening of the scope of drama. The development opens to London theatres the rich and immense field of the middle classes untilled hitherto because it was thought to be unprofitable and unattractive.[29]

Two one-act plays followed: *The Master of the House* opened 26 September 1910 at the Gaiety along with *Independent Means*;

although styled as a comedy Brighouse viewed it as an interesting but faulty experiment in the gruesome ... a 'grimly ironical tale, which makes rather mechanical play with a corpse'.[30]

The action is set in a parlour where two persons are seated in silence – Mr Ovens, supposedly asleep, and his second wife, eagerly awaiting the arrival of a solicitor who is due to bring a new will which should leave her all her husband's goods. Mr Ovens, however, is not sleeping, but dead. Fred, his ne'er-do-well son and heir by an earlier will arrives, turns his stepmother summarily out of the house and gloats at how he is now the Master of the House. His good fortune, he thinks, must be celebrated with a drink at the pub. The play-script continues:

> (The front door bangs. FRED shivers and moves to the front of the table and sits on the edge. He laughs quietly.)
> FRED: Pleasant night. Why shouldn't I? (To MR OVENS.) You won't interfere with me. I'm not afraid of you. What is there to be afraid of? (He looks round fearfully and his eye again returns to MR OVENS' figure.) You can't turn me out of doors now. I'm boss here. (The figure does not take any notice. FRED shivers again.) I'll go round to the King's Arms and have a drink, there'll be company there. (To MR OVENS quickly.) But I'll come back for the night, mind you. You'll not drive me away. (He goes to the gas and turns it out, leaving the room in perfect darkness. He gropes his way to the door. Here he pauses.) I've no money. (He thinks.) They always used to keep some money in the sideboard drawer. (He gropes his way to the sideboard on the extreme right and stumbles against a chair.) Can't see a thing, and I've no matches. Wait a minute. (He crosses to the window and pulls up the blind. Bright moonlight strikes through the window. He crosses to the sideboard and easily finds the drawer, opens it and searches. There is no money to be found. He takes a cash-box and turns towards the window with it to examine it carefully. As he turns he comes full on the silent figure of MR OVENS, sitting rigid in his chair, shrouded in white, ghastly in the glare of the moon. FRED starts back with an oath and drops the

cash-box.} You can't frighten me. You shan't turn me out, I tell you. I'm master of the house. (He sits on the edge of the table looking at the figure for a long space. Then he speaks in a low strained voice.) Don't look at me like that. Don't look at me like that! I didn't know you were dead when I cursed you. (Another pause: he shudders and covers his face with his hands.} God! I can't stand it. (He steals silently out of the room. MR OVENS sits in his shroud in the moonlight, master of the house. The front door is heard closing.)

(THE CURTAIN DESCENDS VERY SLOWLY.)[31]

Times change. In 1973, Allardyce Nicoll considered this 'sorry stuff, contrived and forced'. Today it might be thought of as a precursor of Beckett's short, bleak theatrical pieces.

Houghton's next play, *Fancy Free* (6 November 1911) written in March 1911 reputedly in a single evening, fell flat at first, both with audience and press. The Examiner of Plays found it 'Mildly cynical, & unmoral but harmless.'

It's set in the writing-room of the Hotel Cosmopolitan, 'a tall, hand-some apartment, exquisitely furnished.' Fancy with her lover Alfred by her side is writing to Ethelbert her husband (whom she believes to be in Scotland) to tell, him she has left him for ever. She goes upstairs to finish her letter and Ethelbert enters. He and Alfred happen to be old friends, and so Alfred reluctantly breaks the news that he has just run away with Fancy. Instead of getting angry, Ethelbert consoles his friend, suggesting that he will now have to deal with Fancy's extravagant life-style. Ethelbert is not, however, alone: he is with Delia, a lady he met in Edinburgh. The four then sit down and discuss the situation and one another's shortcomings. Finally, Fancy returns to her husband while Delia starts to flirt with Alfred. The Examiner of Plays found it, 'Mildly cynical, & unmoral but harmless.'

The *Manchester Guardian* critic C.E. Montegue wrote, 'Except for a slight touch of jauntiness, which pervades the treatment, not very happily, the author gives us a rather cold, dry, impersonal representation of two men and two women morally not far removed from a state of canine promiscuity ... A weak piece and a step backwards ... '[32]

Gerald Cumberland recalled interviewing Houghton the day after the bad reviews.

> He must have felt the criticism sorely, but when I met him next day he pluckily treated it as a matter of no consequence whatever.
>
> 'A reasonable man cannot expect always to be understood,' said he, 'and I suppose the *Manchester Guardian*, which has always been very good to me in the past, has a right to scold me if it thinks fit.'
>
> 'A scolding, Houghton? Why, you were thrashed.'
>
> 'Well, I s'pose I was. But I can stand it.'[33]

As Cumberland himself had once remarked:

> I remember Captain James E. Agate, a most original and brilliant colleague of Houghton's on the *Manchester Guardian*, once saying to a group of people: 'Don't you make any mistake about Houghton. He's not such a fool as he appears.'[34]

Notes

[1] *Manchester Courier*, 20 July 1912.

[2] Houghton, letter to Annie Horniman, 13 August 1912, Rylands Library

[3] Brighouse, *Autobiography*, p58.

[4] Harold Brighouse, 'Introduction', in *The Works of Stanley Houghton,* 3 vols. (Constable, 1914). vol. 1, pp. ix–lix.

[5] Ibid.

[6] Gerald Cumberland, *Set Down in Malice* (Grant Richards, 1919).

[7] Brighouse, Introduction to *The Works of Stanley Houghton*.

[8] A.S.W., review in *Manchester Guardian*, 17 May 1921.

[9] 'Stanley Houghton: A Man and his Work', *The English Review* (January 1914)

[10] Brighouse, Introduction to *The Works of Stanley Houghton*.

[11] Cumberland, *op. cit.*

[12] Brighouse Introduction to *The Works of Stanley Houghton*.

[13] *Daily Mail*, 3 December 1912.

[14] Letter to Monkhouse, 3 December 1912.

[15] *Manchester Guardian*, 23 July 1907.

[16] Cumberland, *op. cit.*

[17] *Manchester Courier*, 20 July 1912.

[18] *Daily Mail*, 12 September 1912.

[19] Brighouse, Introduction to *The Works of Stanley Houghton.*

[20] *The Referee*, 13 June 1909.

[21] *The Nation*, 3 July 1909.

[22] Pogson, *op. cit.*, p84.

[23] *Manchester Courier*, 20 July 1912.

[24] *Manchester Chronicle*, 2 July 1914.

[25] Brighouse, Introduction to *The Works of Stanley Houghton.*

[26] The *Observer*, 17 November 1912.

[27] *Manchester Guardian* (22 November 1910).

[28] *Times Literary Supplement* (24 July 1914).

[29] 'Family Plays', *Daily Mail*, 2 September 1912.

[30] Brighouse, Introduction to Houghton plays.

[31] Stanley Houghton, *The Master of the House*, play text.

[32] *Manchester Guardian*, 11 November 1911.

[33] Cumberland, *op. cit.*

[34] Cumberland, *op. cit.*

16

Hindle Shakes Up the World

The message of *Hindle Wakes* is therefore of inestimable value, inasmuch as it dispels the fog of the silly sentimentalism and disgusting bombast that declares woman a thing apart from nature – one who neither does nor must crave the joys of life permissible to man.[1]

There are plays about mill-girls – you will see the mill-girls on the posters walking about in the snow with a baby – but they are simply good old melodrama ... they are of the soporific or eupeptic school ...[2]

ACCORDING TO BRIGHOUSE, HOUGHTON WAS A fast worker. 'From the moment of deciding on his subject, progress was extraordinarily rapid. *The Younger Generation* was written in two months, *Hindle Wakes* in three ... First, Houghton caught his idea, then came a period of incubation, during which a small notebook was carried for the jotting-down of constructive points and scraps of dialogue. The full scheme of *Hindle Wakes* was sketched on a few scattered papers of a penny notebook. From the scenario he wrote the dialogue, rarely rewriting, and never more than once.'

The play was written in the October, November and December of 1911 and completed well before the Christmas of that year. It was offered to Miss Horniman, who accepted it for production in Manchester during the following autumn.

The very first mention of it comes in a long letter Houghton had written to Allan Monkhouse in mid-October 1911. After signing off he added a postscript on a small piece of rough paper:

> P.S. I had almost forgotten to tell you that I have been for some time working upon a play called *Hindle Wakes* about Lancashire people, in which the mill-owner's son seduces the daughter of one of his employees, and the mill owner insists on the young couple marrying. The theme you see is almost identical, only your treatment (in *Mary Broome*) is comedy and mine is an attempt at simple realistic drama.[3]

That the bulk of the letter had been praising Monkhouse for the latter's play, *Mary Broome*, is ironic. *Mary Broome* had failed to make an impact in London. *Hindle Wakes* would cause something of a sensation.

The story is a simple one, skilfully told. The play opens with the parents of mill-girl Fanny Hawthorn discussing their daughter's whereabouts. She has been on a Wakes Weekend trip to Blackpool with a friend but she is late returning. They discuss a postcard she has sent them but it's clear something is wrong. They guess that she's not being honest with them but they are unsure why.

Fanny finally arrives and they question her. She is indignant and has an alibi – the testimony of her friend Mary. The parents reveal to Fanny (and to us, the audience) that Mary has drowned in a boating accident. Fanny is thus forced to confess that she has been in Aberystwyth, not Blackpool, and that she has spent the weekend with a man, Allan Jeffcote.

Allan is the son of a wealthy millowner, Nathaniel, an old-time friend of Fanny's father Christopher. (The two fathers were once fellow workers. Now Nat is the employer and Chris the employee,

(1931 *Hindle Wakes* film advert)

but they retain their old friendship). Chris decides he must tell Nathaniel and settle matters.

In Scene two the two old friends discuss the issue. Once established that their son and daughter have spent a weekend together, the two men decide that marriage is the only respectable option, despite the fact that Allan is already engaged to Beatrice Farrar, daughter of another wealthy mill-owner, Sir Tim Farrar. Nat decides to tell Tim and both men agree that the wedding must be cancelled. Beatrice confronts Allan (who insists he can still marry her despite their parents' wishes) but she insists he marries Fanny, for religious reasons. He reluctantly agrees.

In Act Three, all is explained to Fanny and arrangements are set in place for the marriage. Finally, Allan asks Fanny what she thinks. She replies with what was at the time the show-stopping line: 'I was just wondering where I come in.'

She is clearly indignant: 'It doesn't suit me to let you settle my affairs without so much as consulting me.' Her mother replies: 'Consulting you! What is there to consult you about, I'd like to know? You want to marry Allan, I suppose, and all we're talking about is the best way to bring it about.'

'That's just where you make the mistake,' says Fanny. 'I don't want to marry Alan.'

The parents are dumbfounded and outraged but she is adamant. When left alone with Allan to discuss it, she simply explains that she doesn't love him and that the whole weekend away was a bit of fun.

> FANNY: Don't you kid yourself, my lad! It isn't because I'm afraid of spoiling your life that I'm refusing you, but because I'm afraid of spoiling mine! That didn't occur to you?

Fanny remains unmoved by Alan's appeals to her sense of duty – that if she refuses to marry him, he will lose his inheritance – and to her presumed feelings of love – that since she slept with him, she must have loved him.

> ALAN: But you didn't ever really love me?
> FANNY: Love you? Good heavens, of course not! Why on earth should I love you? You were just someone to have a bit of fun with. You were an amusement – a lark.
> ALAN (shocked): Fanny! Is that all you cared for me?
> FANNY: How much more did you care for me?
> ALAN: But it's not the same. I'm a man.
> FANNY: You're a man, and I was your little fancy. Well, I'm a woman, and you were my little fancy. You wouldn't prevent a woman enjoying herself as well as a man, if she takes it into her head?
> ALAN: But do you mean to say that you didn't care any more for me than a fellow cares for any girl he happens to pick up?
> FANNY: Yes. Are you shocked?

Fanny then tells Alan in even more direct language, 'You're not man enough for me ... We've enjoyed ourselves proper! But all good times have to come to an end, and ours is over now. Come along, now, and bid me farewell.' Thus, in a dramatic tour de force, Fanny chooses her own integrity over marriage and wealth.

When the parents are told the wedding is off, Fanny's mother says she will be thrown out into the street. Fanny remains unmoved.

> FANNY (smiling): ... I shan't starve. I'm not without a trade at my finger- tips, thou knows. I'm a Lancashire lass, and so long as there's weaving sheds in Lancashire I shall earn enough brass to keep me going. I wouldn't live at home again after this, not anyhow! I'm going to be on my own in future. (To Christopher) You've no call to be afraid. I'm not going to disgrace you. But so long as I've to live my own life I don't see why I shouldn't choose what it's to be ...

The play doesn't end on that high-note. Fanny leaves for an uncertain future, while Mrs Jeffcote reveals to her husband that Beatrice will marry Alan after all

Edyth Goodall, Eccles-born actress as the original Fanny
in *Hindle Wakes*, the role that made her name (1912)
(*Author's collection*)

JEFFCOTE: There's no accounting for tastes! (He ruminates,) So Beatrice loves him, does she? Eh! but women are queer folk! Who'd have thought that Fanny would refuse to wed him?

MRS JEFFCOTE: It is strange. It makes you feel there is something in Providence after all.

THE CURTAIN FALLS[4]

Though *Hindle Wakes* was already guaranteed a production at the Gaiety, Houghton was keen for the play to find a London venue. An astute businessman, despite his sometimes diffident image, he retained the rights to the play beyond Manchester, something AH was unaware of. Having had a refusal from one theatre manager, Houghton then wrote to his London agent, Anthony Ellis in December 1911:

> I have just finished a three-act play, rather serious and of more ambitious quality than some of my recent efforts, called *Hindle Wakes*. It is about Lancashire people and is practically in dialect, though not barbaric. It will be of no use to you for London, but I suppose you would like me to send you a copy to read. Tell me if you don't want one and I will not trouble. It is of no use to anybody but the Gaiety here.[5]

He also offered it to Liverpool Repertory Theatre and, although recommended for production by their then adviser, Lascelles Abercrombie (along with director Basil Dean), they declined the play as being 'too strong meat' for the Liverpool public.

But then fortune smiled on Houghton. In June 1912, the Gaiety Company was in London mounting a repertoire season at the Coronet Theatre in Notting Hill. AH was asked by the Stage Society to provide the last production of their thirteenth season, the play to be new and preferably *Lancashire*. Thus it was that, on 16 June 1912 at the Aldwych Theatre, directed by Lewis Casson and played by the Gaiety ensemble, *Hindle Wakes* had its premiere.

As we have seen, the Stage Society was often a springboard to greater things. It had already supplied the Gaiety with several plays over the past couple of years, particularly by women writers. It was an influential, groundbreaking society that boasted a membership of around 1,700 including? Barrie, John Drinkwater and Bernard Shaw. Previous Stage Society productions had been Ibsen's *Pillars of Society* and Shaw's *Mrs Warren's Profession* – evidence of a tendency to promote equality of the sexes and to expose and condemn the injustices of the sexual 'double standard'. *Hindle Wakes*, with Fanny at its heart, looked to be perfect Society material. It was an instant, overwhelming success.

Every major daily newspaper sent critics to review it and, almost without exception, they were complimentary, even adulatory. The *Daily Telegraph* ('a very remarkable performance of a very remarkable play ...'); *The Times* ('it is refreshing to get away from the familiar stage morality and stage language'); the *Daily Mail* ('the author has a keen eye for a dramatic situation and can cap a good line with a better without sacrificing truth to mere verbal cleverness'); these and many, many more extolled the play's humour, its dialogue and its freshness.

The *Times Literary Supplement* was particularly impressed by Houghton's clever use of dialect to delineate character: 'Jeffcote could be paralleled by a hundred Lancashire manufacturers who, with thousands a year to their name, lapse into dialect the moment they are excited, go about their luxurious houses in shirt-sleeves, discard the use of the dining room and take 'high tea' in place of dinner and live on affectionate terms with cotton operatives who have been their workmates in bygone days.'[6]

Houghton also utilised the Lancashire dialect to dramatise the mutual respect and long-term friendship between Nat and Chris, two economically differentiated characters suggesting that in the play community values ultimately trump economic and class interests.

There were some quibbles concerning its length ('the story is perhaps rather a slight one to cover three acts') and its apparent similarity in theme to other plays staged by the Society ('the plot itself a shade too familiar'), but overall it was considered a remarkable piece of work and clearly destined for a longer run elsewhere in the capital.

After some complicated, not to say shrewd, manoeuvrings by Houghton, it did eventually transfer to the Playhouse where it ran until the end of September. It was then moved to the Court Theatre for another three weeks before ending its triumphant London run on 19 October 1912. By that time it had made both Houghton and AH a considerable amount of money. Preparations were then made for its transfer to Manchester and the Gaiety itself, an event that apparently caused Houghton some apprehension.

In the *London Evening News* he'd written an article entitled 'Dialect Plays – are they successful at home?' in which he tried to answer the question whether or not particular social classes liked to see either their own class or another represented on stage. He concluded that Lancashire audiences rarely liked to see plays reflecting their own daily lives and mused, 'How will Lancashire like *Hindle Wakes*?'[7]

He need not have worried. The play was once again an immediate success, Houghton having to respond to several curtain calls on the first night. The *Manchester City News* declared that, 'the supreme test (of the play) had to be made in Manchester,' and that 'we regard *Hindle Wakes* as a masterly work.'[8]

Despite the drama critics' almost universal acclamation, the play caused a great deal of consternation in the country at large. 'It is difficult to remember with complete understanding,' L. du Garde Peach later wrote, 'the wave of indignation which literally swept over the country when *Hindle Wakes* burst upon an outraged public.' He continued: 'Not only scandalised playgoers, but persons who had never been inside a theatre and who were never likely to visit one joined in the general outcry. This was a wicked and immoral play which should never have been allowed to soil the stage.'[9]

If one considers that Mary Broome's decision to leave her husband and seek a new life abroad with another man was thought of as daring, a sign of unsettling, changing times, then one can understand how Fanny Hawthorn's disdain for and rejection of the offer of a lucrative marriage and subsequent 'respectability' was considered shocking, particularly by working-class audiences.

In his article on dialect, Houghton suggested, 'It may be argued that Manchester (ie The Gaiety) does not provide a true working-class audience and that is correct to some extent ... The proper thing would be to go to real manufacturing towns like Oldham and Blackburn and find out what they think of work-class drama ...'[10]

In November 1912, a reporter from the *Manchester Courier* took him at his word. 'WBC' visited a theatre in a small, unnamed cotton town where *Hindle Wakes* was being played (By now at least four versions of the play were on tour). The title of the piece was *Hindle in the Looking Glass* and subtitled *Fanny in Disfavour*.

The audience, according to the writer, was exclusively working-class and its first reaction was to marvel at the 'reality' presented on stage, with fictional characters apparently springing from their everyday life.

'"What's ta doin' theer, Bill?" enquired my right-hand neighbour of a friend.' He continued, 'Then I knew why all the cotton town had come to see this thing. For – this was the joke – this cotton town was Hindle and this play, Hindle in the looking glass!'

As the play progressed, the audience reacted volubly: 'Mrs Hawthorne shook Fanny by the shoulders. "Yer tellin' lies, that y'are!" – then, "'Ave yer been with a feller?"'

'Sad to relate, Hindle shrieked and then applauded as Fanny was allowed to go off to bed.'

Jeff Northcote was apparently the hero of the hour, 'for in the stalls were several of him with wives and eldest sons'. When Northcote tells his son he must marry Fanny, 'he was cheered to the echo by virtuous Hindle.' When the curtain fell on this scene, 'I half fancy many of the audience thought the play was at an end. For what more could there be? Allan was to make amends, Fanny was to be made an "honest woman. Surely – 'God Save The King' and "exit"'.

> This sequence of events not happening, at this moment Hindle became uneasy. Beatrice entreating Allan, her lover, because of her love for him and his love for her to marry another girl because that girl had 'a better right to him'. Hindle found this sorely puzzling. On that scene the curtain descended amid a frigid silence. A matron near me declared in a contemptuous voice, 'Oh Come on! It's soft!' and led her infant son out by the hand. Many followed; some came back ...
>
> It was in the last scene that the storm burst – a storm of inarticulate disapprobation, let me add. Fanny was welcomed back with applause but when she said, 'W'eer do aw coom in?' Hindle laughed uneasily. 'E-e-e! Oo is a thick "un"!' exclaimed a woman closed to the writer.
>
> Then came Fanny's calm refusal to be made an honest woman. Hindle laughed incredulously. There was a joke somewhere, although they could not see it. The audience agreed with Fanny's mother ('Y'are a fool! It's sinful!').

The writer concluded, 'The subtleties that charmed Manchester and amused London are lost here. To Hindle this pig-headedness is wicked, sinful. Fanny's retort that it seemed foolish to have to marry Allan to make *him* an honest man shocked Hindle more than anything else.'

'The curtain fell and Hindle left the theatre, silent and scandalised. My fellow pittites as I passed into Hindle's street were conversing.

"Eh," drawled Mr H, "Aw canna see as there's any moral i' it. Yer dunno even if she'll live straight a-fter".'

"'E—e-e," declared Mrs H with vehemence, "Oo's bad through and through!"'[11]

Though clearly written up to make an amusing piece, the reportage rings true and is rare. Oddly enough, the American writer Willa Cather who reviewed *Hindle Wakes* when it came to America in early 1913, duplicated the sentiment expressed by the departing 'Mr H'. Cather praised the play as being

> ... the only play given in New York this season that touched upon the feminist movement or the industrial position of women at all vitally... It is written in the quiet tone popular among the younger English dramatists, who are so determined not to be artificially conclusive that they are sometimes more inconclusive than they need be ...

Cather concluded,

> It would have been comforting to the conventional-minded if Mr Houghton could have added another act showing us where we would find Fanny in, say, five years – whether she was really able to live up to her liberty, whether she recovered from her indiscretion as a young workman would, kept her head, and made the most of her life and her skill. Probably Mr Houghton would say: 'Here is the situation; I don't know where it's leading any more than any one else does.'[12]

For Emma Goldman, writing in 1914, the play was a bold and skilful piece of writing that challenged contemporary mores:

> *Hindle Wakes* is a much needed and important social lesson, not because it necessarily involves the idea that every girl must have sex experience before she meets the man she loves, but rather that she has the right to satisfy, if she so chooses, her emotional and sex demands like any other need of her mind and body. When the Fannies become conscious of that right, the relation of the sexes will lose the shallow romanticism and artificial exaggeration that mystery

has surrounded it with, and assume a wholesome, natural, and therefore healthy and normal expression.[13]

Du Garde Peach, writing in 1958 from the perspective of one who was there at the time, summed the play and Houghton's achievement up thus:

> Fanny was not sweet and she did not come to a bad end. On the contrary, she walked out of the Jeffcote house and the play with all the honours of war. That was what the public and some of the press could not forgive ...

Peach continued, 'Fanny was a modern independent girl with unconventional views on sex equality mixed up in a play which had not altogether got rid of the theatrical tradition of the 1880s. Lines which Pinero might have written jostle with lines which Shaw *had* written.'[14]

Houghton, according to Peach, had already shown himself to be a mild rebel in 'The Younger Generation' but his youthful play-going had been in the theatre of Pinero and Henry Arthur Jones ... When he wrote *Hindle Wakes* he had not entirely shaken off the influence of either.'

Hindle Wakes, he concluded, was that most interesting thing, 'a transition play'.

Sadly, Houghton would not live to complete that transition.

Notes

[1] Emma Goldman, *The Social Significance of Modern Drama* (Gorham Press, Boston, 1914).

[2] Stanley Houghton, 'Dialect Plays', *London Evening News*, 20 August 1912.

[3] Houghton, letter to Monkhouse, October 1911, Rylands Library

[4] Following quotations all from *Hindle Wakes* play text

[5] Houghton, letter to Anthony Ellis, December 1911 (from Brighouse, *Autobiography*, p178.

[6] *Times Literary Supplement*, 24 July 1914.

[7]*London Evening News*, 20 August 1912.

[8]*Manchester City News*, 2 December 1912.

[9]*Manchester Guardian*. 17 September 1958.

[10]Houghton 'Dialect Plays'.

[11]'Hindle Through The Looking Glass', *Manchester Courier*, 19th November 1912.

[12]Willa Cather: 'Plays of Real Life', *McClure's Magazine*, 40 (March 1913), 63–72.

[13]Goldman, *op. cit.*

[14]LL. Du Garde Peach, 'Hindle With Its Edges Softened', *Manchester Guardian*, 17 September 1958

17

The Theatre's Tragic Loss

The future of the English drama has sustained a great loss, for Stanley Houghton had the ability to write great plays about great people in ordinary life ... I write this with deep regret that we should have lost him.[1]

THE FINANCIAL SUCCESS OF *HINDLE WAKES* and the London production of *The Younger Generation* enabled Houghton to leave the cotton trade, after which he spent an unproductive year in London. He first took a flat in Charing Cross Road, but found, after a few months spent in discovering London that its central position, if convenient for him, was convenient for others to come and interrupt him. Steady work was impossible to a man who found himself lionised by society, caricatured by Max Beerbohm, badgered by editors, tempted by commissions from managers (most, but not all of which he declined), and courted by his own profession. The whirl for a time amused him, but it did not satisfy him.

After returning briefly to Manchester, he moved to Paris, where he began a play, *The Weather*, and a novel, *Life*.

I am quite absorbed in it, and work at it as I haven't done at anything since *Hindle Wakes*. One has the feeling that nothing can ever spoil the work when you've done it, no worry of rehearsals and actors can ever come between your effect and the public. Of course I don't mean that I shall stop writing plays ...[2]

Neither play nor novel would be completed before successive bouts of influenza and appendicitis forced him on to Venice, where he underwent two botched surgical operations. He returned once more to Manchester where, on 10 December 1913, he died of meningitis at the age of thirty-two.

Sadder still, for posterity's sake, the work he produced in those final, hectic twelve months was largely undistinguished due in part to his lingering illness, in part to trying to fulfil the impossible demands that sudden fame and his own apparently unlimited energy, brought.

Phipps was a one-act play written in October 1912 for actor-manager Arthur Bourchier and his wife Violet Vanbrugh. It opened on 20 December at the Pavilion Glasgow for just two performances.

Trust the People fared better, opening on 6 February 1913 at the Garrick Theatre and lasting 44 performances. However, it gained little praise. The *Illustrated London News* review concluded that the play's political satire was implausible and objected to the 'monstrous notion' of a prime minister who attempts to use party funds to silence a blackmailer. The review added that Houghton was, 'too ambitious in breaking from the provincial environment in which he moves with such ease', and that it was, 'not wise of him as yet to try to do without the help of Lancashire'.[3]

The Perfect Cure was written in ten days and produced in June 1913 by Charles Hawtrey. *The Times* praised the well-performed portrayal of a remarkably selfish father as consistent with Houghton's familiar theme of the younger generation's revolt against the old. The *Illustrated London News* meanwhile described the play as a 'true and delightful comedy' and noted that it was set in a London suburb, disproving the reviewer's previous notion that

Houghton was 'helpless without a Lancashire setting'. It was, however, withdrawn after four nights.

After his untimely death, his fellow Manchester playwrights were quick to defend both his legacy and the possibilities that were now dashed: 'The platitudes of depreciation,' wrote Allan Monkhouse, 'were inevitable, but nobody who knew Houghton had any fear that he was at the end of the tether, or near it. He was neither overcome nor soured, and if his prospects were momentarily overclouded, he had yet an abundance of present accomplishment and fine prospects.'[4]

To the charge that Houghton had 'abandoned' Manchester for London and Paris, Harold Brighouse countered, 'He had no immediate intention of representing "metropolitan life".' The novel he had begun was about Manchester. He made in Paris notes of two plays, a country house comedy and a Lancashire play. 'Lancashire interested Houghton; London did not.'[5]

Guardian colleague C.E. Montague wrote in 1914:

> 'He gave the theatre the first modern play, of any quality in which Lancashire character and manners have been faithfully observed and skilfully made vividly curious and exciting to playgoers in all parts of the English-speaking world. It was a definite thing waiting to be done, and was worth doing, and he did it. By doing it he not only did a service to Lancashire, but he helped on the modern movement towards the right kind of localization in imaginative literature ... [6]

The success of *Hindle Wakes* proved to be a seminal moment both where the Gaiety itself was concerned and for the 'Manchester playwrights' in general. It would prove to be the theatre's most profitable venture but its London run undermined the ethos of the company by luring away some of the Gaiety's finest actors and actresses. The old unity would never be fully recaptured, it seems.

Added to that, according to Pogson, AH had been given a taste of West End success, 'and ever afterwards she could not altogether take her eyes off London. There was, from that point, a certain decentralization of power.' Criticism of the theatre, its plays and its very *raison d'être* would accelerate, 'the effect of which was to dissipate the unique spirit and achievement of the early Manchester seasons'.[7]

Houghton's legacy would ultimately be secured via an art form that at one time appeared to threaten the very existence of the theatre. The Gaiety itself would close in 1920 and be turned into a cinema, yet it would be the cinema that would perpetuate and even enshrine Houghton's quintessential Manchester play.

When *Hindle Wakes* had first appeared there had been some confusion in the capital as to exactly what a 'Wakes Week' was. In the *Evening News* Houghton wrote to explain the term for the benefit of London audiences. He also touched on the economic situation of those mysterious creatures, northern mill-girls.

'Wakes in Lancashire,' he said, 'are simply the annual holidays observed by certain towns. There is no regular date common to the county as a whole, though of course the summer months are always the chosen ones. The period lasts a week or ten days, and during that time each town not only suspends all commercial activity, but is actually almost deserted. It is not a holiday; it is a migration.'

'All the year the man or woman ... pay so much a week into a 'Going-away Club'. By the time Wakes week comes round each person has a considerable own saved up, and the total amount drawn out by the combined workers at the same time is quite enormous. In Heywood (near Rochdale) for instance, a comparatively small town, over £15,000 [£390,000 in 1981] ill be drawn out of the clubs this week and distributed amongst the merry-makers.'[8]

He explained that the money was solely for the purpose of a good holiday, to be spent on the lodging-house keepers, the public houses, the variety entertainments, the dancing halls and, 'the towers, palaces and empires of the great Northern watering places', and most significantly, 'upon Blackpool, Douglas and Morecambe, but above all, upon Blackpool. The man who has not seen Blackpool promenade on a hot August Bank Holiday has something left to live for. Two solid miles of humanity, slowly circulating, perspiring ... '[9]

Which brought him to Fanny, and her famous declaration at the end of the play: 'I'm a Lancashire lass, and so long as there's weaving sheds in Lancashire I shall earn enough brass to keep me going. I wouldn't live at home again after this ... I'm going to be on my own in future.'[10]

Financial independence for a mill worker, especially for women, was often underestimated, but Houghton knew full well that Fanny 'was a skilled and well-paid worker in a cotton mill ... ' as long as she was *in* work, of course. What's more, 'they can spend it, these pale-faced weaver lassies ... They know how to enjoy themselves better than anyone in Great Britain. The money is there *and it has got to be spent* ...The festivity endures as long as the money lasts, and often things are cut very fine towards the end. It is rather a point of honour to be "spent up" as they call it, on the last day....Before you went away you will have carefully placed a few shillings on the mantelpiece underneath the clock. That has got to last you until next payday.'[11]

All of this remained latent in the play; it was a backdrop that could only be referred to indirectly but which explained so much about the occasion, about the economics of the situation, about Fanny herself. When film-makers came to render the play for cinema screen, the straitjacket of the proscenium arch could be dispensed with and Fanny's back-story developed.

Hindle Wakes was first filmed in 1918 as a 'silent' directed by Maurice Elvey, one of the most prolific film directors in the history of the British film industry. Although it had been a box-office success, he was reported to have been unsatisfied with the way the 1918 version turned out and, believed he could do better. ('There are too many static situations and here we miss the spoken word, the pungent Houghton dialogue.')[12]

He thus directed a remake in 1927, producing what is now regarded as a classic of British silent cinema. Its skilful use of location gave the film a documentary realism very unusual in British films of the period and in many ways decades ahead of its time, foreshadowing the Northern 'kitchen sink' realism of the 1950s and 1960s.

Elvey admired Houghton's original play greatly, telling film historian Denis Gifford that he thought it was, 'the finest English play ever written ... a really great play; it is really about something.'[13]

The 1927 film would cost between £8,000 and £10,000 to produce, while the two stars, Estelle Brody (Fanny) and John Stuart (Alan), had played the leads in Elvey's preceding 1926 World War I movie, *Mademoiselle from Armentières*.

Elvey was keen to open the play up and so took his cameras outside, filming in the Monton Mill in Manchester, in streets and by canal-sides in Eccles, at various Blackpool locations, as well as overlooking the sea at Llandudno.

To ensure that the two young actresses playing Fanny and Mary, who were neither born nor bred in Lancashire, appeared authentic in the mill scenes, a foreman was recruited to advise them how to handle cotton bobbins and machinery ('how to stand between the roving frames like real "tenters"')[14]

The film begins with shots of the working mill, with men stoking the boilers, the workers starting their shift, the banks of looms moving backwards and forwards, the factory clock and whistle, all of which serve to convey the regimented nature of the factory workers lives. ('Elvey makes poetry out of the mundane, using images of clocks and machines and paralleling views of his

Estelle Brody in *Hindle Wakes*
(1927)

Belle Chrystall (centre) on the set of *Hindle Wakes* in Preston with local mill girls(1931) (*Alamy Stock Photo/Everett Collection*)

Two actresses who found fame playing Fanny in *Hindle Wakes* on the silver screen. Belle Chrystall also starred in a film version of *Hobson's Choice* that same year.

characters' behaviour and routines to set up the vice-like class inequity of the time.') But when the location shooting switched to Blackpool, it took on an exhilarating spontaneity reflecting the escapism of those same workers on their short holiday.

The Blackpool scenes are one of the highlights of the film, with shots taken up Blackpool Tower and on the Pleasure Beach Helter Skelter and Big Dipper rides. Elvey is said to have shot fifty-one scenes at the Pleasure Beach and Tower Ballroom in ten hours over the course of one day.

In the Tower Ballroom, Elvey filmed an ambitious dance sequence, which led to the film being advertised in Blackpool as 'starring Estelle Brody and 5,000 local artistes'. (Actually 6,347, 'the largest ballroom crowd ever filmed') He didn't restrict himself to grand location shooting, however. He also turned his camera's attention to the minutiae: the shoes of the workers as they trudge into work, the feet and legs of the mill-girls as they change out of their work shoes and into their holiday ware or the whirling feet on the ballroom floor.

The film was well received on its release. Caroline Lejeune, writing in the *Guardian* called it, 'The best advocate we have yet seen for the promulgation of British films' and said that Elvey had, 'made time and space and madness whirl before us on the screen ... Elvey has successfully borrowed from the Germans what is apt to his own needs, shaped it to his hand, and made it for the time being his own.' She went on to name it as one of her seven best films of the year (31 December, 1927).[15]

For *Kinematograph Weekly* Lionel Collier said that Elvey, with his colleague Victor Saville, the co-director who would go on to make a sound version of the same film in 1931, had, 'produced the best picture he has ever made, and an outstanding British triumph.'[16]

Even *Variety* – not known for its praise of British cinema – felt that it was a film that, 'did more to establish the birth of the British industry than any other'[17]

Houghton's funeral was held at Manchester Crematorium on Saturday 13 December 1913, conducted by the family clergyman, the Rev J. Pullein Thompson who had also baptised Houghton. Apart from immediate family, there were present people who had known and worked with Houghton: former employers, theatrical managers, local theatre folk as well as his *Guardian* colleagues A.N. Monkhouse, C.P. Scott and probably his closest contemporary writing friend, Harold Brighouse.

Brighouse would play an important role in securing Houghton's memory. Within days of the funeral, he was asked by the Houghton family to arrange for publication of the bulk of Houghton's work, this to be accompanied by a lengthy Introduction, which would serve as a biography of sorts.

The result wasn't admired at the time. James Agate wrote:

> Where we chiefly fault Mr Brighouse's introduction is that it gives little clue to the personality of the man, to that diffidence and charm, that obvious pre-occupation with the best-intentioned in life and art which conquered all of those critics who knew him intimately ... In this introduction Houghton is only a name and there is no indication as to the manner of man he was.[18]

Brighouse would later resist any attempts by biographers to write his own story, preferring to produce a laconic, somewhat elliptical autobiography, so perhaps he felt obliged to do the same for Houghton. Brighouse never suffered fools gladly and was somewhat contemptuous of literary 'outsiders'. There is also a suspicion that he wished to protect his friend's memory from intimations (by others) of Houghton's possible homosexuality.

(He later made a novel out of *Hindle Wakes* and wrote, 'Somebody, it seemed, was going to do this: I had a loyalty to Houghton and a feeling that if I did not do it, it would be done worse.')[19]

Whatever its faults, however, the Introduction remains the only significant contemporary memoir we have of Houghton and a key document in understanding the Manchester Playwrights in general. Brighouse was well positioned to write it. The two men had been close friends and colleagues ever since schooldays. They were both ex-Manchester Grammar School pupils, Houghton being a year and a half older than 'Brig', as he called him. Both worked (and hated to work) on Manchester's Cotton Exchange, and both were Swan Club regulars.

The two men had also shared a dogged determination to make good in the theatre. They'd even worked together on a play, *The Hillaries*, finished by Brighouse after Stanley's death and performed in 1915.

Brighouse suggests the moment their friendship was 'sealed' was when Houghton wrote to him following the production of Brighouse's first full-length play *Dealing In Futures* at the Gaiety (August 1910). In the letter (1 September 1910), Houghton outlined what he liked about the play, and compared it to one by Galsworthy: 'It is not a bit fair to compare *Strife* with *Dealing in Futures*. You concentrate on the people and Galsworthy on the social problem. And your way is the more correct – the finer one – though the extraordinary force and generalship which Galsworthy has exhibited make *Strife* the greater play ... '[20]

Brighouse commented, 'That, from a man implicitly identifying himself as a rival, is handsome ... '[21]

Houghton had also said, 'We are the only two Manchester men whose plays are likely to be worth anything ... ' and at that point, both were well on their way: Houghton with the *Dear Departed*, *Independent Means* and *The Younger Generation*; Brighouse with *Dealing in Futures*, *The Doorway* and the *Price of Coal*. They would also share a Gaiety bill in 1910, when *Dealing in Futures* played alongside Houghton's one-act *Master of the House*.

However, as we'll see, Brighouse's writing career would not be as closely tied to the Gaiety as Houghton's had been. Brighouse explained: 'The three plays that were to write Houghton's name large upon the world map of drama were produced under Miss Horniman ... for Monkhouse, as for me, repertory was the ante-room ...'[22]

Notes

[1] Annie Horniman, letter to the *Manchester Courier*, 13 December 1913.

[2] Harold Brighouse, 'Introduction', in *The Works of Stanley Houghton*.

[3] *Illustrated London News*, 6 February 1913.

[4] Brighouse, 'Introduction', in *The Works of Stanley Houghton*.

[5] Ibid.

[6] *Manchester Guardian*, 9tJune 1914.

[7] Pogson, *op. cit.*, p134.

[8] *London Evening News*, 9 August 1912.

[9] Ibid.

[10] Ibid.

[11] Ibid.

[12] *Manchester Guardian*, 10 September 1918.

[13] British Film Library, Gifford Collection.

[14] *Manchester Guardian*, 28 October 1926.

[15] Ibid., 5th February 1927.

[16] *Kinematograph Weekly*, 10 February 1927.

[17] *Variety*, 13 October 1931.

[18] *Manchester Playgoer*, 2/1 (July 1914)

[19] Brighouse, 'Introduction', in *The Works of Stanley Houghton*.

[20] Stanley Houghton, letter to Brighouse, 1 September 1910.

[21] Brighouse, *Autobiography*, p178.

[22] Ibid., p57.

18

Brighouse Plays the Game

In all Harold Brighouse's plays there is in the acting more laughter than one could expect from the reading. The actors invariably experience a sense of surprise and pleasure when they discover in performance that the public finds far more humour in their parts than they themselves were aware of during the period of preparation.[1]

Why am I writing a play about football, you ask? It is because I do not think any sport attracts more attention than football.[2]

Harold Brighouse was born on 26 July 1882 at Inglewood, 25 Ellesmere Avenue, Eccles, Lancashire, to John Southworth Brighouse, a manager in a cotton-spinning firm and his second wife, Charlotte Amelia (née Harrison), a schoolteacher and headmistress. Harold and his sister Hilda (b. 1884) were technically illegitimate, his father having married Charlotte, his deceased first wife's sister, in an unrecognised ceremony in Montreux in 1881.

Brighouse's home was a happy and secure one, on the surface at least. There was a very large garden in which he and his sister played riotous games of hide and seek and hares and hounds with the neighbourhood children, not to mention numerous cousins (Brighouse senior was one of 13 children; there were 24 cousins and regular large family gatherings.)

Of significance for Brighouse's writing future are two chapters in his autobiography *What I Have Had*. The first concerned his mother's brother, Edwin Harrison. A brilliant Balliol scholar, a colleague of the poet Swinburne and Benjamin Jowett, he died young, unfulfilled and in straightened circumstances.

Brighouse's mother, according to Harold, 'adored' her brother and had hopes that her son might match Edwin's academic brilliance. Brighouse reacted against the pressure and spurned the chance to go to University. His mother's entreaties made no difference to him. (As Gerald Cumberland noted: 'I was used to Brighouse for, from the age of eleven to thirteen I had been at the same school with him, and I remembered how enormously sensitive and how self-contained and how stubborn he was.')[3]

There was another factor where that decision was concerned. His second chapter is entitled 'My Father's Cashbook'. He had become aware as a boy that it was his father's relentless toil and generosity that made their (and their extended family's) comparative prosperity possible. His largesse where various family members were concerned cost him dear. 'Very well: here surely, cotton-spinner, house-owner, lender, and in his degree public figure, was a man in full enjoyment of economic security. But he wasn't.'[4]

The firm Brighouse Snr worked for, Holdsworth and Gibb, was all but ruined by one of the partners, which entailed John Brighouse taking over. 'He had till then been the grossly underpaid miracle-worker who, despite Walter Gibb, had enabled the firm to survive.'[5]

Brighouse clearly admired his father's dedication and abstemiousness immensely. He also became acutely aware of the pounds shillings and pence of everyday existence and of the necessity of hard work. His brilliant uncle Harrison had died penniless. 'When Harold's father asked him what he wanted to be, he said, "Like you, a businessman". I think that he was pleased.'

Harold Brighouse   (*Salford Library*)

(Cartoon *Author's collection*)

Brighouse added, 'And obscurely, with ludicrous wrong-headedness, I was jealous on my father's behalf of my mother's love for her brother.' He thus left grammar school 'without regret'.[6]

Later, in 1909 when his mother lay dying of cancer, his first one-act play was produced at the Gaiety. It gave his mother enormous satisfaction, 'wildly, pathetically disproportionate to the unimportance of the event. Her dream for me, taking its own way, had conquered. She saw me as veritably the nephew of Edwin Harrison. These mothers! Those fond adorable mothers!'

Brighouse later attributed key aspects of his writing to his parents and his childhood. 'I stood and stand, dramatically, for simplicity of statement. Delving speculatively, I find origin for this in the plain living of my parents, combined possibly with boyhood attendance at a Congregational Chapel from which ritual was banished. The Lord's Prayer, if I remember rightly, was the only set-piece in the service.'[8]

The uncle's shadow, however, did not disappear completely, it was merely replaced by another: Gerald Cumberland noted: 'Now, such are the influences that one man may have upon another, it came about that the more successful [Stanley] Houghton became, the harder worked Brighouse. Said Brighouse to himself, I imagine: "If Stanley can do all this, why not I?" So he worked desperately, sloggingly, overwhelmingly.'[9]

It's perhaps significant how each of the three major Manchester playwrights developed an interest in the drama because it was reflected in their work and its wider reception. Monkhouse was first a newspaper critic: he sat at a distance and judged. Houghton was first an actor: he learnt much about the stage by standing on it. Brighouse was primarily an onlooker. As he put it, 'Gallery first-nighting had invaluably prepared me for play writing. The actual impulse, the command to write, came slowly.'[10]

As a cotton fabric salesman, he worked in Whitworth Street in a shipping merchant's warehouse just around the corner from Manchester's theatre-land on Oxford Road, which was where he spent whatever spare time and cash he had.

Brighouse enjoyed seasons of Shakespeare at the Royal, including the famous F.R. Benson company; Richard Flanagan at the Queen's Theatre; along with all the top music hall turns then appearing in the city such as Marie Lloyd, George Formby (Snr), Vesta Tilley, and George Robey.

In 1902, rather fortuitously, Brighouse was sent to London by his firm to run a small office on Broad Street: 'In 1902, at twenty, with £150 a year, London belonged to me.'[11] The work was undemanding and Brighouse became a West End theatre 'first-nighter'. He visited the Court Theatre and saw the famous Barker-Vedrenne seasons; he saw plays at the Adelphi, the Apollo, the Lyric: 'it was a rich, random, unpremeditated first apprenticeship to playwriting, though I had no thought of myself as a potential playwright ... '[12]

It was in London that he also met his wife, another first-nighter, Emily Lynes, assistant to Lala Charles, a leading photographer for society magazines. They married in Lillington, near Leamington Spa, on 7 February 1907. He then returned to Manchester and resumed work – this time for his father's firm, but it had been in London that he had at last started writing. He claimed that he had seen 'an outrageously bad play' and thought, 'surely it could not be impossible for me to write a play not worse than the poor thing I had just seen.'[13]

He did write a play and he sent it to a well-known play-reader who sent it back suggesting it was too long and that he, 'try one-acters first – write the life you know'. Brighouse took the advice and wrote *Lonesome-like*, a one-act play about a Lancashire woman whose poverty and age demand that she move to a workhouse. It was his first, 'and I think my best one-act play'. It was bought by a

West End management but not produced until 1911.

Brighouse now started to write in earnest. Gerald Cumberland observed: 'Every afternoon Houghton and Brighouse would close their ledgers, or petty-cash books, or whatever it was they did close, and rush off home – Brighouse to catch, perhaps, his six-five p.m. train to Eccles, and Houghton to jump gymnastically (he played hockey, I believe) on to a passing tram bound for Alexandra Park. After a hurried meal, out with the MSS., the notebooks, the typescript and to work! And how hard they did work!'[14]

Of the two friendly rivals, Brighouse would always appear to be the more 'clubbable': pipe-smoking, beer-drinking ('you know, the conventionally British pint he will have in a pewter mug, as Gerald Cumberland observed[15]), he formed friendships far more easily than Houghton and although just as ambitious yet was perhaps more realistic, more open-hearted.

At the Court Theatre in London Brighouse had been a member of a young and boisterous crowd who sat on coconut-matting on concrete, crushed up against one another, 'first-nighters' who, in the intervals, indulged in heated discussions concerning the productions until eventually ejected by theatre 'chucker-outers'. Brighouse also clearly loved the Swan Club, forming strong bonds with disparate characters such as Jack Kahane and Ernest Marriott. Houghton, by contrast, tended to veer away from such close associations.

Brighouse's progress as a playwright, following as he did in the footsteps of Houghton, was also more gradual and less spectacular. As we have seen, by 1908 Brighouse had three plays he could send to Iden Payne: *Lonesome-like, The Price of Coal* and *The Doorway*. Brighouse recalled:

> 'Certainly I'll do one of them,' Payne said. 'I haven't decided which.'
> He did *The Doorway* ... in popularity potential it was by streets the
> weakest of the three plays. Later I sent, *Spring in Bloomsbury* to

> Payne. 'They'll hate it but it will do them good.' They did hate it,
> actors and audience. Payne retorted by repeat performances ...'[16]

It seems odd, in retrospect, that Payne passed over the classic *Lonesome-like* at first. In fact, after *The Doorway*, it was Glasgow Repertory that took Brighouse's next two plays, the three-act *Dealing in Futures* and *The Price of Coal*, all in 1909, and Glasgow would also premier *Lonesome-like*.

All three of Brighouse's first plays were set in bleak, industrial situations. *The Doorway* (produced on 10 April 1909 alongside *The Feud* by Edward Garnett, and later in the year at a benefit for the Hebrew Bread, Meat & Coal Fund, 6 December 1909) consists of a dialogue between two down-and-outs, a man and a woman, strangers to each other who meet by chance in the shelter of a factory door. (The latter said to be based on Brighouse's father's firm premises).

They find mutual comfort in telling over their misfortunes and their past adventures as they huddle together in the biting cold in the small hours of a winter's morning. A policeman tries to move them on but the woman pleads to be allowed to stay until the nearby parks open. The man offers to be taken back to the police station to be locked up in her place; the policeman accedes and they slowly wander off, leaving the woman in the doorway. It was considered both 'sympathetic and humorous', and not set in Manchester but in London.

Dealing in Futures (7 October 1909), the play that cemented Brighouse's and Houghton's friendship, was not a comedy but was set in a cotton mill with a conflict of interests at its heart. Charlie, an industrial chemist and engaged to the factory owner's daughter (somewhat against his will) resists the old-fashioned owner's blandishments and threats because he feels the factory is run dangerously with too many fatal accidents.

He tries to instigate a strike, but Jabez, the owner, outwits him and buys everyone off. Jabez's daughter comes to Charlie's rescue, however, insisting that they marry and together fight for a better future together. Critics considered it somewhat didactic and moralising, but Brighouse commented:

> ... But character must have something to be characteristic about – in one word, plot – and into my plot making there was apt to come a touch of didacticism. I couldn't help it; my mother, in her youth, was a school's headmistress, and the better plays of her son are 'about something', usually about the superficial somethings of a moderate optimist.[17]

The Price of Coal (15 November 1909) also has an industrial setting, originally of Lancashire. Accepted for performance at Glasgow Repertory Company, a Scottish journalist assisted Brighouse in translating the Lancashire dialect of his original script into Lanarkshire for the Scottish premiere. Iden Payne described it as 'a swift little play depicting in bold colours the uncertainties and hazards of the miner's life adding gentle humour to brighten the serious mood'.[18]

Jack Tyldesley proposes to his beloved Mary in the wee hours of the morning but she refuses to give him her answer until he returns from work. An accident happens at the mine – Jack might never come back to hear Mary's answer. Jack's mother and her neighbour, Polly Livesey, who know the risks and dangers of Jack's work, try to calm the distressed Mary, keeping their own feelings bottled up.

In *The Polygon, or Graft*, (5 February 1911) Brighouse depicted unscrupulous middle-class business mores in a play concerning municipal corruption. A self-made alderman tries to make a deal with a local council by forming a company to buy up land in order to sell it back to the council for development at a profit. The *Sunday Times* reviewer in 1911 was dismissive of the plot, suggesting that such schemes 'would not hold water these days ... '[19] It was produced by the Play Actors at the Court Theatre in London, but failed to make an impact.

Simultaneously, his very first play, *Lonesome-like*, (6 February 1911) made its debut at the Royalty in Glasgow. Iden Payne considered it 'a masterpiece in miniature'.[20]

> A shy young engineer, his sensitive and unconsciously poetic nature stunted intellectually by the rough atmosphere of factory life, is suffering from loneliness since the death of his mother a year before. Failing in his all too clumsy love affair, he turns to an old woman, disabled by rheumatism and about to be taken to the poorhouse, and 'adopts her as his mother.' This is all, but the story is told so winningly, the dialogue so vibrant with natural humour ...

Lonesome-like introduced a character-type that would feature in Brighouse's most successful plays – and *Lonesome-like* was very successful. The 'shy young engineer' is Sam Horrocks, described in the play-text thus:

> A hulking young man of a rather vacant expression. He is dressed in mechanic s blue dungarees. His face is oily and his clothes stained. He wears boots, not clogs. He mechanically takes a ball of oily black cotton waste from his right pocket when in conversational difficulties and wipes his hands upon it. He has a red muffler round his neck without collar, and his shock of fair hair is surmounted by a greasy black cap, which covers perhaps one-tenth of it.

Here is his first encounter with the young woman he wishes to wed:

> EMMA (rising and facing him. Sam is behind corner table and backs a little before her): What's tha gettin' at, Sam Horrocks? Tha's got a tongue in thy faice, hasn't tha?
> SAM: A suppose so. A doan't use it much though.
> EMMA: No. Tha's not much better than a tongue-tied idiot, Sam Horrocks, allays mooning about in th' engine-house in day-time an' sulkin' at 'ome neeght-time.
> SAM: Aye, A'm lonely sin' ma moother died. She did 'ave a way wi' 'er, ma moother. Th' 'ould plaice 'as not bin t' same to me sin' she

went. Day-time, tha knaws, A'm all reeght. Tha sees, them engines, them an' me's pals. They talks to me an' A understands their ways. A doan't some'ow seem to understand the ways o' folks like as A does th' ways o' them engines.

EMMA: Tha doesn't try. T'other lads goes rattin' or dog-feeghtin' on a Sunday or to a football match of a Saturday afternoon. Tha stays moonin' about th' 'ouse. Tha's not likely to understand folks. Tha's not sociable.

SAM: Naw. That's reeght enough. A nobbut get laughed at when A tries to be sociable an' stand my corner down at th' pub wi' th' rest o' th' lads. It's no use ma tryin' to soop ale, A can't carry th' drink like t'others. A knaws A've ways o' ma own.

EMMA: Tha has that.

SAM: A'm terrible lonesome, Emma. That theer 'ouse o' mine, it do want a wench about th' plaice. Th' engines is all reeght for days, but th' neeghts is that lonesome-like tha wouldn't believe.[21]

Compare Sam with Zack, the eponymous central character of a Brighouse comedy that opened on 30 October 1916 in Syracuse Theatre (New York):

Zack enters. He is younger than Paul, but neglect makes him look middle-aged. He wears spectacles and a beard and is dressed shabbily with a carpenter's apron on. Under his left arm is the wedding-cake model.

ZACK: 'I used to go until my clothes wore out well, they weren't mine at all properly speaking. They were father's when he was alive and then I had them, but I'm hard on clothes somehow. I'm a great expense all ways there are, with being a big eater and all. And when my dress coat gave out at the seams and got that shiny you could see your face in it, mother wouldn't buy me another, and so I don't go now. It's been a sorrow to me, too. I used to take a lot of pleasure in seeing others enjoy themselves. But I wasn't any use, not real use.'

PAUL: You'll have to make allowances for Zack, Jenny.

VIRGINIA: Is he a little ... ?

PAUL: We don't let it go beyond the family, of course.

VIRGINIA: I hope I'm one of you.

PAUL: He was born lazy. That's what's the matter.

ZACK (returning to table, sitting and eating. Zack can talk and eat at once): I've done a job of work today and chance it. Mended that pig-stye at Ballbrook farm.

PAUL: Did you? I daresay there was all of ten minutes' work in that.

ZACK: Took me a couple of hour.

MRS MUNNING: Then I hoped you charged according.

ZACK: I charged a shilling.

MRS MUNNING: For a couple of hour! It's worth half a crown.

ZACK: I charged what I thought fair.

MRS MUNNING: What you! Oh well, it's done now. Where's the shilling?

ZACK (feeling): Oh, it's in my other coat. (He is about to rise.)

PAUL: All right. All right. That'll do later.

ZACK: But I can see I've done wrong thing again. It's like this, Miss Virginia, there's some folk born to do right. They can't do the wrong thing if they tried. Like mother and Paul. I'm different. It's just the other way with me. I can't do right.[22]

And finally Willie Mossop, his most famous creation, from *Hobson's Choice*:

[He] comes up trap. He is a lanky fellow, about thirty, not naturally stupid but stunted mentally by a brutalised childhood. He is a raw material of a charming man, but, at present, it requires a very keen eye to detect his potentialities. His clothes are an even poorer edition of Tubby's. He comes halfway up trap.)

MAGGIE: You're a natural born genius at making boots. It's a pity you're a natural fool at all else.

WILLIE: I'm not much good at owt but leather, and that's a fact.

MAGGIE: When are you going to leave Hobson's?

WILLIE: Leave Hobson's? I, I thought I gave satisfaction.

MAGGIE: Don't you want to leave?

WILLIE: Not me. I've been at Hobson's all my life and I'm not for leaving till I'm made.

MAGGIE: I said you were a fool.

WILLIE: Then I'm a loyal fool.[23]

Sam, Zack and Willie are extremely good at their respective trades but they are all socially, if not intellectually, challenged. They are painfully shy with women and appear to lack any form of ambition. The three plays revolve around them and there is a clearly defined theme to the action: the importance of kindness and of the underdog winning. As Brighouse said: 'In play-writing I put character first. "For mark you, Lady," says John Tanner, "the artist's work is to shew us ourselves as we really are." Quite so: truth is beauty ... '[24]

It can be no coincidence that these three roles have been seized upon by different actors down the years, sensing the possibilities each offers for powerful character development. They can at times descend into the maudlin and embarrassing, but Brighouse was extremely fortunate in originally having two actors who seemed born to play them: Whitford Kane and Herbert Lomas both played Willie and Sam, while Lomas also played Zack. However, Brighouse's range was wide and in 1913 he created, in Jack Wetherall, something quite unique for the British stage – a fictional professional footballer.

He would later explain his reasons in an article for *The Era*. Football was the 'national spectacular sport of modern democracy', he wrote, 'It is the chief concern of the clerk and the warehouseman alike ... '[25]

The Game, which opened on 19 November 1913 at the Liverpool Repertory Theatre, Playhouse was a 'human comedy' according to Brighouse, 'aimed at making people laugh.'

A star professional centre-forward, Jack Wetherall, is placed in an invidious position when his club's chairman first sells him to a powerful rival and then immediately attempts to bribe him into 'throwing' a crucial match between the two teams that would ensure the survival of his old club. The matter is complicated by the fact that Wetherall is about to marry the chairman's daughter – against the wishes of his own mother. He refuses to be bought, even when it is made clear that permission to marry said daughter is dependent on his acquiescence in the crooked arrangement.

During the crucial match, however, he breaks his arm and has to leave the field. With his old club now leading, it appears to many spectators that the injury has been contrived and that he is indeed 'throwing' the game, despite his earlier refusal. Indignant, he forces his way back onto the pitch and heads the winner. The final act sees his mother relenting to the marriage and all ends happily.

The play came and went briefly and appeared not to have been reviewed but in 1920, on the back of Brighouse's worldwide success with *Hobson's Choice* and with a prestigious British film company busy turning *The Game* into a major feature film (re-naming it *The Winning Goal*), Brighouse re-worked the play for a London premiere prior to a nationwide tour. As we'll see, however, the film would eclipse the stage version in certain crucial respects.

When *The Game* reopened at the King's Theatre, Hammersmith in September, 1920 the reviews were lukewarm. The *Manchester Guardian* found the acting 'curiously amateurish', while 'the dialect spoken on the stage has no local habitation.' The principal problem for a number of critics was the central character, Jack Wetherall.

Brighouse wrote: 'In writing a play about a footballer one has the same initial advantage which attaches to a popular figure in history – a Drake or a Disraeli. Everybody has heard of him and everybody likes him and interest is already created before the curtain rises.'[26]

Jack was a flawed individual, an 'erudite professional footballer' with aspirations beyond the field of play. He wanted to improve his mind by reading classics such as Ruskin, Carlyle, Browning and even Plato but was preyed upon by others whose demands conflicted with those aspirations.

His fiancée, on the other hand, being an educated middle-class girl, eschewed such effete strivings, insisting that the raw excitement of football was more to her taste. Why, she asks him, do you want to waste your time on such boring subjects as literature and philosophy when you have the thrills and spills of professional football to enjoy?

His determination to 'play the game' and resist the temptations offered (winning the girl and saving his old club) arose from a sense of his own integrity as a professional player. Brighouse had afforded the professional footballer his debut as an acceptable dramatic hero.

It was an interesting clash of the social classes with the heroine having the majority of the good lines, but Jack ultimately comes across (à la Zack, Willie and Sam) as something of a mother's boy, a lion on the football pitch but a lamb when it comes to making love to a high-spirited, liberated young 1920s 'flapper'. Set in the context of what the *Observer* saw as a traditional melodrama, the complicated tug-of-love seemed out of place. *The Stage* reviewer concluded that, while there was much to please the average playgoer, 'those who go with memories of *Hobson's Choice* will feel a twinge of disappointment.'[27]

As the curtain fell in Hammersmith and *The Game* set out on its tour of regional theatres, however, less than a mile away in his Richmond film studios, film-maker George Berthold Samuelson was busy putting the finishing touches to his celluloid version of the Brighouse's story.

Samuelson was a pioneer of the British film industry and *The Game* would be one of a number of sporting movies his company would make in the early 1920s. Without the finances to employ top film stars, Samuelson relied on his regular group of players when casting for the film. These included the strikingly attractive young Maudie Dunham to play the girlfriend along with experienced actors Haidee Wright (as the disapproving mother) and Tom Reynolds.

Where the question of Brighouse's incongruous 'thinking footballer' Jack Wetherall was concerned, however, Samuelson made an astute move: selecting a prominent professional player called Harold Walden for the role.

Walden was no ordinary footballer. Born in India where his father was serving with the Cheshire regiment of the British army, he concealed his true age in order to enlist in his father's former regiment when he was only 14 years old. Upon leaving the army he was signed up by Bradford City, but under FA rules of the day he was not allowed to turn professional for twelve months. He was thus free to play as an amateur for the Great Britain team at the 1912 Olympics where he scored six goals in one match and a total of eleven in the tournament, establishing a British Olympic scoring record which remains unbeaten. After further army service in the First World War he briefly joined Arsenal before returning to Bradford where he ended his playing career.

By then he'd started a new life in the music halls as a variety performer. He developed an act called the 'Anaemic Footballer' in which he came on stage sporting a kiss curl above a pallid white face wearing the claret and amber shirt of Bradford City and carrying a small football. His outsize 'long shorts' were at half-mast and his football boots looked much too big for him. He would launch into some simple comic patter before singing one of the musical pieces he'd penned for the ukulele, such as 'Only Me Knows Why', which became his signature tune.

When *The Winning Goal* was released, Walden turned out to be the star-turn. Although the *Bioscope* felt that, 'Mr Harold Walden scores more by his prowess on the field than by his histrionic talents,' everyone else felt that he was perfect for the part. The *Kinematograph Weekly* commented: 'Harold Walden makes a quite unusual hero – a nervous young man who allows himself to be made love to – but his performance suits the part,' and *The Times* critic agreed: 'The part of the footballer hero is very well played by an heroic footballer, Mr Harold Walden, and this idea of employing somebody who really knows something of the kind of part he is called upon to play seems worthy of encouragement provided, of course, that he knows how to act as well.'[28]

Walden was helped, of course, by the fact that, it being a silent film, he wasn't burdened with the task of delivering lines or adopting any sort of accent. Aiding and abetting him, meanwhile, were no less than twenty-two top class professional players, including Chelsea centre forward, England international, war hero, dandy, amateur singer and noted socialite Jack Cock.

Others to feature were seven of that season's title-winning West Bromwich Albion team including top League scorer Fred Morris; two from the season's FA Cup winners Tottenham Hotspur, plus popular international stars Dickie Bond, Sam Hardy, Alf Quantrill, Frank Barson, Harry Hampton and Ted Vizard.

Samuelson had employed them for the climactic football match which he had directed himself from the centre of Brentford FC's Griffin Park ground using a megaphone. It was a 'Samuelson Super Production', clearly designed to exploit football's burgeoning popularity, and the change of emphasis from the stage play was obvious in the retitling and as the focus switched from the confines of the theatre to the open spaces of the football arena.

By and large the film appears to have been a success. 'Brilliantly cinematographed', said the *Biograph* while the *Times* enthused, 'The football match is unusually well done and the employment of professional players who know their business has meant the absence of stupid details which make some football films impossible.' It was, 'a real football match on a real football ground with a real football crowd and real football teams.'

However, it's hard to assess the overall quality of the film as no prints remain. Samuelson was not noted for subtlety. In fact, his cinematic style was already considered out-of-date and his fondness for spectacle was regularly undermined by cost-cutting and poor technique. Although the *Kinematograph Weekly* declared it 'A winner without any doubt', the same critic still felt that the film lacked 'visual appeal' and that the climax was marred by 'the irritating intrusion of close-ups.

Brighouse himself was not particularly impressed, restricting himself to the simple comment in his biography that Samuelson's creation had been 'workmanlike'.

By then, the First World War had ended and the Gaiety Theatre had closed. However, out of the chaos of the conflict Brighouse's finest play would emerge, one that would, by 1920, completely transform his life and career.

Notes

[1] Iden Payne, Introduction to *Hobson's Choice*.

[2] 'Football at the Footlights', *The Era,* 24 August 1921.

[3] Cumberland, *op. cit.*

[4] Brighouse, *Autobiography*, p23.

[5] Ibid., p24.

[6] Ibid., p19.

[7] Ibid.

[8] Ibid. p182.

[9] Cumberland, *op. cit.*

[10] Brighouse, *Autobiography*. p38.

[11] Ibid., p32.

[12] Ibid., p35.

[13] Ibid., p38.

[14] Cumberland, *op. cit.*

[15] Ibid.

[16] Brighouse, *Autobiography*, p53.

[17] Ibid., p182.

[18] Iden Payne, Introduction to *Hobson's Choice*.

[19] *Sunday Times*, 12 February1911.

[20]Iden Payne, Introduction to *Hobson's Choice.*

[21]Harold Brighouse, *Lonesome-like* play text

[22]Harold Brighouse, *Zack* play text

[23]Harold Brighouse, *Hobson's Choice* play text.

[24]Brighouse, *Autobiography*, p182.

[25]'Football at the Footlights', *The Era*, 24 August 1921.

[26]Ibid.

[27] *The Stage.*

[28]For football film references see John Harding, 'Reel of Fortune', *The Blizzard*, 16 March 2015.

19

Hobson's Choice

In *Hobson's Choice* the curtain is raised not merely on the interior of a little Salford shoe shop, but on an epitome of Lancashire life, or, at any rate, upon that great stratum defined in England as 'the lower middle class,' that class which Henry Horatio Hobson would proclaim as The Backbone of society[1]

H AROLD BRIGHOUSE'S PRODIGIOUS OUTPUT OF plays would continue as the First World War unfolded but, as he acknowledged, the audiences were no longer interested. His tale of cotton and of the machine-wrecking riots of 1820, *The Northerners*, was produced at the Gaiety Manchester on 27 August 1914: ' ... in the week, that is, of the Retreat from Mons. "The show must go on." *The Northerners* went on; it kept faith with the playbills announcing it, and in that week playgoers, if there were any, cared less than a brass farthing for the troubles of weavers in 1820 ... '[2]

Brighouse had, in fact, found himself engulfed in the conflict without warning. He had travelled to France in June 1914 to help adapt translations from an original Sanscrit manuscript for use in a music drama to be called *Chandra* by the American composer and diplomat Blair Fairchild. They worked, first in Paris and finally at Houlgate on the Normandy coast, then a discreet, wealthy 'hydrotherapy' resort.

The first Brighouse knew that war was declared was, 'when a military monoplane landed on the beach and when, within the next two hours, twenty-two families left the Grand Hotel, partly those of army officers recalled from leave by the airman, partly those of others responding to the belief that holiday-making was inappropriate. That was on the Tuesday; by the Thursday Houlgate was stripped of French visitors, and I bathed solitary, feeling myself to be scandalous.'[3]

> As I wrote the last words of the last revision of *Chandra*, the mobilization order was being posted, with it a proclamation warning foreigners to leave. From proprietor to scullion every male in the hotel was called up; almost they kicked me out. Fairchild, domiciled in France, was unaffected by the orders to foreigners. His car and his chauffeur, both mobilized, had left for Paris; he loaded me with small change and led me towards the station. A train was remotely possible.

Brighouse eventually found his way onto a bus:

> The bus by which I went that Sunday morning from Houlgate to Havre was not a bus on ordinary run; it was a conscript bus; its driver was taking it and himself to report at, luckily for me, Havre, and he was taking friends, including three women who for seven hours hardly ceased to weep.
>
> Here in the raw was shown me what war meant to the common men and women of a conscript nation. Anxiously, desperately anxiously, as that bus passed through countryside and villages where women stood on doorsteps they plied me with questions I couldn't answer. 'What is England doing?' 'Why isn't England in?'
>
> 'Tomorrow,' I said, guessing correctly as it happened, and they accepted me as, potentially, an ally: at the Seine Ferry they decanted me at Havre.
>
> The Channel steamer was chaos: an overcrowded refugee-boat, an early and a mild example of what more seriously and so often happened later. Americans, not then air-minded, travelled with heavy

luggage. Rumour ran riot: the British and German Navies were
fighting; firing had been heard. Food and, worse, water were
exhausted. Ingenuously, we thought that slow crossing terrible.[4]

This experience, Brighouse later claimed, was the 'inspiration'
for his play, *Hobson's Choice*.

'That bus collaborated with me in writing *Hobson's Choice*.
Emotional experience is written off by an author in a form which
may bear no resemblance to the originating disturbance. There is,
too, the saying that one best sees one's own country by seeing
another. To see Salford go to Paris ... More significant was the
general churn-up of emotion; the bus, symbolizing for me the
France which in the first days of the 1914 War behaved with dignity,
stayed with me for months.'

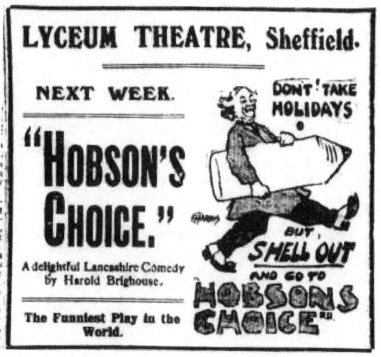

(1917 *Hobson's Choice* play advert)

Brighouse was eventually passed fit for home service and spent the war writing propaganda for the fledgling RAF in 'an attic linen-cupboard of the Hotel Cecil. That was my war.'

'I was a writer with an emotional load to get rid of, and at sharp tangent from the bus to Havre I recollected Salford, where in Cross Lane my father was born, and I wrote *Hobson's Choice*. Once started it came rapidly, too rapidly till a useful influenza compelled reflective pause. Influenza saved the last act of *Hobson's Choice* from being – just a last act; its clothes of 1880 had something to do with saving it from evanescence.'[5]

There are conflicting versions of how Brighouse came upon the title for his famous play. According to Iden Payne, in 1908 Houghton, Brighouse and Payne met in the American bar of the Midland Hotel across the road from the Gaiety where the two playwrights were bemoaning the poor quality of acting in their plays. Iden Payne remarked that it was simply *Hobson's Choice.*

'No sooner had I said this than it occurred to me that the phrase would make a good title for a play. I said so and Houghton and Brighouse agreed. A friendly argument arose as to which of them should be the author of the hypothetical Hobson's Choice. I suggested that they toss a coin. This they did and Brighouse won.[6]

According to Brighouse, however, Houghton had won and Brighouse decided, years after Houghton's death, that 'It seemed to me necessary to do something about it.'[7]

Brighouse's version attests to the strength of feeling that existed between the two young men: his most famous play carries Houghton's title.

Henry Hobson is a widower and owner of a prosperous shoemaking shop in Salton, a fictional suburb of Manchester. While Hobson drinks with his fellow Masons at a nearby pub, he forces his three unmarried daughters: Maggie, Alice and Vickey, to work at the shop for no pay. Hobson lectures his daughters on their 'uppish' ways and claims that they are trying to control him. He complains that if Alice and Vickey continue to act in this way, he will marry them off. However, he considers Maggie, the eldest, to be too old to marry. What's more, he needs her to be at home to care for him and run the shop. However, when made aware of costly marriage settlements by a friend, he temporarily discards the idea.

Mrs Hepworth, one of the shop's wealthier patrons, now enters and demands to know who made the shoes she recently bought. Hobson admits it is Willie Mossop an exceptionally talented but simple-minded bootmaker whom Hobson treats badly, hardly paying him much at all. Mrs Hepworth is so impressed with the work that she demands that all her and her daughter's boots now be made only by Mossop.

When Hepworth and Hobson leave, Maggie questions Willie on his future aspirations and learns that he intends to stay in her father's business since this is where he learnt his trade so well. Maggie suddenly proposes marriage to Willie; she believes that with his boot-making skills and her excellence in managing the shop, they could make a successful business and life together. When the staggered Will confesses that he is already engaged to Ada Figgins, his landlady's daughter, Maggie swiftly puts an end to that relationship.

Maggie then tells her sisters of her intentions but they are horrified at her proposing to wed someone much lower than her own status. When Hobson returns and scathingly refuses to accept Maggie's decision, he calls Willie to the shop floor threatening to beat him. Will holds firm and after Hobson strikes him, Will kisses Maggie, declaring that if Hobson intends to beat either of them again, they will immediately leave the shop for good. Hobson is bewildered and undecided what to do next.

A month passes and Maggie and Will have left Hobson's shop.

Alice and Vickey are trying to manage the business but without Maggie's help they are struggling. Will and Maggie's wedding day has arrived. Meanwhile, Hobson has been spending even more time at the Moonraker's Inn. In a state of inebriation he has managed to somehow fall into the cellar of Beenstock, the local corn merchant. When he finally arrives home he is served with a summons for trespassing, spying, and damaging Beenstock's property. Maggie has engineered all this, utilising the skills of the fiancés of her two sisters: Freddie Beenstock, son of the corn merchant and Albert Prosser, a trainee solicitor. A 'fine' will have to be paid by Hobson in order to keep the case from going to court.

The scene now moves on to Maggie and Willie's wedding dinner where, in the cellar of their lodgings, they are enjoying the company of Vickey and her suitor Freddie, and Alice and Albert. Hobson arrives and Maggie quickly ushers all her guests into the next room. Hobson is in desperate need of her help in dealing with the court summons and terrified of the public scandal that would come with it. Albert Prosser emerges from his hiding place to suggest a settlement of £500 to be paid to prevent the case from proceeding further. Hobson eventually realises this money is intended to be used to set up Alice and Vickey's marriages. Maggie has clearly been instrumental in manipulating the entire situation. He is disgusted by his daughters and declares that he disowns them all and looks forward to his own freedom. He predicts a desolate life for their future husbands. After everyone has left, Maggie and Willie are alone on their wedding night. Although Willie tries to avoid the inevitable and settles down on the sofa, Maggie emerges and gently takes him by the ear and leads him into the bedroom.

A year has passed and Hobson has been drinking excessively and precipitated a breakdown in his health. As a consequence, the business has suffered greatly and there is little to do since there are no customers. His doctor, Mr MacFarlane, visits and recommends abstinence, and that Maggie returns to live in the house to look after him. Maggie is insistent that the decision as to whether to return must be made by Willie. Both Alice and the now pregnant Vickey are so accustomed to their sophisticated lifestyles that they refuse to look after their father. They assume it to be their elder sister's role. Willie arrives and examines the shop's stock and informs them all that the business is worth very little. Hobson makes Willie an offer saying that he can return and be a boot-hand again, but Willie explains that he already possesses most of Hobson's customers and is only prepared to come back if Hobson allows him to become an equal partner in the business. Hobson himself must accept the role of 'sleeping partner'. Willie also states that the shop must called 'Mossop's'. Maggie, somewhat startled by Willie's assertive nature, insists on 'Mossop and Hobson'. Hobson has no choice but to agree to the terms offered. Willie has become a successful and confident businessman while Hobson has been defeated.

So many themes, many from the pantomimes of Brighouse's youth, contributed to charming and entrancing audiences, ultimately leaving them happy and smiling as they exited.

There is the Fairy Godmother – Mrs Hepworth who first recognises the true worth of Willie beneath the grime, thus opening Maggie's eyes; and it is she who loans the money to allow them to escape.

There is Cinders – both Willie and Maggie are excluded from the limelight; both go to the Ball; while the Ugly Sisters, despite being beautiful are also vain, snobbish and as hard-hearted as their father. Hence the King Lear parallels, with Hobson a deluded King in his small kingdom of daughters.

Then there is Beauty and the Beast: with War being the original Beast for Brighouse, horrified as he was by the world and its mechanical monsters; also the violence that Hobson metes out to a simple soul and Beauty being the human love that trumps it.

There is sexual awakening, the ultimate form of human love, presented in so gentle and heart-warming a manner in the play that hard-boiled critics down the century have all fallen for what, in clumsy hands, might have looked like something a little strange – a misogynistic fear of women, perhaps?

One of the play's themes – an assertive young woman challenging the social orthodoxy of an overbearing patriarch – had already been dealt with a little earlier in a different context by Bernard Shaw in *Pygmalion* and Maggie certainly drives the play along, having the vision to see that Willie Mossop's craftsmanship can, with her help and encouragement, be turned into something much more valuable.

But there is also an element of defencelessness to Maggie, a fear that Willie will reject her at a certain point. After all, she was poorly equipped for the task she sets herself. She had lived a very sheltered life. Her mother had died when she was very young, she'd never had a boyfriend, had never been kissed by a man. She has been working in the shop since she was ten, having to look after her father as well as bringing up her much younger sisters almost as a surrogate mother. She has had to grow up very quickly and Willie represents her last chance for independence.

'The spirit of command is never in doubt yet there is also about her a hidden vulnerability that makes both her father's unwilling dependence on her and her husband's visibly deepening love utterly believable and heart-warming ... ', wrote Jack Tinker in the *Daily Mail* as late as 12 May 1995.[8]

There is another intriguing element to the play: that there is initially a difference in social class between the two main characters. Maggie comes from a relatively comfortable background, whereas thirty-one-year-old Willie not only earns a pittance in her father's workshop but also is the son of a man from a workhouse. Not only is he illiterate but also painfully gauche with no experience of women.

Thus, it is a play with a set of intriguing characters, two men and a woman, any one of whom could become the primary focus of the action. Down the years, Charles Laughton as Hobson, Norman Wisdom as Willie Mossop, and Penelope Keith as Maggie – to name but a few – have turned the play into his or her own vehicle.

In 1915, however, London managers refused to mount the play, wanting something immediately successful. Perhaps borrowing a leaf out of his late friend Houghton's book, Brighouse had, sent a copy to Iden Payne, then working in New York on Broadway, who placed it with the New York theatre operators Shubert Brothers. Payne would go on then to direct the first production, a supremely ironic twist. In addition, it would be an ex-Horniman company actor, Whitford Kane, who would be selected as the first Willie Mossop.

In his book of memoirs, *Are We All Met?*, Kane detailed the hazardous journey the play them made to the New York stage. In the Shubert office, the manuscript of *Hobson's Choice* was liked by the women readers, disliked by the men. Lee Shubert thus cautiously took an option and, using remnant scenery and costumes, tried the play out in Atlantic City.

'I don't know,' wrote Kane, 'what, after Atlantic City, kept the company together during those long months of waiting, but there must have been something magnetic in the play to keep us banded side by side ready to go on at the first glimmering of a notice. We gave up any offers of engagements to keep free for the time when *Hobson's Choice* would be put on. At last we were suddenly sent to Albany in late October. From there we were routed back to New York, and finally we opened at the Princess Theatre on November 23 1915. For once the awful agony of waiting was justified; the criticisms read like an actor's dream.'[9]

In the event, they got their New York run, with further appearances in Boston and Chicago, with the play then setting out on two simultaneous tours. It came to London in 1916 at that time besieged by Zeppelin bombing raids:

> For the greater part of its London run *Hobson's Choice* was played at daily matinees, with evening performances (for the braver sort?) on Wednesdays and Saturdays. Thus handicapped, it ran for 246 performances at the Apollo and Prince of Wales Theatres; 246 performances in such circumstances might, the actors told me, fairly be rated prestige-equivalent to a two years run in normal times.[10]

Brighouse helped with the London production alongside the actor Norman McKinnel. He recalled, 'Not many years, it seemed to me, had passed since as gallery first-nighter I saw Veronique at the Apollo. Now I sat in the Apollo by McKinnel's side, helping to direct rehearsals ...

'McKinnel was McKinnel, physically Herculean, the player who in the Court Theatre days I had admired and had identified as forceful first among virile and natural actors in Shaw and Galsworthy. He was producing and acting in my play, and he was, on occasion, deferring to me. No wonder that I was agitated. And Edyth Goodall – Peggy to her friends – read and reread Maggie to me, she who from Miss Horniman's company after her famous performance in *Hindle Wakes* had gone on and up to be a London leading actress.'[11]

Like *Hindle Wakes*, *Hobson's Choice* would be seized on by early film-makers. It was first produced in 1920 by Percy Nash for Master Films, and a remake – (an early talkie version) – appeared in 1931, produced by the leading British company of the time, British International Pictures at their studios in Elstree. Sybil Thorndike would make only her second talkie appearance in it but the film itself is now lost.

The play eventually became the source of an extremely successful David Lean picture in 1953 starring Charles Laughton, one of the centrepieces of which would be Laughton's drunken encounter with a huge, puddle-reflected moon and his subsequent tumble down a coal-chute. The film would receive a gala premiere in Eccles, attended by the Mayor and many local dignitaries. Strangely, however, the play itself was never produced at the Gaiety Theatre.

As we we'll see, it might have made all the difference to the theatre's ultimate fate.

Notes

[1] Iden Payne, Introduction to *Hobson's Choice*.

[2] Brighouse, *Autobiography*, p94.

[3] Ibid., p61

[4] Ibid., p62.

[5] Ibid., p63.

[6] Iden Payne, *op. cit.*, p125

[7] 'Hobson – Our Choice', *John Bull*, 12 June 1932.

[8] *Daily Mail*, 12 May 1995.

[9] Brighouse, *Autobiography*, p65.

[10] Ibid., p67.

[11] Ibid., p68.

20

The End of the Gaiety

A night in a repertory theatre was almost as cheerful as a night in a morgue.[1]

It was disheartening to find the playwrights of the Manchester School stigmatised as drab-minded practitioners of excessive naturalism. I spit upon the accusations equally of greyness and of datedness.[2]

IN 1953 IN HIS AUTOBIOGRAPHY HAROLD Brighouse revealed the initial financial box-office takings for *Hobson's Choice*. 'Experts of today will smile at the 1915-16 figures of *Hobson's Choice*; receipts in the highest week of its New York run were $7558 and in the highest week of the London run were £1033.'[3]

Such figures would have been welcomed at the Gaiety Theatre during those years when it was experiencing a steady but sharp decline in audience numbers. Why the play never made it to Manchester or was offered to the Gaiety remains a puzzle. It's not as though Brighouse had severed connections with the either the city or AH. His one-act play *Followers* opened on 19 April 1915 at the Prince's Theatre, Manchester while another one-act play, *Converts* opened on 23 August 1915 at the Gaiety Theatre itself. *Converts* was then produced by Miss Horniman's Company at the Duke of York's Theatre in London on a double bill with *Hindle*

Wakes for 33 performances in September 1915.

Perhaps AH couldn't afford it. It would certainly have gone a long way to turning the rising tide of criticism concerning the apparent 'drab' nature of much that was being staged there.

Criticism had begun as early as autumn 1912 concerning the apparent lack of adventure and experiment in the selection of plays mounted. In that month's issue of the *Manchester Playgoer* the editor, Oscar Drey, beneath the headline 'The Failure of our Repertory Theatre', condemned the Gaiety:

> 'Perhaps the burden of our complaint is that Miss Horniman's theatre is not in advance of its time. But that, artistically, is the deadliest judgment that can be delivered against it. It is smug, it is mediocre, it is dull. All these things are worse, far worse, than stupidity.'[4]

AH retorted that the Gaiety had not set out to be, 'in advance of its time', and 'What we suffer from most is the habit people have

Brenda De Banzie, Charles Laughton and John Mills in David Lean's 1954 version of *Hobson's Choice*. (*Alamy Stock Photo*)

of labeling us, without taking trouble to find out whether they are labeling us correctly or not.'[5]

What's more, she felt that some people were misusing the word 'repertory' which by 1913 carried connotations of something avant-garde, if slightly, 'dull', 'rather improper', or 'improving'.

Cecil Chisholm, writing in the *Manchester Courier*, agreed with some of the complaints Oscar Drey had made about the Gaiety and agreed that Manchester seemed to be missing out on some of the best new plays; but for the rest he discounted Drey's article as destructive rhetoric and thought that the Gaiety would do no harm to alienate the, 'choice spirits', as he described the people who wanted an experimental theatre.

'The Gaiety', said Chisholm, was not 'a faddists' laboratory,' and: 'were its advisers so foolish as to make it a laboratory for testing the weird and strange works the playgoers' would like, it would become a mausoleum of dead hopes and frustrated activities within a week.'[6]

When interviewed by the *Manchester Courier*, Miss Horniman defended herself stoutly against her critics. Protesting that she, 'didn't want a freak theatre for the joy of the cranks', she claimed that people were jealous and that she was paying the penalty of success.

She also defended herself against another criticism; that she was a rich woman who used the Gaiety as some kind of hobby. She denied this and pointed out that the theatre needed to be profitable as her financial resources were by no means limitless. She was unrepentant about the choice of plays. She would continue, she said, to give Lancashire light comedy and, although she could not afford the rights to certain London successes, she promised a Greek play and Granville Barker's and Laurence Houseman's *Prunella* for the 'superior' people in Manchester.[7]

By the end of 1913, however, Chisholm blamed success for the failure of the repertory theatres. Writing in *TP's Weekly* in December 1913, he asserted, 'where the Repertory Theatres have sown, the Managers have reaped,' and he instanced playwrights like Houghton and Harold Chapin who, with various actors, had gone to work for London managements after they had made their name in repertory.[8]

1913 did see the end of a cycle of pioneering actors, actresses and playwrights who had begun with Manchester, Glasgow and Liverpool but who were now tiring of the repertory theatres and looking for better-paid work with more overtly commercial managements, usually in London.

Other observers thought that Miss Horniman had made a mistake in siting her theatre in Manchester in the first place, as a suitable audience did not exist in the city. James Agate and Alan Monkhouse, for example, blamed the 'insipid' audiences and the lack of a 'smart set' in the stalls for the theatre's ills.[9]

Others were more brutal and claimed that it was 'time we admitted that Manchester's reputation for appreciation of the drama is as mythical as Manchester's musical reputation.'[10]

AH claimed that the reason London managements could poach actors and writers, was the size of the salaries they could pay. If she had more support from Manchester, she could afford to pay such salaries and she dismissed James Agate's suggestion that she should conciliate the 'smart set'.

'I thought', she said 'that all the inhabitants of Manchester, with a few exceptions, were respectable middle-class folk like myself, and the territorial nobles from beyond never came within six miles of Albert Square.'[11]

When the First World War began, AH was determined to keep her theatre open and decided to 'ignore the war', refusing to be made: 'nervy, just because a lot of men are rushing at each other's throats'. She resolved to produce plays which would 'keep the public

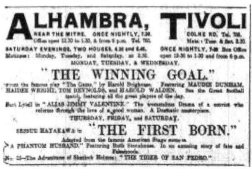

(1920 *The Winning Goal* film advert)

in good heart', denying, however, that this in any way detracted from the Gaiety's first principles:

> There has been absolutely no change of policy. But, as a matter of commonsense during the war I am avoiding such plays as would be likely to depress people. I have certainly had some revivals of rather old-fashioned plays ... but I have no thought of altering my policy in any way at all ... As to the idea of closing down the Gaiety, my compliments to people's imaginations![12]

In the summer of 1917, however, the Gaiety ceased to be run as a repertory theatre. On the face of it, it seemed a strange decision, as the *Sunday Chronicle* pointed out:

> The rumour ... that Miss Horniman's repertory company was to be disbanded is confirmed. It has a melancholy interest when one recalls the high hopes and ideals of its originators and the tremendous amount of spadework they contributed. However, I understand from Miss Horniman that she hopes and intends to revive it ... presumably after the war.
>
> Curious this development should occur just when certain managements are advocating stock or repertory companies as a means of coping with the current difficulties of travelling and dearth of good attractions.[13]

The Gaiety repertoire was definitely becoming rather lacklustre, however. In the last two and a half years of its existence, 26 new plays,[14] many of them one-act plays, were performed, almost all of them weak, some never even published. The rest of Miss Horniman's selections consisted largely of comedies by Pinero, Sutro and other successful West End playwrights.

Though she denied it, she was losing too much money, and when Entertainment Tax was introduced in 1916, this must have added to her overdraft. In 1917 she decided to keep the Gaiety open as a 'lodging house' theatre for touring shows and put her business manager in charge. She never again ran the theatre as a repertory venture.

On 31 December 1920, the *Manchester Guardian* announced that the Gaiety had been 'Sold For A Kinema'. Interviewed, AH said:

> I have nothing much more to say beyond a few words of good advice to the very young people of Manchester and that is that as they grow older they will wish they had a Gaiety Theatre to go to as their elder brothers and sisters had. Then perchance Manchester will realise that it could perfectly well afford to have the finest theatre in Europe. And how I shall chuckle if some other city comes to its sense and shows Manchester the way to build and subsidise a great municipal theatre. Is that rude? But I shall chuckle.[14]

When Miss Horniman was asked if she would be attending the final performance at the Gaiety replied, 'Of course ... every corpse must attend its own funeral,'[15]

By 1920, Harold Brighouse and his wife had moved permanently from Manchester to London to live in a house at 67 Parliament Hill, Hampstead. Brighouse only left Manchester after his father had died. 'Had he lived, I should probably have returned to the house in Eccles next door to his. Voluntarily to separate from him would have been beyond me.'[16]

In the post-war years, though never a great fan of the cinema, he saw his football play *The Game* filmed in 1920, was scriptwriter for a Paramount silent called *The Children of Jazz* (a film version of his play *Other Times*), and in 1929 he was even offered a job as a screenwriter by Irving Thalberg, head of MGM. He turned it down ('I did not like films and did not like Hollywood').

In August 1913 he was asked to provide his first *Manchester Guardian* 'back-pager', as he called it, and he continued providing the paper with essays and short stories, plus travel sketches of Canada, USA, where he went with his wife during the inter-war years.

He continued writing plays although the success of *Hobson's Choice* would never be matched. During the 1920s he responded to the burgeoning amateur dramatic societies of the Village Drama League and the Women's Institute with such anthologies as *Plays for the Meadow* and *Plays for the Lawn* (1921) and *Open Air Plays* (1926), which were light, even fey, compositions, far removed from the realism of *Hobson's Choice*. He served as chairman of the Authors' Society dramatic committee from 1930 to 1931.

After 1931, however, Brighouse never wrote another full-length play. In his autobiography, he writes that he 'wilted' and speaks of a 'domestic tragedy' (possibly concerning his wife's health) that continued for twenty years and discouraged him from writing.

He lived from 1919 onwards in Hampstead Garden Suburb and continued to contribute articles to the *Manchester Guardian* until 1949. He collapsed in the Strand on 25 July 1958 on the eve of his 76th birthday and died the same day in the Charing Cross Hospital

Brighouse was always a stout defender of the Manchester playwrights. He admitted that the ' Manchester School ' was never conscious of itself, that it came upon the authors unexpectedly, as even something a little preposterous, to be taken seriously, to be labelled, 'heaven knows by whom', the ' Manchester School,' as if they had a common aim.

What had happened, he concluded, was that AH, by putting on

a series of Repertory plays which had no likelihood of being seen in the provinces under the touring system, demonstrated that drama was a living art, and in the light of that demonstration, 'there outcropped spontaneously, un-self-consciously, the body of local drama now known as the "Manchester School".'[17]

This brought variety where variety was needed, 'particularly when it travelled to London and introduced to Londoners authentic representations of natives of their country.'

The Lancashire plays possessed 'the significance of localization. Stimulated by Miss Horniman's catholic repertoire, local authors sought to express in drama local characteristics.' However, he insisted that the Lancashire writers avoided local dialect as, in the first place, impracticable, and in the second place, disused, except (to quote Houghton) 'amongst the roughest class in the most out-of-the way districts.'[18]

Accent, Brighouse explained, is not dialect. It didn't exist in Lancashire:

'Dramatically correct dialect is literally incorrect; it is highly-selected dialogue which indicates, but does not obscure, and the true dialect dramatist is not the man who exactly imitates the speech of a district, but he who most skilfully adapts its rhythms and picks out its salient words.'

Brighouse pointed out that Synge had 'invented an Irish dialect which is false in detail and infinitely true in broad effect'. The Manchester School tried to do the same, 'using local idioms to indicate that the speech of Lancashire has a well-marked individuality'.[19]

The puzzle was, he mused, why other provincial theatres failed to produce such a considerable body of local drama as emerged from Manchester. 'Must the conclusion be that the Manchester atmosphere has, with its soot, a vitalizing dramatic principle? Possibly; but a less fantastic theory is that Manchester had Miss

Horniman, and other Repertories had not.'

'The type of play preferred by Miss Horniman's Company, let us call it realistic comedy, happened to be the type by which the life of Lancashire could be best expressed in drama and the future authors of the 'Manchester School,' most of them of an impressionable age, some of them already fumbling their way to dramatic expression, seized avidly the type and the opportunity. It is putting the case without hyperbole to say that Miss Horniman's Company was an inspiration.'[20]

He summed his own achievements up thus: 'Optimism in the time of my pre-1914 formative years did not offend against common sense, and perhaps I dared to be a Henry. "What great cause is he identified with?" demanded Councillor Barlow at the end of *The Card*. "He's identified," was the reply, "with the great cause of cheering us all up."'

'And a fig for the libellous reputation of the Manchester School!'[21]

Notes

[1] St John Ervine, *Twentieth Century Drama* (Harrap, 1950), p46.

[2] Brighouse, Autobiography, p181.

[3] Ibid., p186.

[4] *Manchester Playgoer*, 2/1 (September 1912) 18-19

[5] *Manchester City News*, 6 September 1912.

[6] *Manchester Courier*, 9 September 1912.

[7] Ibid., 12 September 1912.

[8] *TP's Weekly*, 26 December 1913.

[9] *Manchester Guardian*, 10 December 1912.

[10] Ibid.

[11] Ibid., 17 December 1912.

[12] Ibid., 12 January 1914.

[13] *Sunday Chronicle*, 5 August 1917.

[14] *Manchester Guardian*. 31 December 1920.

[15] Pogson, *op. cit.*, p175.

[16]Brighouse, *Autobiography*, p89.

[17]Brighouse, 'Introduction', in *The Works of Stanley Houghton*.

[18]Ibid.

[19]Ibid.

[20]Ibid.

[21]Brighouse, Autobiography, p182.

EPILOGUE

The Gaiety's (Lancashire) Legacy

I don't think it [the Gaiety] produced any great dramatists or any very great plays but it had an individuality.[1]

The Manchester School lost its home ground, but its plays persisted and persist, outlasting two wars and a social revolution.[2]

BRIGHOUSE'S COMMENT IS A FAR MORE accurate summary of the School's achievements than Monkhouse's typically parsimonious assessment of both himself and his fellow Manchester writers. Brighouse, of course, had the advantage of living into the 1950s when he witnessed a resurgence of interest in his own work in particular. In his 1953 autobiography, he wrote:

In 1951, Blackpool, Lancashire's popular holiday resort, the show-town which has forgotten more than Coney Island ever knew, gave surely final rebuttal to the accusation that the Manchester School playwrights wrote, depressingly, 'grey matter' plays. The attraction – and attract it did – at Blackpool's Grand Theatre was *Hobson's Choice,* or, to put first things first, Wilfred Pickles in *Hobson's Choice.*[3]

Pickles was one of the country's most popular radio stars and also a very good actor. He'd decided to mount *Hobson's Choice* during the peak season playing Willie Mossop with Derek Oldham of the D'Oyly Carte Company as Henry Hobson, and Lally Bowers playing Maggie.

'The result was that Lancashire on holiday savoured a Lancashire play and that *Hobson's Choice*, some thirty-six years old, was for the first time "in the money".'[4]

Two years later came David Lean's film with the great Charles Laughton as Hobson, and ever since then the play has never been too far away from either stage or screen. Major stars such as Leo McKern, Martin Shaw, Anthony Quayle and James Harcourt have relished playing the comic-Lear character Henry Hobson, while John Mills, Trevor Peacock, Michael Caine and John Barrie have essayed Willie Mossop. Penelope Keith, Anne Stallybrass, Patricia Routledge and Brenda de Banzie have taken on the Maggie Hobson role with some relish. Norman Wisdom starred as Mossop in a musical version called *Walking Happy* with lyrics and music by Jimmy Van Huesen and Sammy Cahn made in 1966. In 1991 the Birmingham Royal Ballet performed a ballet version. In 2003 the Young Vic gave the play an Asian makeover transposing it to modern-day, multiracial Salford and in 2014 it was up-dated to the 'Swinging Sixties'. There has even been an Americanised CBS televised version in 1983 set in 1914 New Orleans, starring Sharon Gless as Maggie ...

This undoubted phenomenon might well have confirmed Brighouse in another assessment he made of both himself and his great friend Stanley Houghton: 'In the long run, if one-act plays can be ignored, Houghton and I are one-play men.'[5]

Like Monkhouse's judgement, this too is proving wide of the mark. In 2010, Brighouse's play *The Game* was successsfully revived by the theatre company Northern Broadsides. Director Barry Rutter said, 'Its themes include: class divisions, the immoral effects of rich idleness, the moral value of having to work and social trends in the society of that day. It's very funny, but also heartrending with a real Chekovian, bittersweet ending. For a play written nearly a century ago, *The Game* is bang up to date about football. People will think we've added in dialogue. There's a moment when Elsie says: 'They can raise a decent crowd at Chelsea nowadays.' It's nearly 100 years old, that line. We're not changing a thing. And the chicanery over money, the financial disaster of relegation – that's all here too.'[6]

More surprising was the revival of *Zack* in Manchester in January 2011 with stand-up comedian Justin Moorhouse playing the lead. With *Lonesome-like* and *The Price of Coal* being mounted in 2015 at the Finborough Theatre, Brighouse's work has lasted well and continues to be popular. As he put it in typically droll fashion in his *Autobiography*,

'A play's vital statistic is its number of recorded performances ... money talks, and unrefined as its speech may be, money – that is, fees received – is the sure indication of a play's vitality.'[7] For Brighouse's work, money still talks.

On that 2015 Finborough bill with Brighouse's two short plays was Stanley Houghton's one-act *The Old Testament and the New*. Houghton's work has also regularly been restaged down the years with *Hindle Wakes* inevitably leading the way. It was a favourite of Joan Littlewood's, and her Workshop put it on at the Theatre Royal, Stratford in April 1953. It was in production in Manchester the night the IRA destroyed the Royal Exchange theatre in 1996, and appropriately it was the first play to grace the rebuilt Royal Exchange in 1998. In 2012 the Finborough Theatre mounted the first London performance of the play in 30 years, while in 2015 it was produced to great acclaim at the Octagon Theatre Bolton.

Perhaps one might have expected Brighouse and Houghton to continue as popular favourites, but Allan Monkhouse might well have been surprised to see his own work gradually resurfacing onto the country's stages.

His short 'war' play *Night Watches* was on that same Finborough bill in 2015, while *Mary Broome*, the first of the major Manchester plays to gain a reputation, was revived in March 2011 at the Orange Tree, Richmond. Critics were taken with Leonard, describing him as a fascinatingly disruptive character, alternating between dazzling charm and mutinous sulks, a 'subversive saboteur at the bourgeois hearth' 'unreachable and irresponsible in his nature.' The following year the same production appeared at the Mint Theatre New York City.

Even more impressive, his major war play, *The Conquering Hero*, was mounted at the Orange Tree, Richmond in May 2012, the *Guardian*'s Michael Billington writing, 'I cannot recommend too highly this play. Written in 1923, five years before R.C. Sherriff's infinitely more popular *Journey's End*, it strikes me as superior to the latter in every way: less emotionally reliant on public-school attitudes and more politically radical in its scepticism about war. It can be ranked with O'Casey's *The Silver Tassie* as among the finest anti-war plays.'[8] In May 2014, the Brand New Music Theatre transformed the play into an opera: *King and Country* for the Brighton Fringe ...

Brighouse, Houghton and Monkhouse were not the only ones to have an influence on succeeding generations of playgoers, however. Writing to Miss Horniman in 1920 when he had heard of her intention to leave Manchester, John Masefield said:

> Looking at it now, you must see that it has been a glorious success, for all over England, in towns and villages, the theatre is springing up with quite new wonderful life. Troupes of village players are everywhere, often doing sound work and quick with new ideas. 'The end men look for cometh not.' It may not have been the end any expected, but it is a living consequence of your first establishing the theatre here; and no man can tell how far this new movement, now beginning from the ground up, may grow. I hope that you may see it reach every height you have hoped and striven for.[9]

Masefield was alluding to the upsurge in interest in amateur dramatics, in local communities creating small theatrical ventures that fed upon the one-act play, a speciality of the Gaiety. Harold Brighouse saw this trend as a by-product of the First World War, and from the disbanding of the troops after 1918:

> They had sat in garrison theatres and had seen plays sent to those theatres by the Canteen Board, they had sat in overseas theatres and had seen the plays performed in those theatres by the Lena Ashwell organisation under the YMCA, and, returning to the villages and towns with a new-born appreciation of drama, they determined to continue for themselves and to pass on to others the pleasure they had derived from plays.[10]

There were other factors: a change in life-styles for many British people, with reduced working hours, new pastimes, new towns. In many of the latter, drama was one of the activities that helped bond people together. The local church, tennis club or community centre was likely to produce a dramatic section, and in winter months this provided a suitable indoor focal point for socialising as well as performing. One-act plays would be the staple fare of such institutions.

In his autobiography, Brighouse commented on the phenomenon:

> But *is* the Manchester School outmoded? A satisfying 'No' comes from the Repertories, the BBC, and, above all, the amateurs, to whom I owe especial thanks for their continuing use of one-act plays.[11]

Brighouse would write over 50 one-act plays during the interwar period, some specifically designed for outdoor performance. *The Price of Coal* was always extremely popular and *Lonesome-like*, by 1953, had reached over 3,000 performances! Where the fledgling medium of radio was concerned, during the year 1928, Brighouse had the following items produced at studios in Manchester, Cardiff and London by the 'Station Repertory Players': *Followers*, a Cranford Sketch, *Lonesome-like*, *Maypole Morning*, *The Paris Doctor*, *Hobson's Choice* (with ex-Gaiety actresses Hilda Bruce-Potter and Edyth Goodall in the cast), *Fossie for Short*, *The Maid of France* and *Dealing in Futures*.

But he wasn't the only ex-Gaiety playwright to contribute to this amateur dramatic phenomenon. Sackville Martin, Allan Monkhouse and Michael Arabian also continued writing for the amateur theatre well into the 1920s and two men in particular, whose plays had been produced by AH in the years just preceding the war, went on to become prolific one-act playwrights, their influence on inter-war drama far outweighing their initial productions.

Harold Frederick Rubinstein (1891-1975) was educated at Cheltenham College and was both an English solicitor and playwright, in fact, the only Jewish writer to emerge from that cultured Manchester community that contributed so much to Manchester society prior to the war.

His play *Consequences* (produced at the Gaiety on 9 February 1914) was heralded as a bold attempt to grapple with the issue of mixed marriages, but what in fact looked at first to be a problem comedy turned out to be a farce of sorts.

A young couple, Rosalind Collins a 'Gentile' and Benjamin Lipsky, a Jew, meet at a suffragette demonstration and decide they love one another. Being young radicals, they decide to challenge their parents, who they are sure will object. The outcome is not what they expect as, for differing reasons, both sets of parents agree.

The Referee critic wrote 'It is a rather clever stroke of irony that Mr Rubinstein could make business the solvent of Christian prejudice and sport the solvent of Jewish prejudices,'[12] while the *Jewish World* felt: 'The young author hasn't had the courage to describe the qualities of his own race without compromise. That is to say all the Jewish characters in *Consequences* might quite easily be Christians with the exception of the amusing boy who is a characteristic Jew.'[13]

His next play, *Over The Wall*, was not a success. He attempted a similar kind of reversal technique, this time involving two sets of children living next door to one another with parents holding diametrically opposed views on how to bring them up. Harold Brighouse was clearly unimpressed, considering it 'a farce with a good idea but a good idea drenched in words', and felt that the play, 'could be classed with those artistically negligible plays which often make enormous successes in London when expensively cast with popular players ... '[14]

Nonetheless, Rubinstein went on to have a long and distinguished theatrical and literary career, becoming one of the most prolific one-act playwrights of the inter-war period. He pursued a wide range of historical and literary themes, and was deeply interested in philosophical and religious issues (he was a member of the Religious Drama Society in 1929), writing several sets of probing plays about characters from both the Old and New Testaments. He said, 'sensing deeply the basis of an ultimate reunion between Jew and Christian.. I shall go on asking my questions ... while I remain on earth.'[15]

Rubinstein also founded a well-known London law firm (Rubinstein, Nash & Co Solicitors) specialising in literary cases and dealing with authors such as Rafael Sabatini, Bernard Shaw, H.G. Wells, Anthony West, J.M. Barrie and George Orwell. His brother-in-law was the publisher Victor Gollancz for whom he routinely evaluated proof copies of manuscripts for potential libel.

Laurence Du Garde Peach had his first play, the one-act tragedy *Wind O' the Moors*, produced at the Gaiety in September 1913 on same bill as Monkhouse's *Mary Broome*. C.E. Montague reviewed it, feeling that the author had 'absorbed a lot but was not yet able to make something entirely of his own ... ' His present tragedy was, 'not so tragic as it would be if its fatal turn has less of a curious accident about it, but it was still cordially received.'[176]

By then Peach (yet another alumnus of Manchester Grammar School) had already taken up a postgraduate position at the University of Göttingen in 1912, later earning a PhD at Sheffield University in 1921 for a thesis on the development of drama in France, Spain and England in the 17th century. He married in 1915 and served in military intelligence during the First World War, reaching the rank of captain.

Peach claimed in 1933 that of the three great institutions in Manchester he'd attended: the Grammar School, the University and the Gaiety – 'it was what he learnt and saw and experienced at the last of these three that remained with him.'[17]

From the early 1920s, he began regularly writing humorous pieces for *Punch* and other magazines and, after a period as a lecturer at the University College of the South West of England, Peach left academia to become a full-time writer.

His one-act plays became a mainstay of the fare offered by small drama groups in England in the 1930s and 1940s. They were well-crafted pieces, often based on historical documentary evidence, and always within the acting compass of inexperienced players. They were frequently developed from radio scripts and thus usually relatively brief. Indeed, a major outlet at the time was the then new medium of radio for which Peach wrote his first play in 1924.

Much of his work for radio dramatised history and biography and became a staple of the *Children's Hour* strand for younger listeners. Today he may be best remembered as the author of over thirty books for Ladybird's Adventure from History series of non-fiction children's books, which was published from 1957 until his death, was the largest series Ladybird ever produced, remaining in print until 1986.

He was also a great supporter of local theatre, running a group at Great Hucklow. In the mid-1930s the Great Hucklow players were known for performing their plays at full moon because it was known to light the audience across the moors.

From 1934 to 1936, he wrote screenplays for a number of films, ranging from horror and musical comedy to serious drama adaptations. He was made an OBE for services to literature in 1972, and recognised with an honorary DLitt from Sheffield University in 1964. He died in 1974.

Other Gaiety alumni would influence the course of theatre and cinema throughout the inter-war period.

After leaving Manchester in 1912, Iden Payne travelled to the United States the following year to begin a long and distinguished career in American theatre, first organising a season of modern plays for the Chicago Theatre Society, a pioneering community theatre, and thereafter in Indianapolis to produce plays for the Drama League of America. In 1914 he joined the School of Drama at the Carnegie Institute of Technology where he worked from 1914 to 1950. He would direct professionally in New York City on Broadway, while form 1935 to 1943 he directed the Stratford Memorial Theatre Festival in Stratford-upon-Avon. He retired as Professor Emeritus of Drama at the University of Texas in Austin in May 1973 where an award in his name for outstanding contributions to theatre is annually bestowed. He died in 1976.

His successor at the Gaiety, Lewis Casson, spent much of his career as a theatrical director overseeing the glittering career of his wife, Dame Sybil Thorndike. In 1939 he led an Old Vic tour around the Mediterranean and in 1940 he directed John Gielgud in *King Lear* at the Old Vic. During the Second World War, Casson organised tours of the Old Vic company to the South Wales valleys. He was president of the British Actors' Equity Association from 1941 to 1945 and was knighted in 1945. He died in 1969, aged 93.

In 1911 Basil Dean became the first director of Liverpool repertory theatre and in 1918 was awarded an MBE for his services to national entertainment during the First World War. Over the next ten years he rose to be one of the most influential theatrical producers and directors in the country, responsible for London and New York productions of new plays by John Galsworthy, Somerset Maugham, Noël Coward, Dodie Smith, Clemence Dane and J.B. Priestley.

He later moved into the film industry and in the early 1930s founded Associated Talking Pictures which later became Ealing Studios, publicising and working with many great British entertainers. (In a strange twist of fate, Charles McEvoy, one of the old Gaiety's original hopes, would have a hit in the 1920s in the West End with a cockney comedy play called *The Likes of 'Er*. It was produced by Dean who in 1931 would transform it into a film called *Sally of Our Alley* making northern music hall actress Gracie Fields into an international star.)

When World War II started Dean left the film industry and became the head of ENSA, the government-sponsored body responsible for bringing live performances to the armed services. He remained an influential figure in the theatre until shortly before his death from a heart attack on 22 April 1978.

Postscript

AH died in London on 6 August 1937. In 1959 the Gaiety Theatre was demolished to make way for offices. The *Manchester Guardian* reported, 'No tears need be shed over its disappearance ... It had had an up and down career of more than twenty years as a music hall under the name of the Comedy Theatre ... Since Miss Horniman sold it nearly forty years ago it has been a cinema theatre (and) as a relic it had long lost any air of sanctity which may have lingered with her going. Yet if anyone spoke of 'the Gaiety' he was at once understood to be speaking of the Gaiety of 1908 to 1914; the long years before and after dissolve like a cloud from the mind ... '[18]

Notes

[1] Allan Monkhouse *Manchester Guardian*, 17 June 1932.

[2] Harold Brighouse, *Autobiography*, p185.

[3] Ibid., p185.

[4] Ibid.

[5] Ibid., p179.

[6] Barry Rutter 'A Playwright of Two Halves: Barrie Rutter on Harold Brighouse', *TheArtsDesk.com* , 14 September 2010.

[7] Brighouse, *Autobiography*, p182.

[8] *Manchester Guardian*, May 2012.

[9] Pogson, *op. cit.*, p197.

[10] Harold Brighouse, *Autobiography*, p184.

[11] Ibid., p183

[12] *The Referee*, 10 May 1914.

[13] E.A. Baughn 'The Jewish World', *Drama* , 13 May1914.

[14] *Manchester Guardian*, 3 November 1914.

[15] Rex Walford and Colin Dolley, *The One-Act Play Companion* (A.&C. Black, 2006), p126.

[16] *Manchester Guardian*, 2 September 1913.

[17] *Manchester Guardian*, 6 October 1933.

[18] *Manchester Guardian*, 9 July 1959.

APPENDIX ONE

The Actors

Nobody wore evening dress, and when an actor must he wore it gauchely, with a shirt that wasn't too clean. The actresses' clothes made dressmakers weep.[1]

The actors were the friends of the audience and we still take a friendly interest in them, scattered as they are.[2]

THE SUCCESS OF THE GAIETY – AND the plays produced there – clearly relied on Payne being able to recruit suitable actors.

'My first task was to gather a company together. Miss Horniman, after consultation with me, restricted the total sum for actors' salaries to a figure that would have precluded my engaging actors with established reputations, even if I had wished to have them, which I emphatically did not. Instead I sought a group of capable actors, skilful and dedicated to their art. In this search I had the advantage of having toured in several provincial companies myself, so I was able to choose on the basis of personal observation.'[3]

AH had her own ideas concerning who might be suitable:

'As far as my own company is concerned, I never take the raw beginner. Everyone who comes to me must have been trained and had experience. As far as their place in the plays performed at the

Gaiety Theatre is concerned they must be prepared to act any part that is assigned to them, however humble it may be. I believe in discipline in the theatre as well as an all-round experience. This fits them late for any opening that may be offered to them and gives them the training that is necessary for every person who aspires to act well.'[4]

Payne's success in recruiting sufficiently talented actors was made easier by the fact that, compared to conditions elsewhere in the acting world, working at the Gaiety was an attractive proposition. The lure of London for a performer might be great, but conditions there, unless one had reached or was approaching the 'star' circle, were, at best, very uncertain indeed. To be cast for a West End show meant rehearsals without salary and a possibility that the play might be withdrawn after a brief run. There was no Equity at that time, and salaries, again outside the charmed circle, were often miserably poor even in London, where the cost of living was higher than in the provinces.

By contrast, the Gaiety agreement gave greater security than was usual in the theatre. There was an assurance of a settled weekly salary for forty weeks of the year and, as during most years Miss Horniman was playing in London in the 'off' season or was running a summer company at the Gaiety or elsewhere, there was usually opportunity given for her permanent company to play during that time, so that they could have a complete year's security if they so desired.

AH also paid salaries which were above the average. The youngest, least experienced earned about £1 15/- a week compared with £4 for a more experienced actor and £7 for Lewis Casson as Director. (Payne was thus able to 'poach' Irene Rooke and Milton Rosmer from Glasgow Repertory Company.) These wages compared very well with those of other skilled workers in Edwardian England where the average wage was £80 a year. 'Real wages', says

Paul Thompson in his book *The Edwardians*, 'were stagnant during the Edwardian period,' and the Company's wages bill would not have varied much from the £120 per week for a company of 23 estimated by H.K. Moderwell in 1915 from statistics given by Miss Horniman, probably in 1914 before the expenses of war distorted the economy.[5]

AH did all she could to prove herself the superior of male managers in her treatment of the actors. When the Gaiety was rebuilt she provided well-ventilated dressing rooms and a comfortable greenroom for her company, just as she had done in Dublin. She was also generous in releasing actors for other engagements.

In fact, there were relatively few changes in the company in the early years, and some of those who left, such as Basil Dean, Miss Darragh, Penelope Wheeler and Muriel Pratt, did so to found or to take an active share in similar theatrical undertakings elsewhere. The Gaiety, as the parent of repertory, placed no obstacles in the way of those who wished to spread the good news.

There were, of course, alternatives to London or Manchester. There were the touring companies, either those under regular managements or those collected to tour a particular play, but even in cases where these gave some guarantee of prolonged engagement, constant and tiring travelling, cheap and often unsatisfactory 'digs', in fact, a purely nomadic existence, was all that could be expected. A company like that of the Gaiety could settle themselves in Manchester, and even though some touring was involved, they could, for the greater part of their time, go home to their own beds and feel they had some roots.

Over the course of the next few years, therefore, the Gaiety actors often refused to be tempted away by seemingly better offers; and willingly went on doing work which was far more exacting than they might have found elsewhere. More than one of the old Gaiety

Mona Limerick (*top left*); Sybil Thorndike (*top right*);
Charles Bibby (*bottom left*); Hilda Bruce Potter (*bottom right*)
(*All author's collection*)

Prominent Actors for the Manchester Gaiety Theatre

company told Rex Pogson: 'We never thought of asking for an increase of salary in those days. We were most of us young, we received enough to live on, we were getting wonderful experience, and we felt to be doing something that mattered.'[6]

Many of the Gaiety players had local associations; Charles Bibby, Hilda Bruce-Potter, Edward Landor, Ada King, Louise Holbrook, Edyth Goodall, Henry Austin, Enid Meek and Hilda Davies were all born in or near Manchester, and others such as Milton Rosmer and Herbert Lomas were natives of other parts of Lancashire.

From the management side, the importance of this more settled existence was emphasised some years later by Lewis Casson when he was Director at the Gaiety. In a letter to the *Manchester Guardian* he spoke of 'the immense artistic advantage of having a company of normal human citizens who do a day's work and go home at night, instead of a troupe of wandering mountebanks whose life is the play they are acting.'

Many of the actors lived in the same area of Manchester and there were many stories circulating about this new and 'different' company, as Basil Dean recalled:

> The Horniman players were so unlike their usual lodgers that the landladies of Ackers Street began to spread rumours; we were very peculiar people indeed, 'atheists and I don't know what else, living on nuts and things. In those days we were all looked upon with a good deal of suspicion ... It was even rumoured that we indulged in what was then called 'free love', whereas in point of fact we were just a group of rather high-brow over-earnest young actors and actresses, living on humble salaries and with our noses just slightly tilted upwards since we were, after all, somewhat different from the ordinary run of touring actor, or at least we thought we were. It was due to the persistence of these old wives' tales quite as much as to the left-wing tendencies of our authors that we lived in a state of apartheid for the first year, more so even than the actors who came up from London to play in Shakespeare and pantomime at Christmas.[7]

Dean himself recalled, 'At first I lived in rather dreary lodgings in Ackers Street but I got so tired of the smell of fried fish shops on Saturday nights that when I got my first rise in salary I invested it in a season ticket on the Midland Railway to Chorlton-cum-Hardy and there I lodged for the remaining three years of my engagement with the company. (Actor) Esmé Percy had more money than I had and so he lived one station further on at Withington.'[8]

Dean outlined the work-schedule: 'The routine of work was exacting: we rehearsed from 10.30 to 4 p.m. with only half an hour's interval for lunch, taking a hasty sandwich and a glass of lager beer at the German restaurant opposite the Midland Hotel, which is where the new Manchester Library stands ... then a scamper through the rain to tram or train to one's lodgings, then back though the rain once more for the evening performance. Miss Horniman did what she could to make things easier for her company. It was she who insisted that there should be a break in the middle of the morning for coffee, which she sent in at her own expense from the Midland Hotel. Thus, the established routine of the mid-morning coffee-break during rehearsals owes its origin to Miss Horniman.'[9]

'Another example of her concern comes to mind: *An Enemy of the People* contains a dinner scene in the second act. For the sake of realism, actual food was proposed. The business manager wanted to deduct the cost of the meal from our salaries. Esmé Percy took the matter to Miss Horniman, who calmly replied that no such thing would happen. Thereafter, we ate a hearty meal of hot roast beef with trimmings at every performance, and enjoyed ourselves so much that we forgot our cues, and the prompter gave up in despair.

'Her benign influence is best illustrated by the good feeling that existed among us. I can recall no quarrels or jealousies of any consequence. This unanimity of purpose, which critics noted at the time, enormously increased the company's impact. Possibly it was because of Miss Horniman's utterly selfless motives that the influence of her company extended far beyond the scope and duration of its work.'[10]

The actor and later film-maker Whitford Kane considered that the enthusiasm at the Gaiety seemed to spring from a satisfaction with artistic standards and especially from the high quality of the acting:

'Here everyone seemed to be alive down to the stage doorkeeper. There were many jealousies, of course, but they were healthy and stimulating ones. Everyone in the Manchester Theatre participated, and there was a fine intermingling of actors and authors, quite different from the reserve and aloofness one felt in London. There was an excellent system too, of distributing the work, for Payne divided the company into two units. One company played while the other rehearsed and vice versa. Irene Rooke, a fine actress, was the leading lady of one group while Miss Goodall headed the other. To me the Manchester Theatre was an ideal repertory organisation, as it combined both the creative and the interpretive.'[11]

This unanimity of purpose must have been fostered by AH's stern disapproval of 'star' treatment – no individual curtain calls were allowed, and only reluctantly agreed to one at the end of the show, no names were printed larger than others on posters or programmes, and all actors were under contract to play whatever parts they were given. All the same, there still developed various personality cults at the Gaiety, particularly where the female actresses were concerned.

Edith Goodall, to the displeasure of other members of the company, placed a life-sized photograph of herself in the Gaiety foyer and Irene Rooke and Milton Rosmer developed a personal following which deserted the Gaiety when they left the company. It was also noted that 'factory lasses, who come to the theatre with the greatest regularity on Mondays and Fridays and who are usually seated in the sixpenny gallery – where seats can be booked – are very faithful adherents of their favourites – actresses as a rule and not actors.'[12]

Basil Dean concluded that he'd not had his contract renewed by the Gaiety because of the 'cult' status he had achieved in the role of Jack Barthwick in Galsworthy's *Silver Box*.[13]

He was also certain that 'There can be little doubt that the absence of the "star" system was a handicap, in a financial sense, particularly at the beginning. Playgoers had been brought up to go to the theatre to see some important actor or actress, rather than to see a fine play. Irving might come on his provincial tours with rubbish like *The Bells* and *Waterloo*, but he was Irving, and what he was playing mattered not a jot. This idea was so firmly embedded that it was substantially there for life. "The play's the thing," said the Gaiety and its whole policy and method were based on that assumption.'

'As time went on the inevitable happened. Certain players became objects of popularity and obtained a personal following. When they left, as we have seen, their supporters stayed away. It is often said that the "star" system is imposed on the public, but experience does not entirely support that view.'[14]

Notes

[1] Agate, *op. cit.*, p87.

[2] A.N. Monkhouse, *Manchester* Guardian, 30 April 1921.

[3] Iden Payne, *op. cit.*, p80.

[4] *Daily Mail*, 18 February 1914.

[5] H.K. Motherwell, *The Theatre of Today* (Bodley Head, 1915), pp308–9.

[6] Rex Pogson, *op cit.*

[7] Basil Dean, *Seven Ages*, p51.

[8] Ibid.

[9] Ibid.

[10] Basil Dean, 'Early Days at the Gaiety', *Manchester Guardian*, 25 February 1935; *Autobiography*, p64.

[11]Whitford Kane, *Are We All Met?* (Elkin Mathews and Marrot, 1931), pp80-1.

[12]*Yorkshire Evening News*, 21 September 1910.

[13]Basil Dean *Seven Ages*, p70.

[14]Ibid.

APPENDIX TWO

The Audience

The Gaiety drew a loyal audience to whom the theatre was a spiritual home, almost a church. But the faithful band was too small and the venture failed.[1]

There must be a real use in doing one's best to help people think for themselves.[2]

ONE OF THE KEY ASPECTS IN situating the Gaiety in Manchester was the prospect of providing good theatre for a discerning audience. Whether that audience was thought of as working-class or middle-class mattered not to AH or Payne; but there was a definite 'missionary' sense about the way they went about trying to create it. She also contradicted herself at times.

Though she regularly inveighed against the 'impertinence' of theatres which claimed to 'uplift' people, she did seem to have been guided by similar ethical forces, as when she suggested that, 'there must be a real use in doing one's best to help people think for themselves.'[3]

Repertory theatres should not be thought of as 'superior' she felt (*Yorkshire Post*, 18 November 1913), but she took the credit for the remark that when most people went to theatre they 'left their brains in the cloak-room.'[4]

Iden Payne clearly knew that he had to woo an audience. 'We were ... concerned, of course, with public reaction to the often unfamiliar activities onstage. We did not leave this reaction entirely to chance. On Sunday nights I gave lectures in the many towns surrounding Manchester, spreading the gospel of repertory. This form of propaganda soon led to another, making what we called 'flying matinees' in towns where I had lectured. Railway service was adequate and by leaving early in the morning we were able to return to the Gaiety in time for the evening performance.

'These incursions showed little consideration for the touring companies occupying the local theatres at night. We learned that they would have prevented them if their contracts with the theatre managers had given them legal power to do so. They must have been furiously jealous of the packed houses we attracted.

'Great curiosity had been aroused everywhere with a wide orbit around Manchester. Only in one town, Oldham, though it had a fine new theatre, was there a meagre audience. I asked the theatre carpenter if he could account for it. His answer, typically Lancashire in broad dialect, was, 'It's only to be expected in Oudam. You wouldn't get folk to come to a theayter if you was to give 'em the Crucifixion with the original cast!'[5]

Playgoer James Gregson recalled how the Gaiety caught his attention: 'I was soon jerked out of my provincial lack of enterprise! I knew nothing of Miss H and nothing of her repertory company but I could not help noticing her posters and her day bills which were so different from the usual brand. Her "six sheets", her "twelve sheets", her "double crowns" of cream paper with good bold type in two colours and a border that gave a panel effect and left plenty of blank space never failed to attract the eye and satisfy one's expectations. They made you feel that their theatre was different from the ordinary. It was.'[6]

Gaiety historian Pogson was certain that the Gaiety made a

significant difference to those who were persuaded to sample its, at the time somewhat daring, fare.

'In Edwardian days there were still large sections of the community who avoided the theatre as something sinful or, at least, not quite nice, and some of these people were brought in. The Gaiety had to create its own audience and it did so, in some measure, from those who, in the ordinary way, had not been regular playgoers.

'There were many who came week after week from Huddersfield, Halifax, Sheffield and the Lancashire towns. To those to whom the Gaiety meant anything, it meant almost everything, but there were not nearly enough of them. To many it opened up a new and fascinating world and was an inspiration for their whole lives.'[7]

Exactly who these people were has been disputed: Miss Horniman was, as Lewis Casson said, 'basically a do-gooder',[8] and her theatre attracted an appropriate audience, described in a semiserious article in The Gaiety Annual for 1909:

> The trouble is, that for some mysterious reason, the Gaiety has become known as the home of advanced thought ... and the consequence is that everyone who regards himself or herself as an advanced thinker considers it a duty to go to the Gaiety ... In any ordinary theatre it is usually safe to chat to the man next to you if you are feeling lonesome, but in the Gaiety it is absolutely perilous. You may be asked for an opinion on anything from The Communist Manifesto to Thus Spake Zarathustra or the relative food values of bean and broccoli.[9]

James Agate was even more scathing:

> There was no drink licence, but only the horrid spectacle of intellectuals consuming cocoa. No orchestra, and in the intervals pale young men, who had not gone out to drink cocoa, nodded glumly to one another across Professor Herford's beard.[10]

It cannot be denied, however, that the Gaiety did manage to

create, from the working classes in particular, a new body of people interested in the drama. There is abundant evidence of this. In the years after she left the Gaiety, AH kept up correspondence with many of them and Sybil Thorndike often claimed she regularly heard from several women who, as mill-girls, were regular 'galleryites' at the Gaiety and whose interest in the drama began then and had never flagged.

James Gregson, though not a mill-girl, was emphatic: 'I became a faithful, devoted Hornimanite, regularly booking my two gallery seats each week, and watched a procession of new dramatists as they crossed the magic boards.

'What gorgeous times we had – we gallereyites! What argument during the intervals! We used to go whether we had seen the play before or not, whether we liked it or not – and we would gather together during the intervals thinking furiously in company and aloud.

'And what wonderful acting treasures we had! I wonder whether any English theatre housed such a wonderful company as the one we knew and loved. How well I remember the thrill that the white and red interior gave me. For the first time in my life I had a reserved seat! It was in the gallery and I paid sixpence for it ...[11]

C.B. Purdom noticed, 'a feeling in the audience more like the understanding and affection of a company of friends, than the bored and distant attitude of the usual theatre audience.[12]

Gerald Petrie, writing in *The Gong*, the magazine of the Birmingham Repertory Theatre in the 1920s, remembered sitting in the circle of the Gaiety with a man in dress clothes on one side of him and a man in oily overalls on the other.[13]

Winifred Blatchford, writing in *The Woman Worker* in 1909 was equally enthusiastic. She'd gone to watch Galsworthy's play *Strife* and found the theatre was, 'very well filled and the audience was wonderfully alive and enthusiastic':

The theatre is so cosy and tasteful in its rich crimson hangings and the visitors are so very refreshing after the ordinary jaded theatregoers. Bright young men and women – the real live thing – flock there. They dominate the circles and the pit and one may be certain that they all hold 'views' that would shock their grandparents dreadfully; and one likes them very much and in looking at their intelligent faces gathers hope for the future. For they at least will think and once we can get the people to do that we shall gain a long step in the right direction.[14]

Future Trade Union leader Harry Pollitt recalled going to the Gaiety with his group of socialist, communist young friends: 'Our group was going all "arty". Miss Horniman was running the Gaiety theatre at that time and we were all frequently to be found in the gallery.'[15]

Factory worker Alice Foley wrote enthusiastically: 'These shaping years also included the gay, gracious days of Miss Horniman's reign at the Gaiety Theatre Manchester. As a member of a group of young socialists I hoarded my scanty pocket money amounting at that time to one penny on the shilling of factory earnings, so that I could afford with them the luxury of a monthly matinee.

With a cheap seat in pit or gallery we saw most of the early Shaw and Galsworthy plays followed by tea in the Clarion café in Market Street where I remember there was a fine William Morris fireplace. If the café was crowded we hived off to the Art Gallery and over tea, brown bread, peaches and cream we animatedly argued and discussed the philosophy, art or satire of the production.

The whole outing cost about 5s each but we returned home like exultant young gods, tingling and athirst with the naive faith that if only sufficient human beings could witness good drama and comedy it might change the world.'[16]

All of which makes Alan Monkhouse's comments when the Gaiety eventually closed sound a little patronizing. He wrote that the one great failure of the Gaiety audience was that they were, 'plaguey slow in educating themselves into intelligent receptive playgoers.' Advanced thinkers they may have been, but, according to Monkhouse, 'not only did they not know how to behave in a theatre; there was nothing that could not be laughed through and hardly anything that [could not] be misunderstood.'[17]

When Lewis Casson suddenly resigned as director of the Gaiety in 1914, he too made a point of criticising the audience, or lack of it, citing it as one of the reasons for his leaving. In January 1914 at a dinner given in his honour, Casson made a speech in which his main point was that the Gaiety was not an 'organic' part of Manchester and for that reason it would almost certainly wither away:

> It should be clearly understood that the Gaiety was not Manchester's own theatre. Manchester did not ask for it and did not work for it to any great extent or pay for it ... The Gaiety Theatre was founded with no hope of appealing to the great majority of Manchester people. It was founded because Miss Horniman had a confidence that in Manchester there was a minority ... who would support such a theatre well enough to make it a commercial proposition ...

He went on to attack Manchester's citizens for their utter lack of support for any new experiment, their lack of faith in the Theatre, their smug pride in having such a regime as Miss Horniman's in their great city – 'a pride which they had done little to deserve or claim ...'[18]

In April 1921 under a *Manchester Guardian* headline 'A Splendid Failure' Monkhouse wrote:

> The Gaiety never looked up after Mr Casson resigned. It compromised and failed and it is a pity to do both. Miss H had always done her best to reassure the public and to wean it from the stupid obsession that the Gaiety was the home of gloomy plays. The demand for cheerful plays is about as intelligent as a demand for

cheerful statues would be but it was made. The cheerful masterpieces did not materialize but there was always plenty of comedy, if it wasn't always of the best quality.

But the stupid people had got it into their heads that the Gaiety was gloomy and highbrowed and facts are to no avail to the fixed idea. The Gaiety venture failed because the initial interest and enthusiasm did not create an adequate audience. I don't think it was the fault of the plays; certainly not of the actors. We had not in Manchester a sufficiency of people who could distinguish good from bad or had any real pleasure in attempting to do so ... [19]

Notes

[1] Lewis Casson, *Manchester Guardian*, 6 September 1958.

[2] Miss Horniman, letter to Tom Bass, 27 August 1919, Manchester Public Library.

[3] Ibid.

[4] Miss Horniman, letter to Tom Bass, 11 January 1923, Manchester Public Library.

[5] Iden Payne, *op. cit.*

[6] 'The Playwright's Progress'; James Gregson. *Leeds Mercury,* 11 September 1926.

[7] Pogson, *op. cit.*

[8] *Manchester Guardian*, 8 September 1958.

[9] 'That Audience', Harold Lake, *The Gaiety Annual* (1909), p24.

[10] Agate, *op. cit.*

[11] 'The Playwright's Progress', James Gregson. *Leeds Mercury* (11 September 1926)

[12] C.B. Purdom, *A Proposal for a Town's Theatre* (Arden Press, 1911)

[13] *The Gong.* 1/5 (April 1922), 205.

[14] *The Woman Worker,* 24 November 1909.

[15] Harry Pollitt, *Serving My Time* (Lawrence & Wishart 1941).

[16] Alice Foley *A Bolton Childhood* (1973).

[17] *Manchester Guardian* (9 December 1913).

[18] Lewis Casson *Manchester Guardian,* 12 January 1914; and Russell Thorndike, *Sybil Thorndike* (Butterworth, 1929), pp. 241–2.

[19] *Manchester* Guardian, 30 April 1921, 'A Splendid Failure'.

APPENDIX THREE

First plays by the Manchester Playwrights at the Gaiety

1908

4 May: *The Few and the Many* (H.R. Richardson)

7 September: *Marriages Are Made in Heaven* (Basil Dean)

21 September: *Woman's Rights* (James Sackville Martin)

28 September: *Reaping the Whirlwind* (Allan Monkhouse)

5 October: *Makeshifts* (Gertrude Robins)

2 November: *The Dear Departed* (Stanley Houghton)

1909

10 April: *The Doorway* (Harold Brighouse)

26 April: *Trespassers Will Be Prosecuted* (A. Arabian)

1910

28 February: *The Tallyman* (Judge Parry)

11 April: *Subsidence* (Fred E Wynne)

1911

21 November: *Miles Dixon* (Gilbert Cannan)

1913

14 April: *The Whispering Well* (Frank Rose)

2 September: *The Wind o' the Moors* (Laurence du Garde Peach)

1914

9 February: *Consequences* (Harry Rubinstein)

26 October: *Complaints* (Ernest Hutchinson)

Plays by Manchester Playwrights produced at the Gaiety

Harold Brighouse: *The Doorway, Dealing in Futures, Spring in Bloomsbury, Lonesome-like, The Polygon, Garsides Career, Converts*

Allan Monkhouse: *Reaping the Whirlwind, Mary Broome, The Choice, Nothing Like Leather*

Stanley Houghton: *The Dear Departed, Independent Means, The Master of the House, The Younger Generation, Hindle Wakes*

Harry Richardson: *The Few and the Many, Bringing it Home, Going On Parade, Gentlemen of the Press, The Awakening Women.*

Gertrude Robins: *Makeshifts, The Point of View, Realities, Loving As We Do, The Plaything*

James Sackville Martin: *A Question of Property, Woman's Rights, Cupid and the Styx, The Purse of Gold*

Basil Dean: *Marriages are Made in Heaven, Mother to Be*

Frank Rose: *The Whispering Well, The Hanging of Hey-Go-Mad-Jack*

Judge Parry: *The Tallyman, Katawampus, Charlotte on Bigamy, The Captain of the School, Disraeli.*

Fred Wynne: *Subsidence*

Gilbert Cannan: *Miles Dixon, Mary's Wedding*

Harry Rubinstein: *Consequences, Over the Wall*

M.A. Arabian: *Trespassers Will Be Prosecuted*

L du Garde Peach: *Wind o' the Moors*

Ernest Hutchinson: *Complaints*

Kahane, Forrest, Iden Payne – one one-act play each

APPENDIX FOUR

from *Leeds Mercury* 28 April 1913

GIRL – MOTHER AND HER LOVER PERSIST IN REFUSING TO MARRY HIM

HINDLE WAKES IN REAL LIFE

A case curiously reminiscent in some of its features of the well-known play *Hindle Wakes* has been heard at Heywood, Lancashire.

The plaintiff, Miss Selina Schofield, a weaver in a cotton mill earning 25s a week had, it appeared, had an illegitimate child, but declined to marry the father, Robert Harold Hilton, though he had repeatedly asked her to do so.

In cross-examination Miss Schofield admitted this, but said that she wanted to stay with her parents for a few years longer. Then, again, her lover said he could only furnish the house on the hire system.

Colonel Hall (for defendant): Well, isn't that better than having an illegitimate child?

Plaintiff: Well, I don't see it.

Colonel Hall: You don't see it but all respectable people do.

(1912 *Hindle Wakes* play headlines)

Applicant: All respectable people don't: some have one, two and three and are still respectable.

Colonel Hall: I think that is doubtful. When your lover pleaded with you to be married didn't you tell him that your child if born out of wedlock would be without name and didn't you reply that it would have a name better than any name in Heywood?

Applicant: Yes.

Defendant, in the box, said his fiancée's parents told him when he offered to marry their daughter that she was not 'thoroughly domesticated' but he replied that she would become domesticated in time. He was prepared to make sacrifices in every way to put the girl in a right position and avoid scandal.

Councillor Redmond, who appeared for the applicant asked for an order of 4s a week but Colonel Hall replied that in view of the exceptional circumstances this was too much. As the girl would not marry she ought to be made equally responsible for the child's bringing up.

The magistrates after consulting privately granted an order for 3s 6d a week, but directed each side to pay their own costs.

APPENDIX FIVE

Gilbert Cannan: The Semi-Detached Manchester Playwright

Gilbert Cannan was born on 25 June 1884 in Broughton, Manchester, the son of a Scottish shipping clerk. He went to Manchester Grammar School on a Foundation Scholarship and thence to King's College, Cambridge to study law, but later abandoned the bar in order to write. He quickly gained a foothold in literary and theatrical circles. His first novel, *Peter Homunculus*, was published in 1909, followed by *Devious Ways* (1910), *Little Brother* (1912) and *Round the Corner* (1913). He was also a drama reviewer for the *Manchester Guardian* as well as the *Star*.

By his mid-20s he was moving in the grander London literary circles, with friends including Mark Gertler, Dora Carrington, Ottoline Morrell, D.H. and Frieda Lawrence, Duncan Grant, John Middleton Murray, Katherine Mansfield, Edward Marsh, Edward Garnett and Compton Mackenzie.

He was also on first-name terms with Allan Monkhouse, sending greetings to the latter's children on their birthdays and writing him letters urging him to come to London and be his, Cannan's, manager. In one letter, in March 1908, he suggested it would be, 'good for your soul'. He also shared gossip about meetings with John Galsworthy and Isadora Duncan ('went back to her hotel to eat cold beef and strawberries. Told her family stories until 2am').

In 1909, Cannan caused quite a scandal amongst the literati by running off with the playwright J.M. Barrie's wife. (At one point he arrived at rehearsals in Manchester for his play *Miles Dixon* accompanied by Barrie's dog, the inspiration for Nana in Peter Pan!). When the story broke, however, Cannan wrote to Monkhouse expressing his desire that their friendship 'might not be affected by it'.

Cannan's relationship with others in the Manchester School was less amicable. He appeared to know Annie Horniman quite well, commenting at one point that she had a mind, 'like a fly dancing about on a wall.' However, rather like Gerald Cumberland, Cannan was suspicious of Stanley Houghton, although he seems not to have known him well ('I think he was in form at Manchester Grammar School with my elder brother now in Shanghai. I remember him well enough but I don't think I ever knew him…')

In August 1912 he wrote to Monkhouse: 'It was really disconcerting to see them (critics) calling *Mary B[roome]* blackguaredly … and going blue in the face with enthusiasm over Hindle Wakes which being rather dirty they thought "strong". Houghton sent me a copy of the play the other day with an announcement that he was renunciating the cotton trade in favour of authorship. He'll probably be very successful.'

His own career as a playwright was less so. His one major achievement, *Miles Dixon*, produced in 1910 was short – just two acts – and considered 'symbolic' and 'strange', with characters speaking in an odd Westmorland dialect that many found difficult. It reminded some critics of J.M. Synge's work, and according to Pogson, 'there were likenesses which could not be ignored, apart from the similarity in plot between *Miles Dixon* and *The Shadow of the Glen …*'

The play was well received on a tour of America and Canada, but its 'realistic' dialogue would jar with audiences today:

ELLEN. Why must you come on this wild night?

MILES. 'Tis t' wild night that t'crazy man is craziest and t' thing that calls to 'im calls longest and loudest.

ELLEN. And you'll not be content

MILES. I'll never be content. To sleep cold and lonely out on t' fells, wet and cold under a wall or wet and cold in a ditch, wi' t' scent o'yer 'air and t' touch o'ye in my mind for all t' warmth that I 'ave. By God 'twas a bad night for me when I furst coom to ye.

When Cannan sensed that Iden Payne was ignoring his requests to mount another of his plays, he wrote to Monkhouse in August 1911: 'Plays are an awful nuisance. I have an awful suspicion that he [Payne] has a very strong and sincere love for the second-rate. No aspersion on your house-maid play [*Mary Broome*] but the theatre has that effect on people ...'

On 6 May 1912, a second Cannan play, *Mary's Wedding*, was produced by the Gaiety company in London at the Coronet. It was, 'a tale with a horrible and repugnant theme' – alcoholism. A young woman promises to marry a man if he refrains from drinking for a year. He does so, but turns up at the church reeling drunk. The play then ends abruptly. 'The pity of it all remains, however, and sinks deep' (*Daily Telegraph*).

Thereafter, wrote Frank Swinnerton, Cannan, 'made no progress ... Although opinions multiplied and verbosity increased, the talent remained stationary.'

His wife's affair with a friend and the subsequent divorce triggered a deep depression and in April 1924 he was certified insane and became a patient in The Priory in Roehampton, where he died in 1955.

BIBLIOGRAPHY

Works consulted in addition
to those sourced in the footnotes

Books

Agate, James, *Alarums and Excursions* (G. Richards Ltd., 1922)

Archer, William, *The Old Drama and the New: An Essay in Re-valuation* (Small, Maynard 1923)

Armstrong, James, *Of Obelisks and Daffodils: The Story of Jack Kahane and the Obelisk Press* (Handsack Press, 2003)

Armstrong, James, *One Who Flies the Jolly Roger on the Sea of Censorship Jack Kahane 1887–1939, Publishing History*, 45 (January 1999)

Bankhead, Tallulah, *Tallulah: My Autobiography* (Harper, New York, 1952)

Barker, Clive and Maggie B. Gale, *British Theatre Between the Wars, 1918–1939*, Cambridge Studies in Modern Theatre (Cambridge University Press, 2001)

Bloom, Clive, *Literature and Culture in Modern Britain*, vol. 1: *1900–1929* (Longman, 1993)

Cameron, Alasdair F. *The Repertory Theatre Movement, 1907–1917*. (PhD thesis, University of Warwick.1983), *http://wrap.warwick.ac.uk/id/eprint/55938*

Cardus, Neville, *Autobiography*, reprinted edn (Readers Union, 1949)

Cather, Willa Sibert, 'Plays of Real Life', *McClure's Magazine*, 40 (March 1913)

Clark, Barrett H., 'Contemporary English Dramatists, II', *The English Journal*, 15/10 (1926)

Croall, Jonathan, *Sybil Thorndike: A Star of Life* (Haus Books, 2008)

D'Monte, Rebecca, *British Theatre, and Performance 1900–1950* (Methuen Drama Critical Companions series, 2015)

Demastes William and Katherine Kelly, *British Playwrights 1880–1956* (Greenwood Press, 1996)

Devlin, Diana, *A Speaking Part: Lewis Casson and the Theatre of his Time* (Hodder and Stoughton, 1982)

Dolley, Colin and RexWalford, *The One-Act Play Companion: A Guide to Plays, Playwrights and Performance* (Methuen Drama, 2006)

Eltis, Sos, *Acts of Desire: Women and Sex on Stage 1800–1930* (Oxford University Press, 2013)

Farr, Diana, *Gilbert Cannan: A Georgian Prodigy* (Chatto and Windus, 1978)

Flannery, James, *Miss Annie F. Horniman and the Abbey Theatre.* (Dolman Press, 1970)

Ince, Bernard, 'For the Love of Art: The Life and Work of Percy Nash, Film Producer and Director of the Silent Era', *Film History,* 19/3 (2007)

Frazier, Adrian Woods, *Behind the Scenes: Yeats, Horniman and the Struggle for the Abbey Theatre* (University of California Press. 1992)

Goldie, Grace Wyndham, *The Liverpool Repertory Theatre* (Hodder & Stoughton, 1935)

Grieves, K.C.E., 'Montague, Manchester and the Remembrance of War, 1918–25', *Bulletin of the John Rylands University Library of Manchester*, 77/2 (1995)

Higson, Andrew (ed.), *Young And Innocent? The Cinema in Britain, 1896–1930*, Exeter Studies in Film History (University of Exeter Press, 2002)

Isaac, Winifred, *Alfred Wareing: A Biography* (Green Bank Press, 1951)

Kershaw, Baz (ed.) *The Cambridge History of British Theatre* (Cambridge University Press, 2004)

Kosok, Heinz, *The Theatre of War: The First World War in British and Irish Drama* (Palgrave Macmillan, 2007)

Mallins, Edward, 'Annie Horniman's Practical Idealist', *The Canadian Journal of Irish Studies*, 3/2 (November 1977)

Andrew Maunder, Angela Smith, Jane Potter and Trudi Tate. *British Literature of the First World War*, vol. 1 (Routledge, 2017)

McDonald, Jan, *The 'New Drama' 1900-1914*, Modern Dramatists (Macmillan, 1986)

Miers, Gary (author) and James Armstrong (contributor), *Of Obelisks and Daffodils: The Publishing History of the Obelisk Press, 1929-1939* (CreateSpace Independent Publishing Platform, 2011)

Monkhouse, Allan, *Essays of Today and Yesterday* (George Harrap, 1926)

Mortimer, P., *The Life and Literary Career of W. Stanley Houghton 1881-1913* (PhD thesis University of Salford 1984), *uk.bl.ethos.332472*

Nicoll, Allardyce, *English Drama, 1900-1930: The Beginnings of the Modern Period*, part 2 (Cambridge University Press, 1973)

Pratt, Tinsley, 'The Manchester Dramatists', *Manchester Quarterly*, 34 (1914)

Riley, Patricia, *Looking for Githa* (New Writing North, 2009)

Sutton, Graham, 'The Plays of Alan Monkhouse', *Fortnightly Review* (October 1924)

Sutton, Graham, *Some Contemporary Dramatists* (Leonard Parsons, *1924*)

Trussler, Simon (ed.), *20th Century Drama Great Writers*, Student Library (Macmillan, 1983)

Wyke, Terry, *Public Sculpture of Greater Manchester*, Public Sculpture of Britain (2004)

Wearing, J. P., *The London Stage 1920–1929: A Calendar of Productions, Performers and Personnel* (Rowman & Littlefield 2014)

Wewiora, G., 'Manchester Music Hall Audiences, 1880s', *Manchester Review*, 12 (1973)

Wild J. *The Rise of the Office Clerk in Literary Culture, 1880-1939* (Palgrave Macmillan; 2006)

Woodfield, James. *English Theatre in Transition 1881-1914* (Rowman & Littlefield, 1984)

Yeats, William Butler. *The Autobiography of William Butler Yeats* (Collier Books and Macmillan, 1965)

Archives

Papers of the Manchester Literary Club, *Works of H. Brighouse* (1932)

Newspapers and Journals

AMA Journal

British Medical Journal

Chicago Evening Post

Daily News

Illustrated London News

John Bull

Kinematograph Weekly

Laughter

Leeds Mercury

Leeds Times

Leigh Chronicle

Liverpool Post and Mercury

London Evening Standard

Manchester City News

Manchester Courier

Manchester Dispatch

Manchester Evening Chronicle

Manchester Guardian

Manchester Playgoer

Moving Image

McLure's Magazine

New Age

New York Times

INDEX

DREAMING OF BABYLON
The Life & Times of Ralph Hodgson

John Harding

978-1-906075-00-2 (pbk)
238pp

Ralph Hodgson was already a brilliant graphic artist and innovator in the field of Victorian children's comics when, in the early 1900s, he began producing poetry imbued with a spiritual passion for the beauty of creation and the mystery of existence. Naturally drawn to animals, particularly birds and dogs, he was one of the first major poets of the last century to highlight the threat posed to nature by mankind's greed. His work, according to Pulitzer Prize-winning American poet Philip Levine, 'challenges us to see with more clarity the people and creatures on the margins of our world'. Admired by T.S. Eliot, John Berryman, Stephen Spender and E.E. Cummings, his work has continued to draw praise from more contemporary writers such as Robert Nye, Martin Seymour-Smith and Studs Terkel.

In writing this first-ever biography on Hodgson, John Harding has been able to draw on a wealth of previously unseen documents from libraries and collections on both sides of the Atlantic. In doing so he has brought to life one of England's most intriguing and significant literary characters. Hodgson's close friendships with Eliot, Siegfried Sassoon and Edmund Blunden provide the biography with absorbing insights into contemporary literary history. His life in Japan during the 1920s and 30s and his final years in the United States, when he wrote much of his last, compelling work, will make fascinating reading for both the general reader and literary historian alike. Illustrated with Hodgson's original cartoons and line-drawings, *Dreaming of Babylon* is sure to capture yet another generation of readers for Hodgson's timeless verse.

SWEETLY SINGS DELANEY
A Study of Shelagh Delaney's Work, 1958-68

John Harding

978-1-906075-83-5 (pbk)
204pp

Shelagh Delaney rose to fame following the instant success in 1958 of her first play, *A Taste of Honey*. Lauded as Britain's answer to the controversial French novelist Francoise Sagan, Delaney's work scandalised her home city of Salford but established her as one of the country's most original and exhilarating young playwrights during a period in theatre history when women writers were rare and acceptance hard to achieve.

Delaney has served as an inspiration to countless young artists down the succeeding years. Rock star Morrissey wrote, 'She has always been a part of my life as a perfect example of how to get up and get out and do it.' Novelist Jeanette Winterson claimed, 'She was like a lighthouse – pointing the way and warning about the rocks underneath.'

Sweetly Sings Delaney is the story of her first exciting decade as a writer when she not only produced challenging and dramatic work in prose and on stage but also collaborated with some of the most innovative film and documentary-makers of the decade such as Ken Russell, Tony Richardson, Lindsay Anderson, not to mention actor and fellow Salfordian Albert Finney during his first and only foray as a film director.

OTHER TITLES OF INTEREST

STORY
The Heart of the Matter
Maggie Butt (editor)
978-1-871551-93-8 (pbk) 184pp

W.H. DAVIES
Man and Poet: A Reassessment
Michael Cullup
978-1-906075-88-0 (pbk) 146pp

MILTON'S *PARADISE LOST*
Peter Davies
978-1-906075-47-7 (pbk) 108pp

JOHN DRYDEN
Anthony Fowles
978-1-871551-58-7 (pbk) 292pp

RAYMOND CHANDLER
Anthony Fowles
978-1-906075-87-3 (pbk) 206pp

POETRY MASTERCLASS
John Greening
978-1-906075-58-3 142pp

SWEETLY SINGS DELANEY
A Study of Shelagh Delaney's Work, 1958-68
John Harding
978-1-906075-83-5 (pbk) 204pp

DREAMING OF BABYLON

The Life and Times of Ralph Hodgson

John Harding

978-1-906075-00-2 (pbk) 238pp

SPRUNG FROM DIVINE INSANITY

The Harmonious Madness of Byron, Keats and Shelley

Andrew Keanie

978-1-910996-14-0 (pbk) 206pp

WORDSWORTH AND COLERIDGE

Views from the Meticulous to the Sublime

Andrew Keanie

978-1-871551-87-7 (pbk) 206pp

SECOND WORLD WAR POETRY IN ENGLISH

John Lucas

978-1-906075-78-1 (pbk) 236pp

GEORGE CRABBE

A Critical Study

John Lucas

978-1-906075-93-4 (pbk) 220pp

A. E. HOUSMAN

Spoken and Unspoken Love

Henry Maas

978-1-906075-71-2 (pbk)
978-1-906075-73-6 (hbk) 61pp

ERNEST DOWSON

Poetry and Love in the 1890s

Henry Maas

978-1-906075-51-4 (pbk)
978-1-906075-73-6 (hbk) 48pp

POETRY IN EXILE

A Study of the Poetry of Auden, Brodsky & Szirtes

Michael Murphy

978-1-871551-76-1 (pbk) 270pp

DEREK MAHON

A Study of His Poetry

Christopher Steare

978-1-910996-08-9 (pbk) 232pp

BETWEEN TWO WORLDS

A Survey of Writing in Britain, 1900-1914

Hugh Underhill

978-1-906075-55-2 (pbk) 188pp

To find out more about these and other titles visit
www.greenex.co.uk
www.greenexeducational.co.uk